OVERVIEW OF ADB'S SUITE OF ANNUAL CORPORATE PERFORMANCE REPORTS

The Asian Development Bank (ADB) prepares a suite of three complementary yet distinct corporate performance reports annually. **All three reports share the common goals of learning, and accountability to ADB shareholders and other stakeholders.** This overview summarizes the unique focus, purpose, and value addition of each report. It maps their common areas of focus to cross-refer the reader between the reports for information about common topics.

	FOCUS	PURPOSE AND VALUE ADDITION
Annual Evaluation Review	The Board-required report of the Independent Evaluation Department (IED) is produced to promote accountability and learning. It focuses on the operational performance and results of ADB and provides a synthesis of the evaluations prepared by IED in the preceding year and an in-depth analysis of performance trends of completed operations. It includes a special topic to strengthen results, and reports on Management's acceptance and implementation of IED recommendations.	An evidence-based evaluation of performance that is independent and provides recommendations for improvement.

COMMON FOCUS  performance of completed operations

	FOCUS	PURPOSE AND VALUE ADDITION
Development Effectiveness Review	The review is Management's flagship report on ADB's performance in achieving the priorities of its corporate strategy, using indicators in the corporate results framework as the yardstick. Focusing on operations financed by ADB, it assesses ADB's development effectiveness, highlights actions ADB has taken to improve, and identifies areas where ADB's performance needs to be strengthened.	The findings provide the Board of Directors and ADB Management with performance information to guide ADB's strategic and operational directions and resource planning.

COMMON FOCUS  performance of active portfolio

	FOCUS	PURPOSE AND VALUE ADDITION
Annual Portfolio Performance Report	The report provides a strategic overview and analysis of the performance trends, size, composition, and quality of ADB's active portfolio based on key indicators. It includes all operations and projects, including those funded by special funds and cofinancing fully administered by ADB. It identifies key issues, actions taken by departments to support improvement, and lessons for future ADB interventions, and makes recommendations for improvement to ADB Management.	The report provides ADB Management with evidence-based recommendations grounded in an in-depth analysis, including by region, of ADB's full portfolio of active committed sovereign and nonsovereign operations and projects.

2020 DEVELOPMENT EFFECTIVENESS REVIEW

APRIL 2021

ASIAN DEVELOPMENT BANK

6 ADB Avenue, Mandaluyong City, 1550 Metro Manila, Philippines
Tel +63 2 8632 4444; Fax +63 2 8636 2444
www.adb.org

ISBN 978-92-9262-807-9 (print); 978-92-9262-808-6 (electronic); 978-92-9262-809-3 (ebook)
Publication Stock No. SGP210129-2
DOI: *http://dx.doi.org/10.22617/SGP210129-2*

Notes:

In this report, "$" refers to United States dollars.
The Asian Development Bank's Strategy, Policy and Partnerships Department is the source of all information in tables, figures, boxes, and infographics in this report, unless otherwise stated.
Totals may not sum precisely because of rounding.
ADB recognizes "South Korea" as the Republic of Korea.

All photos are owned by ADB unless otherwise stated.

Cover design by Karmen Karamanian. On the cover: (Clockwise from left): India and ADB are working to provide safe and sustainable drinking water to about 1.65 million people in West Bengal (photo by Amit Verma). Salasika, 8, does her homework at home during the lockdown of schools caused by the spread of coronavirus disease in Jakarta, Indonesia (photo by Afriadi Hikmal). The 53rd Annual Meeting of the ADB Board of Governors (2nd Stage) events were held through virtual meetings and online seminars in September 2020 (photo by Eric Sales). A street vendor selling face masks in Phnom Penh, Cambodia (photo by Chor Sokunthea). The $150 million Rural Infrastructure Sector Project helped improve rural infrastructure to increase agricultural and off-farm production, raise personal incomes, create access to markets and basic services, and reduce poverty in Viet Nam (photo by Ariel Javellana). Tufui Faletau, who leads Policy and Planning with the Ministry of Finance, stands outside the Treasury building in Nuku'alofa, the capital of Tonga (photo by Luis Enrique Ascui). Highways in Rajasthan, India (photo by Amit Verma). The Chaiyaphum Wind Farm, which started commercial operation in 2016, contributes to Thailand's energy security goals by using clean power sources (photo by Zen Nuntawinyu). Finance Manager Joy Isihanua of The Franjti Shipping Co Ltd, whose company holds a franchise for the cofinanced Domestic Maritime Support Project, at the Port in Honiara, Solomon Islands (photo by Luis Enrique Ascui). Nine-year-old Safeen sells face masks during the coronavirus disease lockdown in Pakistan (photo by Rahim Mirza).

CONTENTS

SCORECARD AND RELATED INFORMATION

SIGNALS AND SCORING METHODS

RESULTS FRAMEWORK INDICATORS

TRACKING INDICATORS

LINKED DOCUMENTS

1. ADB CORPORATE RESULTS FRAMEWORK, 2019–2024
2. RESULTS FRAMEWORK INDICATOR DEFINITIONS
3. TRACKING INDICATOR DEFINITIONS
4. TECHNICAL NOTE ON THE DEVELOPMENT EFFECTIVENESS REVIEW RATING SYSTEM

WEB-LINKED RESOURCES

Download the scorecard and related information, and linked documents from
http://www.adb.org/Documents/LinkedDocs/?id=2020-DEFR

FIGURES

BOXES

ABBREVIATIONS

ADB	–	Asian Development Bank
APDRF	–	Asia Pacific Disaster Response Fund
APVAX	–	Asia Pacific Vaccine Access Facility
COVAX	–	COVID-19 Vaccine Global Access
COVID-19	–	coronavirus disease
CPRO	–	COVID-19 Pandemic Response Option
CRF	–	corporate results framework
CSO	–	civil society organization
CY	–	calendar year
DEfR	–	development effectiveness review
DMC	–	developing member country
DMF	–	design and monitoring framework
EGM	–	effective gender mainstreaming
FAST	–	Faster Approach to Small Nonsovereign Transactions
FCAS	–	fragile and conflict-affected situations
GEN	–	gender equity as a theme
IAE	–	internal administrative expense
ICT	–	information and communication technology
IED	–	Independent Evaluation Department
KPS	–	knowledge products and services
Lao PDR	–	Lao People's Democratic Republic
MAKE	–	Most Admired Knowledge Enterprise
MARS	–	Management Action Record System
OP	–	operational priority
PPE	–	personal protective equipment
PPFD	–	Procurement, Portfolio and Financial Management Department
PRC	–	People's Republic of China
PSM	–	public sector management
PSOD	–	Private Sector Operations Department
RY	–	reporting year
SDG	–	Sustainable Development Goal
SGE	–	some gender elements
SIDS	–	small island developing state
SMEs	–	small and medium-sized enterprises
TA	–	technical assistance
UNICEF	–	United Nations Children's Fund
VET	–	vocational education and training
WHO	–	World Health Organization

Urban services improvement. The Urban Services Improvement Investment Program in Georgia seeks to ensure continuous and reliable water supply and safe sanitation services to all urban residents (photo by Eric Sales).

Sustainable transport. The rail network of the BTS Skytrain slices through Bangkok's busiest commercial areas (photo by Lester Ledesma).

INTRODUCTION

The Development Effectiveness Review (DEfR) is the primary tool of the Asian Development Bank (ADB) for monitoring and reporting on its performance in achieving the priorities of its corporate strategy. The 2020 DEfR uses the 60 indicators of the Strategy 2030-aligned corporate results framework, 2019–2024 as its yardstick. It assesses overall development progress in Asia and the Pacific and ADB's effectiveness in delivering development results.

A. OVERVIEW

1. **An annual review exercise.** The development effectiveness review (DEfR) is the primary tool of the Asian Development Bank (ADB) for monitoring and reporting on its performance in achieving the priorities of its corporate strategy. The 2020 DEfR is ADB's 14th annual performance report. Preparing the DEfR is ADB's annual review and reflection exercise. This yearly process enables it to spot and analyze trends in corporate effectiveness, identify underlying issues, and develop actions to improve. The DEfR's findings inform ADB's operational directions and resource planning through the President's planning directions and the 3-year corporate work program and budget framework process.

2. **Corporate results framework structure.** The 2020 DEfR uses the 60 indicators of the Strategy 2030-aligned corporate results framework (CRF), 2019–2024 as its yardstick. The CRF, 2019–2024 covers ADB operations overall and the subset of ADB operations and countries that receive concessional assistance. Its indicators are organized into four performance levels that are arranged in two sections. Section 1, comprising Level 1, tracks the collective regional development progress made by ADB's developing member countries. These regional progress indicators are fully aligned with the Sustainable Development Goals (SDGs). Section 2, containing levels 2–4, assesses ADB's performance in executing Strategy 2030. Level 2 focuses on the results of ADB operations that supported the seven Strategy 2030 operational priorities and were completed over the preceding 3 years. Level 3 tracks ADB's performance in selecting, designing, financing, and implementing operations that align with Strategy 2030 priorities. Level 4 examines ADB's performance in managing the internal resources and processes that support its operations. The CRF indicators are complemented and reinforced by 156 tracking indicators.

B. HOW TO READ THIS REVIEW

3. **Thematic presentation and discussion of results.** The report's main body is organized by theme to reflect the directions of Strategy 2030 and the CRF, 2019–2024. The 2020 DEfR is divided into seven thematic chapters that group indicators according to the priorities and overall objectives of Strategy 2030. Performance signals and key related data are provided graphically alongside brief commentaries on overall thematic performance followed by deeper examination of particular areas and notable results. Chapter 1, the first thematic chapter, focuses on the SDGs (covering all level 1 indicators) and on ADB's seven Strategy 2030 operational priorities (covering relevant indicators from level 2). This is followed by a special chapter detailing ADB's response to the coronavirus disease (COVID-19) pandemic. The six other thematic chapters cluster and discuss results for indicators from levels 2–4 according to theme.

4. **Understanding performance signals.** The use of arrows and check mark symbols and green, amber, and red signals to illustrate the status of performance continues in the 2020 DEfR. These signals indicate the direction of change for level 1 indicators and performance against targets for indicators in levels 2–4. Performance on indicators with 2024 targets is expected to show the progress necessary from the baseline values to reach these targets. Signals for indicators with annual or periodic performance targets reflect performance on meeting the minimum and/or maximum threshold values set for each year during 2019–2024. Performance on some level 2–4 indicators is monitored rather than scored. In these cases, arrow signs indicate any improvement or deterioration, but no color signals are assigned.

5. **Where to find performance results.** The Performance Highlights section and the scorecard summarize performance on all indicators across the four levels of the CRF. The scorecard explains each performance signal. The indicator index in Appendix 1 shows where to find details on performance for each indicator discussed in the report. Some indicators are featured across several chapters.

Levels 2–4 Signals Explained

Scoring Method	Signal	Annual Change[a]
At or above target—performance at or above target	✓ (green)	
On track—performance exceeded desired progress to attain target	↑ (green)	Improved
	■ (green)	Remained constant
	↓ (green)	Deteriorated
On track but watch—performance met desired progress to attain 2024 target but requires close monitoring	↑ (amber)	Improved
	■ (amber)	Remained constant
	↓ (amber)	Deteriorated
Off track—performance fell short of desired progress to attain target	↑ (red)	Improved
	■ (red)	Remained constant
	↓ (red)	Deteriorated
Monitor—no performance assessment	↑ (gray)	Increased
	■ (gray)	Remained constant
	↓ (gray)	Decreased

[a] An arrow indicates a significant (≥ 3%) change from previous performance.

Components of Signal Bands

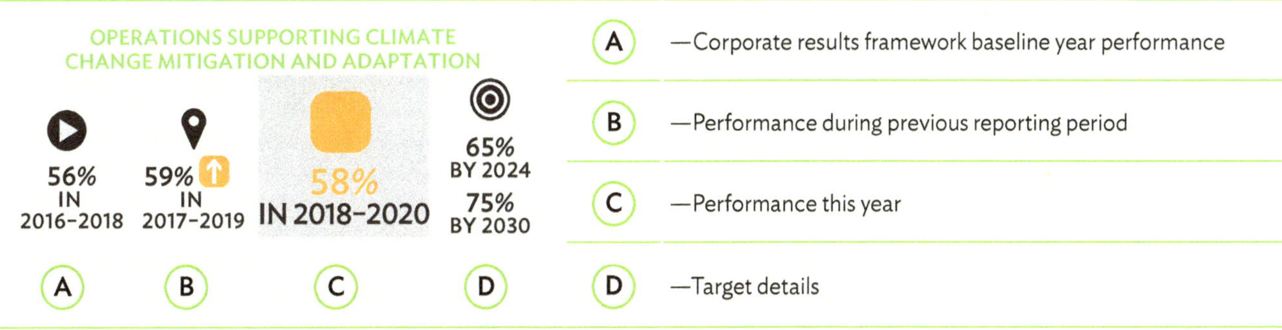

6. **Reporting on actions to address challenges.** ADB identifies and monitors actions for improvement and took important steps in 2020 to address major performance challenges described in the 2019 DEfR. Actions to address challenges that remain relevant to Strategy 2030 priorities are summarized in the penultimate section.

7. **Complementing the two other ADB corporate performance reports.** The DEfR complements and refers to the two additional corporate performance reports—the Annual Portfolio Performance Report prepared by the Procurement, Portfolio and Financial Management Department (PPFD), and the Annual Evaluation Review prepared by the Independent Evaluation Department (IED). The diagram on p. iv of this report provides an overview of the focus and purpose of each review.

Remote learning in Phnom Penh. Distance learning helps minimize disruption to education during the pandemic in Cambodia (photo by Chor Sokunthea).

CHAPTER 1

STRATEGY 2030 OPERATIONAL PRIORITIES

Strategy 2030 envisions a prosperous, resilient, inclusive, and sustainable Asia and the Pacific and reiterates that ADB's future operations will help developing member countries meet the Sustainable Development Goals. To achieve this vision, the strategy introduced seven operational priorities that take integrated, thematic approaches, reflecting the global 2030 agenda and linked to the 17 Sustainable Development Goals. This chapter takes stock of the region's development progress across the seven operational priorities, taking the implications of the COVID-19 pandemic into account. It then highlights results delivered and new efforts initiated for each of the priorities through projects completed in 2020.

A. DEVELOPMENT PROGRESS IN ASIA AND THE PACIFIC

8. **A historic development crisis.** The social and economic shocks, crises, and chain reactions triggered in Asia and the Pacific by COVID-19 disrupted the region's pursuit of the SDGs in 2020. The pandemic highlighted, and in some cases intensified, the consequences of uneven progress toward the SDGs across ADB's developing member countries (DMCs).

9. **Projections fill data gaps on implications for region's development.** Given data reporting time lags and the ongoing complex nature of the pandemic's impacts, it is too soon for the level 1 indicators of the DEfR to reflect the full effects of the pandemic on this development progress. Only two regional progress indicators had 2020 data available at the time of preparing this report. This chapter therefore complements analysis of progress against the regional progress indicators with insights and projections from more current related research and assessments, to put ADB's operations in 2020 in context.

10. **Rise in poverty amid economic contraction.** ADB estimates that economic growth in the region, already slowing in part because of pre-pandemic global trade tensions, turned negative in 2020 for the first time in more than 60 years. ADB research also estimates that poverty has risen in Asia and the Pacific after many decades of almost uninterrupted decline. The latest data showed extreme poverty continuing to ease in the region from 7.2% in 2015 (representing 273 million people living on less than $1.90 per day) to 5.1% (198 million people) in 2017. In the same year, about 24.0%, or 941 million people lived in near poverty on incomes of less than $3.20 a day. This was down from 1.1 billion people living in near poverty in 2015. In September 2020, ADB estimated that pandemic impacts had pushed about 78 million people back into extreme poverty, and that an additional 162 million people are living in near poverty on less than $3.20 daily.[1]

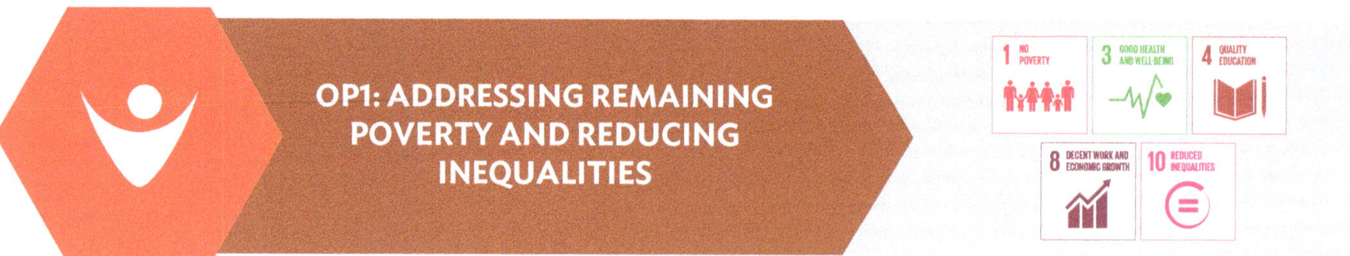

11. **Poorest hurt the most.** The pandemic is expected to hurt the region's poor the most, and its effects will be shaped by inequalities and fragility in social systems and structures. Income inequality, a key indicator, remains high across the DMCs, with the average Gini coefficient standing at 34.44 in 2018, slightly worse than 33.84 in 2016. Data also showed that the income growth rates for the poorest 40% of the populations of ADB DMCs were gradually starting to catch up with the average rates for populations as a whole, although immense disparities persisted.

12. **Learning and jobs disrupted.** Unemployment and underemployment through substantial loss of working hours rose in 2020. Young people have had their prospects for employment and education disrupted, reversing progress made on this front before the pandemic struck, including for women and girls. The proportion of youth not in education or training in the DMCs increased from 22.3% in 2017 to 26.3% in 2019. A greater proportion of enrolled students completed their lower secondary education in 2019 than in 2017. However, school closures interrupted the education of about 1.7 billion children globally in about 187 countries as COVID-19 first spread. By the end of 2020, schools were still completely closed in at least 14 ADB DMCs.[2]

13. **Remote learning filled some gaps, although many at risk of being left behind.** Core challenges with which the DMCs were grappling pre-pandemic can be expected to continue. Despite improved enrollment, educational attainment levels remained inadequate overall—a key issue at the heart of the SDG 4 Quality Education targets.[3] Closure of education institutions has also disrupted access to social support systems (such as access to food and care provided to poorer students through schools) and reduced play and social learning opportunities, taking tolls on the mental and physical well-being of students. On the other hand, the pandemic has forced education systems into hands-on exploration of new and more flexible teaching and learning approaches using information technology. Online learning may not be able to substitute for all dimensions of the learning experience, but it has an important role to play in strengthening these systems. The risk is that the poorest and the most vulnerable students, particularly girls, are likely to be left out. They have less access to the technology and infrastructure needed for distance learning and are the least likely to resume their education once it has been suspended.[4]

14. **Urgent need to widen health care and social protection coverage.** DMC, ADB, and development partner pandemic relief programs worked on immediate financing for stressed health care and health security systems in 2020, but COVID-19 underscored the need for faster progress toward broader and, eventually, universal health care across the region. Health care coverage was improving in 2017 but remained highly uneven and incomplete. The pandemic has also made it even more challenging for women to access the health care services they need.[5] Countries with weak social protection experience an even greater increase in inequality in income and access to opportunities. The most recent data suggested that only about half of the DMCs' overall population had any social protection coverage.[6]

OP2: ACCELERATING PROGRESS IN GENDER EQUALITY

15. **Women's economic empowerment at risk.** ADB is working with its DMCs under Strategy 2030 to empower and harness the capacity of the region's women to help achieve sustainable development. The pandemic has added to this challenge, although there is a dearth of sex-disaggregated data on the impacts of COVID-19. Early though incomplete data suggest that the gap between participation by women and by men in the DMC labor force may have grown in 2020.[7] Women's participation was 48% compared with 81% for men in 2020. Those women participating in the labor force in 2019 were only slightly more likely than men to be out of a job. However, unemployment data from 2020 suggest a greater increase in the unemployment rate for men than for women in ADB DMCs. More women than men in formal employment reported drops in working time, however, even if they did not lose their jobs. Projections also suggest that more women than men may be pushed back into poverty or near poverty, particularly in South Asia.

16. **Gender equality impediments amplified.** Women's burden of unpaid care, already triple that of men, has likely grown as well, as COVID-19 has imposed new and expanding demands at home, including for childcare and schooling support, amid a pervasive absence of family support structures.[8] COVID-19 has driven home the critical importance of such "invisible work" for sustaining societies. A range of evidence suggests increases in gender-based violence in 2020 as well, adding to a pervasive challenge. UN Women estimates that 243 million women and girls aged 15 to 49 have been subjected to violence by an intimate partner in the last year. There have also been severe disruptions in access to reproductive health care for women. Emerging evidence also suggests that in some countries, child marriage and child pregnancy are on the rise.[9] Applying a gender lens to COVID-19 recovery programs and prioritizing measures that enable women's economic and social empowerment will continue to be vital.

OP3: TACKLING CLIMATE CHANGE, BUILDING CLIMATE AND DISASTER RESILIENCE, AND ENHANCING ENVIRONMENTAL SUSTAINABILITY

17. **Climate change, resilience, and environmental issues insufficiently prioritized.** Achieving environmental sustainability in Asia and the Pacific requires accelerated progress toward environmentally focused goals to promote sustainable consumption and production, protect life on land and below water, and take climate action. However, the Yale Environmental Performance Index suggests weakening DMC performance on a variety of environmental issues. The COVID-19 pandemic has highlighted the critical relationship between the health of nature and the health of humans: land degradation, climate change, and biodiversity loss are critical drivers of zoonotic diseases. In addition, in 2020, the use of plastics and the generation of medical waste rose dramatically throughout the region.[10] This trend has added to the severe difficulties of managing waste and marine pollution.[11]

18. **Ambitious climate action essential.** The carbon intensity of the region's economies had been declining in 2018, but greenhouse gas emissions continued to grow in absolute terms. In 2020, despite the dramatic economic contraction associated with the pandemic, carbon dioxide emissions are estimated to have reduced by less than 7%.[12] The number of deaths linked to extreme climate and geophysical hazards increased slightly in 2020 relative to 2019 because of flooding in South, Central, and West Asia. The death toll in concessional assistance countries, including Afghanistan, Nepal, and Pakistan, was particularly significant. Global policy processes are creating opportunities to promote sustainability and increase climate action ambition. In 2020, some DMCs, including the region's largest greenhouse gas emitter, the People's Republic of China (PRC), announced more ambitious climate targets, including greater reductions in carbon intensity. It is imperative that COVID-19 recovery efforts promote low-carbon and environmentally sustainable development.

OP4: MAKING CITIES MORE LIVABLE

19. **Brief respite from urban air pollution.** Although the latest data show the DMCs had moderate air quality overall in 2017, with ADB's concessional assistance countries doing slightly better, they remained home to 99 of the world's 100 most polluted cities in 2019.[13] The dense Asian megacities that have been battling to contain and reduce particulate pollution were also on the front lines of the 2020 pandemic.[14] Poor air quality is strongly correlated with elevated COVID-19 mortality rates.[15] Reduced mobility and economic activity during the pandemic's early months temporarily improved urban air quality, but this respite was short-lived. By November, pollution levels in many South Asian cities, for example, had reached record highs, adding to COVID-19 caseloads.

20. **Uneven access to services in cities.** A primary challenge in ADB's DMCs is access to basic services such as electricity, clean water, and sanitation. The services considered available in large informal and slum settlements, however, may be hard for many residents to access, making it difficult to maintain

the hygiene measures necessary to contain COVID-19.[16] Overcrowding in close living quarters in these neighborhoods poses another livability challenge and heightens the risk of disease transmission. Urban areas are also often home to low-paid migrant workers who are severely exposed to COVID-19 infection in the region's rich and poor cities because of their jobs and living conditions.

21. Food security concerns caused by disruptions to rural–urban food supply chains and the sudden cutting off of income opportunities in cities reversed the traditional flow of migrants to urban areas. Many were forced to return to the countryside. These dynamics have provided renewed impetus for more integrated approaches to urban and rural development.

OP5: PROMOTING RURAL DEVELOPMENT AND FOOD SECURITY

22. **Food scarcity worsening.** Food security and zero hunger (SDG 2) were distant goals across DMCs even before the COVID-19 crisis hit. The Food and Agriculture Organization of the United Nations estimated that more than half of the world's undernourished people lived in Asia in 2019. More than 22.0% of the region's people were experiencing moderate or severe food insecurity, up from 19.4% in 2014.[17] The pandemic exacerbated this situation as the prices of rice, wheat, and other staple foods jumped because of bad weather in poorer countries, production and distribution breakdowns, and panic buying.[18] The poor nutrition that results has continued to stunt the growth and development of 28% of the children under 5 across the region, although these numbers represent an improvement over past decades. Stunting prevalence is particularly high in some Pacific countries and in South Asia. The problem of food scarcity for some is coupled with problems of plenty for others. Obesity is a growing health issue in the DMCs. Avoidable food losses in weak agricultural and supply chains also add to these challenges.

OP6: STRENGTHENING GOVERNANCE AND INSTITUTIONAL CAPACITY

23. **Weak governance.** Strengthened governance and institutional capacity are vital to sustainable development. The region's scores on the World Governance Index, though still negative on a scale from −2.5 to 2.5, improved slightly in 2019 from the year before on all six pillars (Figure 1.1). Political stability has been a relative strength for the region, while the regulatory environment remains a particular challenge. Controlling corruption is a perennial problem. The environment for private sector activity showed some improvement, with the average time needed to start a business cut by a day. Limited institutional capacity and shortfalls in financing public systems through domestic resource mobilization are directly linked challenges. Tax revenue to DMC gross domestic product is among the lowest in the world and is also volatile. It shrank from 13.9% in 2018 to 12.2% overall in 2019 and was as low as 11.6 % in 2017.

Figure 1.1: World Governance Index 2019 Scores for ADB Developing Member Countries

2017
2018
2019

Control of Corruption
0.00
-0.10
-0.20
-0.30
-0.40
-0.50
Government Effectiveness
Political Stability
Regulatory Quality
Rule of Law
Voice and Accountability

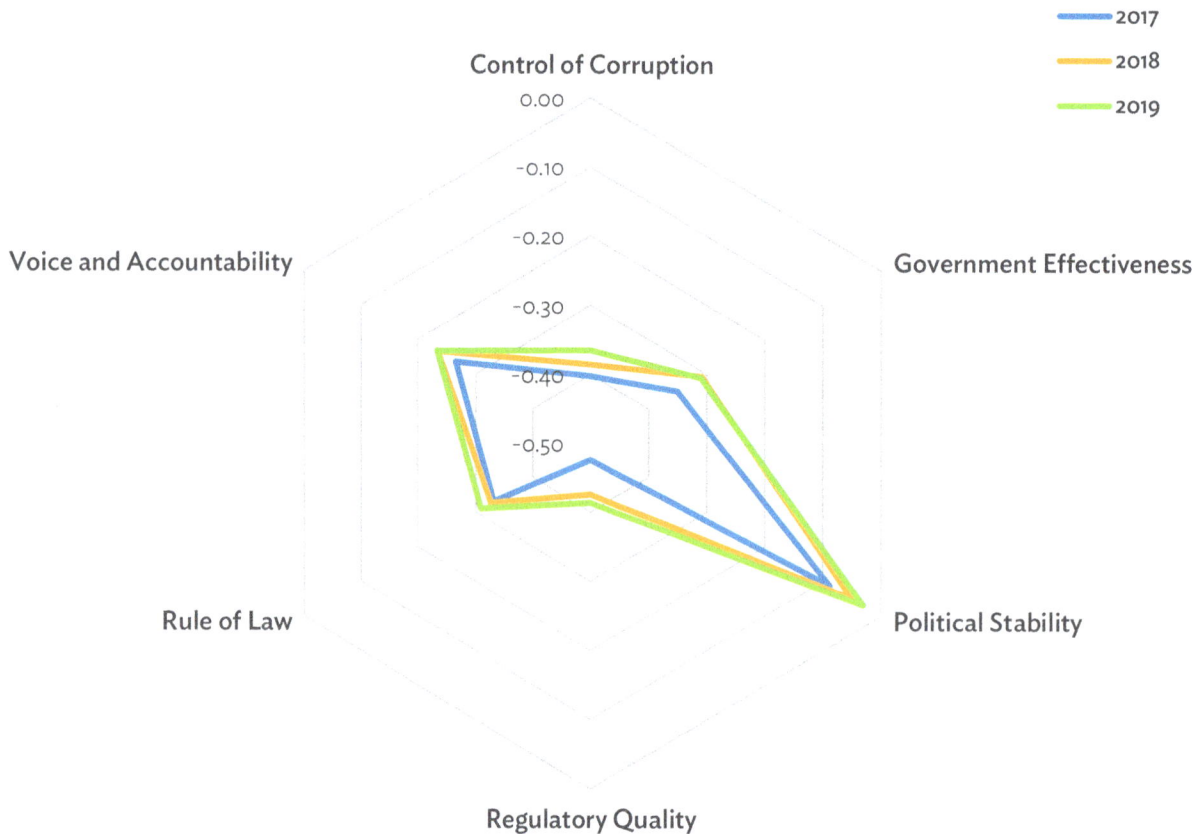

Source: World Bank. *Worldwide Governance Indicators* (accessed 15 January 2021).

OP7: FOSTERING REGIONAL COOPERATION AND INTEGRATION

24. **Countries looked inward despite strengthening foundations for cooperation.** The COVID-19 pandemic has highlighted the inescapable interconnections between countries in the region and the world, as well as the multiple ways developments in one nation can affect many others. Global tensions had weakened Asia's global cooperation through international trade even before the pandemic, although intraregional trade within Asia remained strong. Data for 2018 from ADB's Asia-Pacific Regional Cooperation and Integration Index showed improvements in the region (Figure 1.2). Development of regional value chains was the one exception. Financial and monetary cooperation scores recovered to above the 2010–2015 baseline, including in the six concessional assistance countries for which data are available. When COVID-19 began to spread, countries everywhere, including ADB's DMCs, turned further inward. This hobbled cross-border trade and economic activity, exposing vulnerabilities in crucial global supply chains.[19]

Figure 1.2: Regional Cooperation and Integration Index Scores for ADB Developing Member Countries

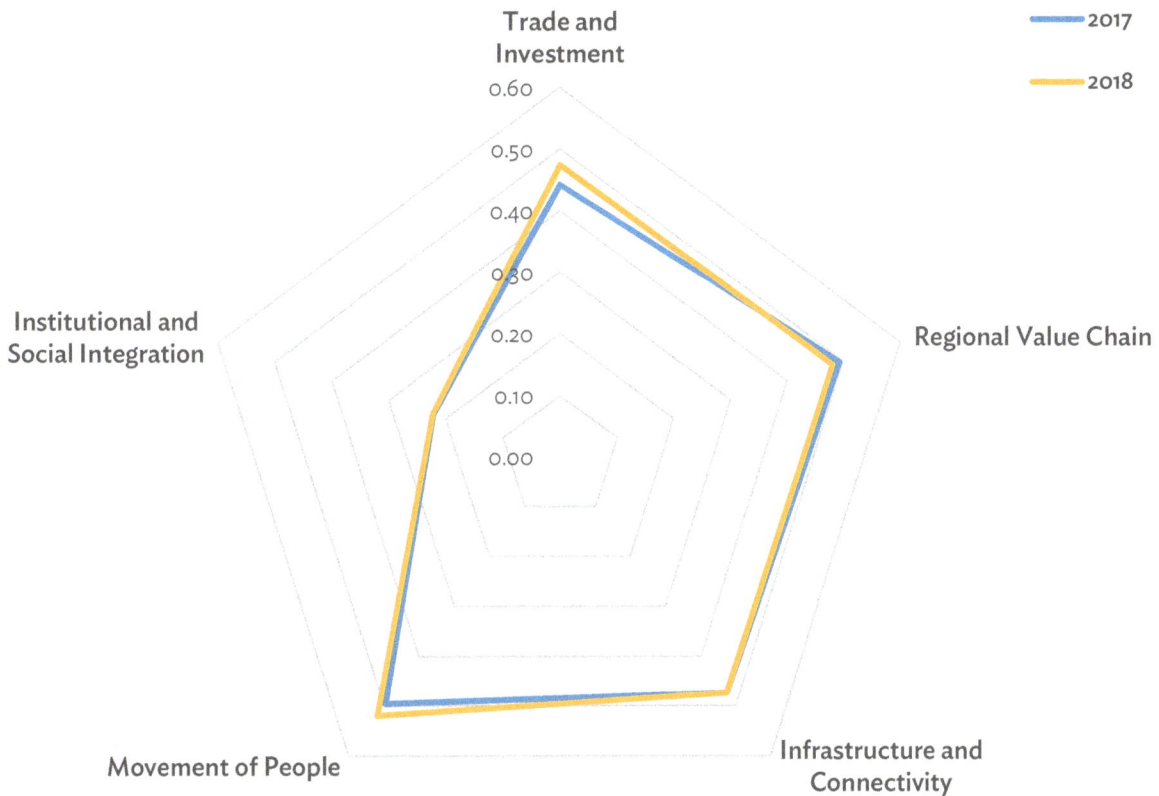

Source: Asian Development Bank. Asia-Pacific Regional Cooperation and Integration Index (accessed 22 January 2021).

25. **Reinvigorating regional cooperation.** A broad and successful economic recovery will require countries to coordinate rather than isolate. Cooperation will be needed to reconnect economies, strengthen inclusion and environmental sustainability, and make the best use of digitalization and innovation.

High-efficiency horticulture. A supply chain project in Yerevan, Armenia, is supporting the development of 30 hectares of greenhouses equipped with drip irrigation to produce tomatoes and bell peppers (photo by Eric Sales).

Sustainable tourism. Women from the Hmong ethnic group in Sapa, northern Viet Nam, have seen a boost in tourism since the completion of an expressway from Ha Noi to Lao Cai (photo by Sean Crowley).

B. SEVEN OPERATIONAL PRIORITIES: HIGHLIGHTS

Asia and the Pacific faces pressing development challenges related to the seven operational priorities of Strategy 2030. This section highlights ADB's efforts to respond to these challenges as it implements its operational priorities. Pages 13–19 provide the results of completed operations and selected project synopses that bring ADB's work to life.

OP 1 ADDRESSING REMAINING POVERTY AND REDUCING INEQUALITIES

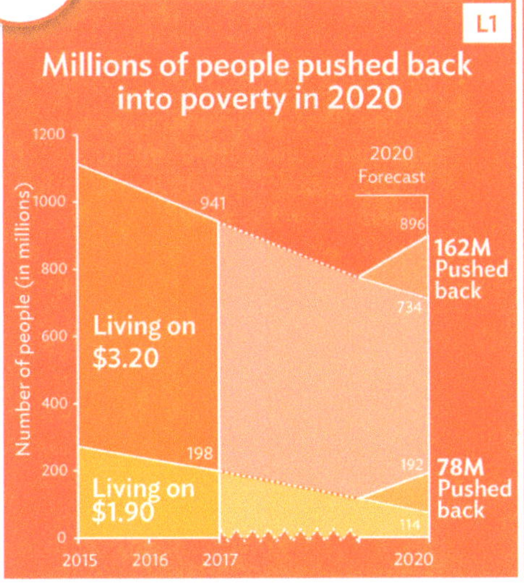

L2

4.9M

People benefiting from *improved* health services, education services, or social protection

11 Health services *established or improved*

7 Social protection schemes *established or improved*

30.5M

Poor and vulnerable people with *improved* standards of living

82,000

Infrastructure assets *established or improved*

1.75M

Jobs directly *generated*

120 Business development and finance sector measures *supported*

4 Models for business development and financing *established or improved*

L1 = Development Progress in Asia and the Pacific, L2 = Results from ADB Operations Completed in 2020, M = million.

Despite substantial progress in expanding access to primary education in Bangladesh, improving learning outcomes remains a major challenge. Many students from the country's poor and remote communities still drop out of school before completing primary education, and a large percentage of those who do complete, leave having learned too little. ADB's $411.6 million support through the **Third Primary Education Development Project** enabled the country to make considerable progress on education access and student achievement by helping train 11,000 teachers; construct 39,000 classrooms; and provide quality, inclusive, and equitable education to more than 2.5 million primary school students. The government's continued mainstreaming of the project's institutional reforms and improvements will help solidify these benefits.

Typhoon Haiyan, known locally as "Yolanda," hit the central Philippines on 8 November 2013 with severe winds and rain that left more than 7,000 people dead, 28,000 injured, and 4.1 million displaced. Damage was estimated at $2.2 billion, plunging more than a million people into poverty.

ADB's $325 million loan through the **KALAHI-CIDSS National Community-Driven Development Project** ensured increased access to basic services and strengthened government capacities. Rubysol Blasé, a student from Siargao Island, is one of about 16.2 million poor and vulnerable people who benefited from improvements in education, road access, water supply, and sanitation. "With the help from ADB, the bridge between my house and my friends was built, and another to the school," she says. "Suddenly, we were connected by more than blood—we were connected by bridges."

ADB continues to pursue the vision of a region free of poverty—addressing the remaining poverty and reducing inequalities in the developing member countries. Investments in infrastructure projects in 2020, complemented by investments in education, finance, health, and agriculture, created jobs and economic opportunities and reduced the vulnerabilities of millions of poor and vulnerable people by connecting them to markets and increasing their access to social services.

OP 2 ACCELERATING PROGRESS IN GENDER EQUALITY

L1

Women more likely to be pushed back into poverty because of COVID-19

48% women participating in the labor force vs. 81% men

3 times as many women not in education, employment, or training as men

women do 3 times as much unpaid care, and demands have grown during the pandemic

L2

67,000 Women and girls *completing* education, and/or training

317,000 Skilled jobs *generated* for women

115,000 Women *represented* in decision-making structures and processes

997,000 Women and girls with *increased* time savings

870 Women and girls with *increased resilience* to external shocks

74% IN 2019

73% IN 2020

80% BY 2024

Completed operations *delivering* gender results

Delivery of gender results on track but watch

Of the 30 sovereign and nonsovereign operations completed in 2020, 21 (70%) successfully delivered their intended gender results, bringing the 3-year average for 2018–2020 to 73%—slightly lower for the third consecutive period. Performance on this indicator remains *on track but watch* to meet the 80% target by 2024. The highest success rates were for operations in agriculture and natural resources, health, public sector management, and industry and trade. The one nonsovereign operation completed in 2020 failed to achieve targeted gender results, underscoring the need to continually engage with private sector clients and borrowers on gender targets and indicators.

COVID-19 = coronavirus disease, L1 = Development Progress in Asia and the Pacific, L2 = Results from ADB Operations Completed in 2020.

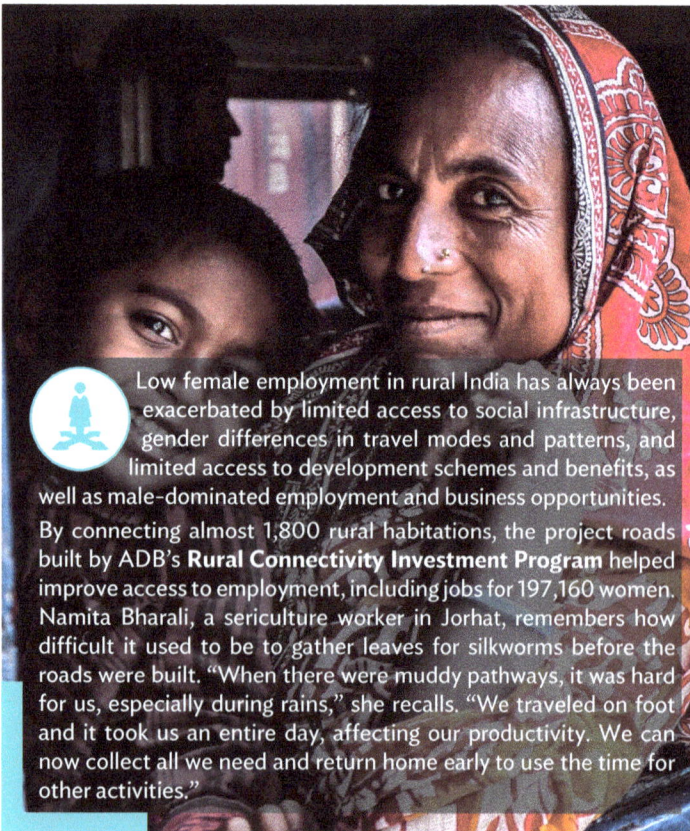

Low female employment in rural India has always been exacerbated by limited access to social infrastructure, gender differences in travel modes and patterns, and limited access to development schemes and benefits, as well as male-dominated employment and business opportunities.

By connecting almost 1,800 rural habitations, the project roads built by ADB's **Rural Connectivity Investment Program** helped improve access to employment, including jobs for 197,160 women. Namita Bharali, a sericulture worker in Jorhat, remembers how difficult it used to be to gather leaves for silkworms before the roads were built. "When there were muddy pathways, it was hard for us, especially during rains," she recalls. "We traveled on foot and it took us an entire day, affecting our productivity. We can now collect all we need and return home early to use the time for other activities."

Nepal made good progress in achieving almost universal enrollment in primary education, but most workers are poorly educated and school leavers lack the skills required by the labor market. The technical and vocational education and training (TVET) system faced key constraints, including insufficient and inequitable access to TVET, poor training quality and low market relevance, and weak institutional capacity.

The ADB-supported **Skills Development Project** helped address the shortage of skilled labor and increase the participation of women and excluded groups in training and employment. Akriti Gurung, 30, is one of 19,378 women who completed training in construction, manufacturing, and services industries. "When I enrolled in the Building Electrician training, I was the only woman among the 19 trainees, so I was very nervous," she recalls. "Now, I work as a building electrician. I feel empowered to have skills in an area where few women work."

Operations completed in 2020 narrowed gender gaps and provided women and girls with greater access to job and livelihood opportunities, increased time savings, and enhanced mobility and access to education, health, and social protection. ADB projects also empowered thousands more women through their participation in decision-making structures and processes, accelerating progress in gender equality.

While overall results in this operational priority were satisfactory, progress toward targets for women represented in decision-making structures and processes fell short in the concessional assistance subset. Only two of the four operations in this group achieved their intended gender outcomes. An unsuccessful gender action plan for a project in Vanuatu lacked sufficient reporting against its gender targets and faced challenges arising from prevailing social norms. The other project, a regional operation in Southeast Asia, did not ensure that women had equal representation in the provincial project management unit.

OP3 TACKLING CLIMATE CHANGE, BUILDING CLIMATE AND DISASTER RESILIENCE, AND ENHANCING ENVIRONMENTAL SUSTAINABILITY

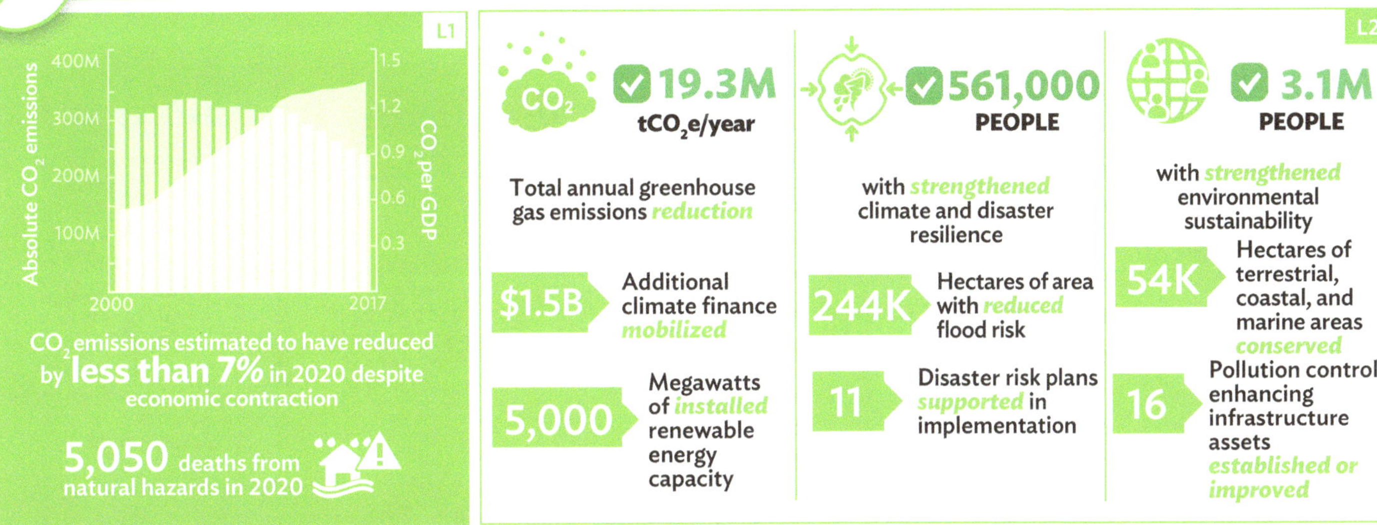

B = billion, CO_2 = carbon dioxide, GDP = gross domestic product, K = thousand, L1 = Development Progress in Asia and the Pacific, L2 = Results from ADB Operations Completed in 2020, M = million, tCO_2e = tons of carbon dioxide equivalent.

In April 2014, tropical Cyclone Ita hit the island of Guadalcanal in Solomon Islands triggering catastrophic flooding that caused 23 fatalities and displaced thousands. Roads, bridges, and other major infrastructure were destroyed and devastated, with losses estimated at $107.7 million—equivalent to 9.2% of Solomon Islands' gross domestic product that year.

ADB's $12.5 million emergency assistance through the **Transport Sector Flood Recovery Project** helped rebuild climate- and disaster-proof roads, culverts, stream crossings, and three elevated bridges, restoring the east–west road link to the capital, Honiara. About 79,150 people benefited from shorter travel times to markets, schools, and health services, and from improved connectivity for businesses. "Communities in the east and west can get to town now even when some of the main rivers are flooded," says Mike Qaqara, a government official. "That means sick people can reach clinics and hospitals in town for treatment during heavy storms."

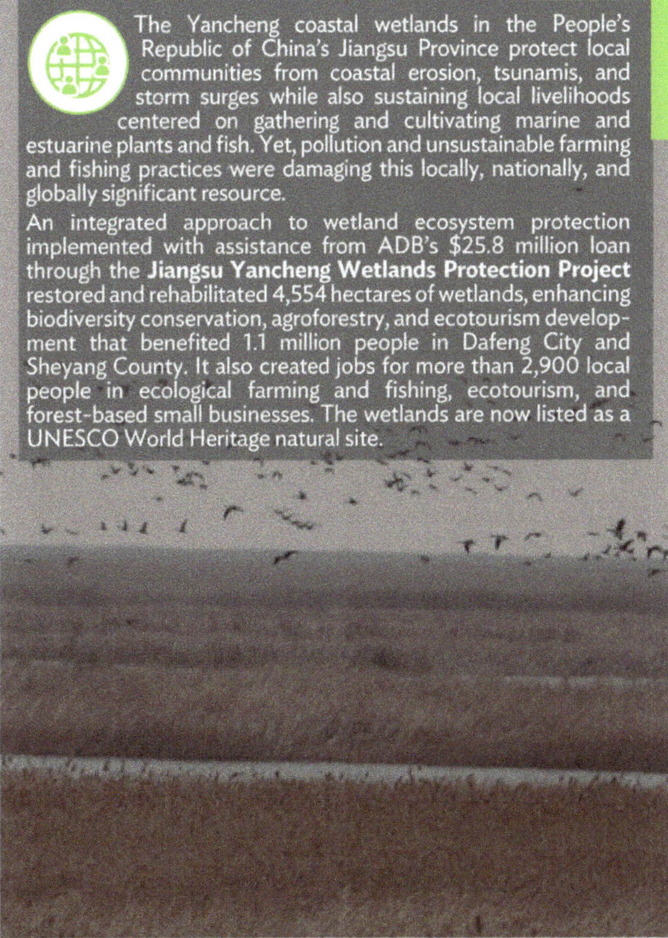

The Yancheng coastal wetlands in the People's Republic of China's Jiangsu Province protect local communities from coastal erosion, tsunamis, and storm surges while also sustaining local livelihoods centered on gathering and cultivating marine and estuarine plants and fish. Yet, pollution and unsustainable farming and fishing practices were damaging this locally, nationally, and globally significant resource.

An integrated approach to wetland ecosystem protection implemented with assistance from ADB's $25.8 million loan through the **Jiangsu Yancheng Wetlands Protection Project** restored and rehabilitated 4,554 hectares of wetlands, enhancing biodiversity conservation, agroforestry, and ecotourism development that benefited 1.1 million people in Dafeng City and Sheyang County. It also created jobs for more than 2,900 local people in ecological farming and fishing, ecotourism, and forest-based small businesses. The wetlands are now listed as a UNESCO World Heritage natural site.

In 2020, ADB scaled up support for clean energy investments, sustainable transport, and climate adaptation in DMCs, making millions of people less vulnerable to environmental degradation and rising levels of water and air pollution, and enhancing their resilience to climate change and natural hazards. Twenty-five operations contributed to greenhouse gas emission reductions of 19.33 million tons of carbon dioxide-equivalent per year in various DMCs.

OP 4 MAKING CITIES MORE LIVABLE

L1

Pollution PM 2.5 of 60.65 mg per m³

Region hosts 99 of the 100 most polluted cities in the world

URBAN COVERAGE

WATER 97%

SANITATION 87%

Crowded conditions and difficulties in accessing services challenge COVID-19 containment

L2

14.2M PEOPLE

Benefiting from *improved* services in urban areas

380 Urban infrastructure assets *established or improved*

670 Service providers with *improved* performance

7 ENTITIES

with *improved* urban planning and financial sustainability

10 Measures to improve regulatory, legal, and institutional environment for better planning *supported in implementation*

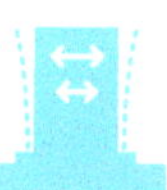

2 ZONES

with *improved* urban environment, climate resilience, and disaster risk management

9 Solutions to enhance urban environment *implemented*

3 Urban climate and disaster resilience capacity development initiatives *implemented*

COVID-19 = coronavirus disease, L1 = Development Progress in Asia and the Pacific, L2 = Results from ADB Operations Completed in 2020,M = million, mg per m3 = milligram per cubic meter, PM = particulate matter.

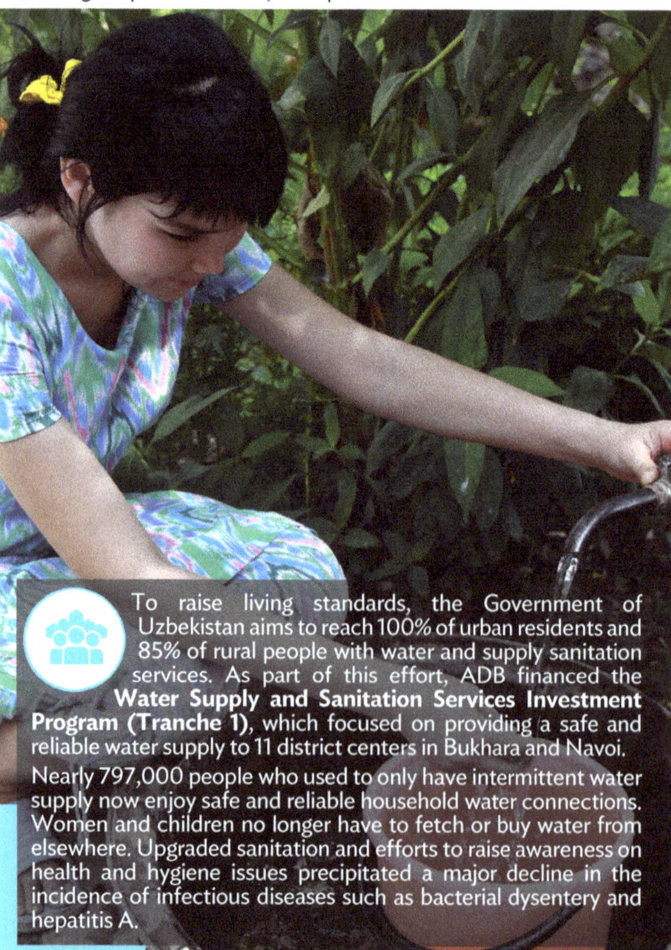

To raise living standards, the Government of Uzbekistan aims to reach 100% of urban residents and 85% of rural people with water and supply sanitation services. As part of this effort, ADB financed the **Water Supply and Sanitation Services Investment Program (Tranche 1)**, which focused on providing a safe and reliable water supply to 11 district centers in Bukhara and Navoi.

Nearly 797,000 people who used to only have intermittent water supply now enjoy safe and reliable household water connections. Women and children no longer have to fetch or buy water from elsewhere. Upgraded sanitation and efforts to raise awareness on health and hygiene issues precipitated a major decline in the incidence of infectious diseases such as bacterial dysentery and hepatitis A.

Sri Lanka's northwestern dry zone suffered from insufficient and poor-quality groundwater supply, and weak resource coordination and planning. More than half of the population in the region lacked access to safe water and sanitation.

ADB's $104.6 million loan and grant assistance through the **Dry Zone Urban Water and Sanitation Project** helped strengthen the regional support centers' capacities in business management, water supply modeling, operation and maintenance, design, systems automation, and service delivery. The institutional reforms, coupled with infrastructure investments, improved septage removal and disposal services, and provided constant water supply to 283,000 people in the districts of Chilaw, Mannar, Puttalam, and Vavuniya.

ADB aims to transform the well-being of city dwellers while helping its DMCs catalyze economic development through increased urbanization. Operations completed in 2020 focused on urban water supply and sanitation management and low-carbon energy sources, as well as solutions to promote sustainable integrated urban development. Urban populations also benefited from improvements featuring upgraded transport systems, disaster risk management, and climate resilience.

OP 5 PROMOTING RURAL DEVELOPMENT AND FOOD SECURITY

L1

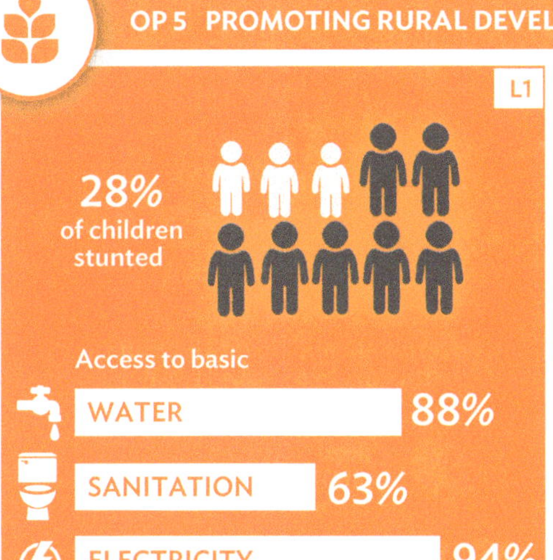

L2

27.6M PEOPLE
benefiting from *increased* rural investment

1,200 Rural infrastructure assets *established or improved*

3 Rural economic hubs *supported*

2,800 FARMERS
with *increased* market access

Agribusinesses *integrating* farmers in efficient value chains

361,000 HECTARES
of land with *higher* productivity

17,000
Hectares of land *improved* through climate-resilient irrigation infrastructure and water delivery services

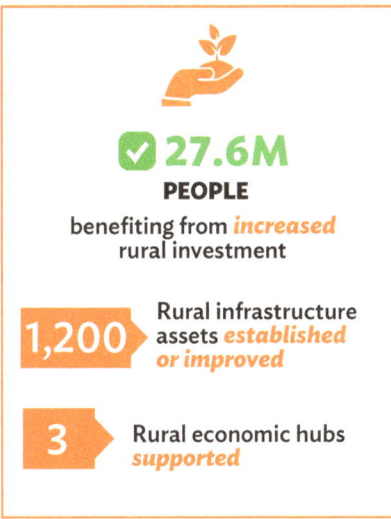

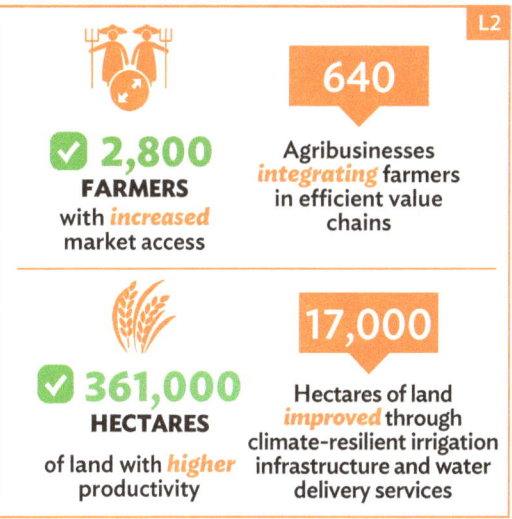

L1 = Development Progress in Asia and the Pacific, L2 = Results from ADB Operations Completed in 2020, M = million.

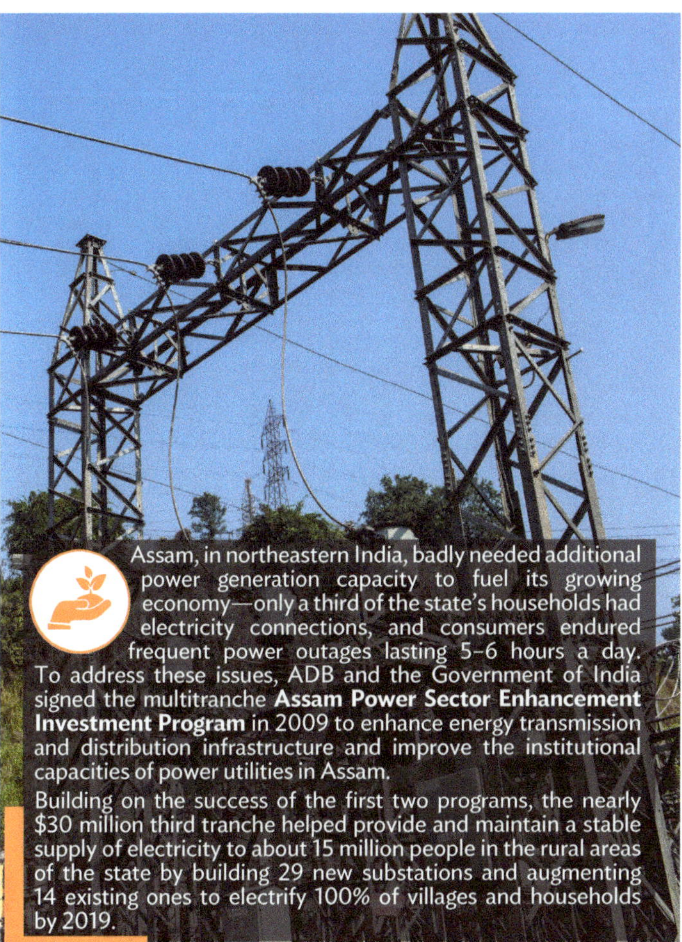

Assam, in northeastern India, badly needed additional power generation capacity to fuel its growing economy—only a third of the state's households had electricity connections, and consumers endured frequent power outages lasting 5–6 hours a day. To address these issues, ADB and the Government of India signed the multitranche **Assam Power Sector Enhancement Investment Program** in 2009 to enhance energy transmission and distribution infrastructure and improve the institutional capacities of power utilities in Assam.

Building on the success of the first two programs, the nearly $30 million third tranche helped provide and maintain a stable supply of electricity to about 15 million people in the rural areas of the state by building 29 new substations and augmenting 14 existing ones to electrify 100% of villages and households by 2019.

In 2014, heavy rains in northern Afghanistan resulted in severe floods that devastated homes and farmlands, irrigation canals, and rural farm-to-market roads. More than 140,000 people were displaced and losses amounted to $800 million, posing a threat to the food security of a country heavily reliant on agriculture.

The $38.3 million emergency assistance grant through the **Northern Flood-Damaged Infrastructure Emergency Rehabilitation Project** helped restore 82,939 hectares of affected farmlands and rehabilitate flood-damaged infrastructure and flood control works in 161,478 hectares of irrigable land in 15 of the worst-affected provinces. "Physical upgrades of the Irrigation system are crucial for improving livelihoods and achieving financial and food security of rural households in Afghanistan," says Hazrat Omar Zakhilwal, Afghanistan's former minister of finance.

ADB's renewed focus on rural development aims to help its DMCs improve infrastructure and provide access to social and economic services in rural areas. Millions of people benefited from operations in the agriculture and natural resources management, transport, and energy sectors completed in 2020 that improved land by providing climate-resilient infrastructure and irrigation services, quality farm inputs, and sustainable mechanization technologies. A regional technical assistance project helped forge public–private community partnerships linking private firms and smallholder farmers to markets.

OP 6 STRENGTHENING GOVERNANCE AND INSTITUTIONAL CAPACITY

L1

−0.28 in 2019

−2.5 | −0.32 in 2017 | +2.5

World Governance Indicators Index scores slightly improved

Tax to GDP Ratios
11.6% in 2017
13.9% in 2018
12.29% in 2019

L2

890 ENTITIES

with *improved* management functions and financial stability

93K Government officials with *increased capacities*

160 Measures *supported in implementation* to promote the private sector and finance sector

320 ENTITIES

government and private institutions with *improved* service delivery

14 Measures *supported in implementation* to strengthen state-owned enterprises' governance

8 Better service delivery standards *adopted*

GDP = gross domestic product, L1 = Development Progress in Asia and the Pacific, L2 = Results from ADB Operations Completed in 2020.

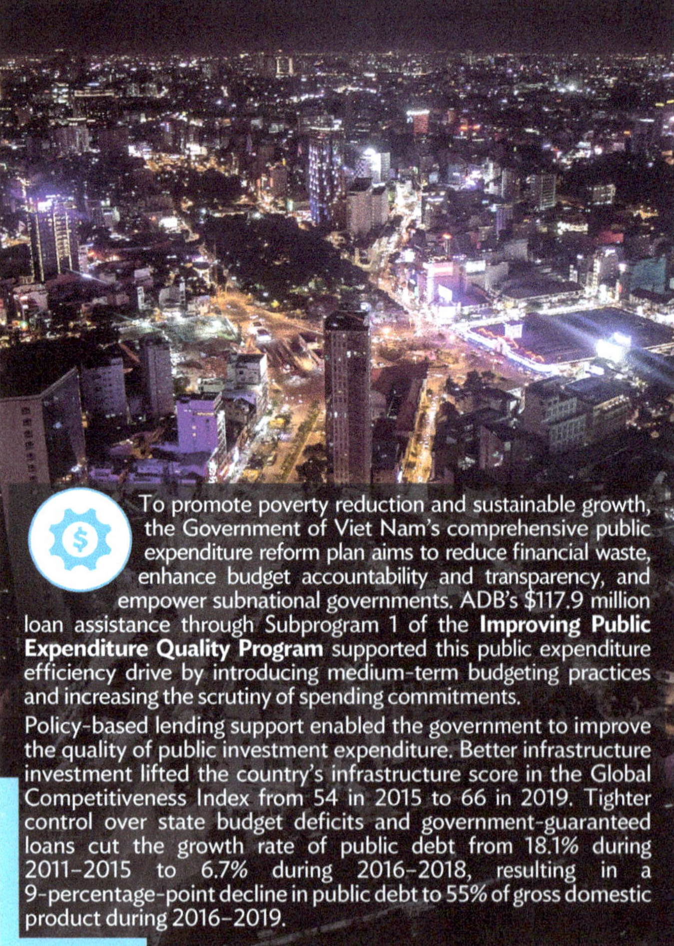

To promote poverty reduction and sustainable growth, the Government of Viet Nam's comprehensive public expenditure reform plan aims to reduce financial waste, enhance budget accountability and transparency, and empower subnational governments. ADB's $117.9 million loan assistance through Subprogram 1 of the **Improving Public Expenditure Quality Program** supported this public expenditure efficiency drive by introducing medium-term budgeting practices and increasing the scrutiny of spending commitments.

Policy-based lending support enabled the government to improve the quality of public investment expenditure. Better infrastructure investment lifted the country's infrastructure score in the Global Competitiveness Index from 54 in 2015 to 66 in 2019. Tighter control over state budget deficits and government-guaranteed loans cut the growth rate of public debt from 18.1% during 2011–2015 to 6.7% during 2016–2018, resulting in a 9-percentage-point decline in public debt to 55% of gross domestic product during 2016–2019.

Despite Sri Lanka's heavy investment in modernizing secondary school infrastructure, poor completion and pass rates and too little science, mathematics, and English teaching in many schools have made it difficult for graduates to move into post-secondary education and beyond. **The Education Sector Development Program**—ADB's first results-based loan—supported the government's secondary school system reforms that aimed to strengthen science, technology, and other applied subjects, and cut youth unemployment after graduation. The $177 million education loan helped upgrade 255 schools with new science and mathematics facilities and equipment, and train teachers, school principals, and education agency staff. By 2018, total enrollments in the 255 schools reached 44,971.

Ruviththa Uthayakumar, a student in Sri Somaskanda College in Puttur, dreams of pursuing an academic career in biotechnology. "My ambition is to become a university lecturer," she says.

The quality of growth, including reduction in poverty and inequality, is strongly linked to effective governance and adequate institutional capacity. ADB commits to help enable the policy environment and build capacities to deliver effective, corruption-free, and gender- and socially inclusive public services within the context of meaningful citizen engagement. In 2020, most of ADB's operations continued to support public and corporate sector reforms that helped DMCs improve governance and create an enabling environment for sustainable growth. Public and private sector entities benefited from improved tax policy and administration and better financial management, and these improvements helped them provide better quality education and health services, more reliable water and electricity supply, and more efficient transport and financial services.

OP 7 FOSTERING REGIONAL COOPERATION AND INTEGRATION

L1

ARCII

ARCII Index

0.45 in 2018

0 | 0.44 in 2017 | 1

Asia-Pacific Regional Cooperation and Integration Index scores improved, but countries prioritized national measures to manage the pandemic

L2

$1.37B INVESTMENTS trade and investment *facilitated*

66 Measures to improve execution of new or existing trade or investment agreements *supported*

8 Measures to develop existing or new cross-border economic corridors *supported*

1 INITIATIVE regional public goods *initiative*

7 Measures to improve regional public health and education services *supported in implementation*

12 Regional or subregional mechanisms *operationalized* to enhance DMC cooperation in trade, finance, or multisector economic corridors

ARCII = Asia-Pacific Regional Cooperation and Integration Index, B = billion, DMC = developing member country, L1 = Development Progress in Asia and the Pacific, L2 = Results from ADB Operations Completed in 2020.

In 2006, about 70% of Azerbaijan's road network was in poor condition, resulting in high transport costs, long delivery times, and traffic accidents. This impeded poverty reduction and growth of the non-oil sector. The government aimed to create an adequate, efficient, safe, and sustainable road network that ensures domestic and international connectivity.

ADB supported the government's efforts through the **Road Network Development Program**, which helped increase the share of roads in good and fair condition from to 56% in 2017 from 10% in 2006. This triggered a 50% rise in road freight, a 30% growth in passenger traffic, and a 43% reduction in road traffic accidents. Improved expressways and local roads linked communities with markets and social services, brightening livelihood prospects and stimulating rural growth. Better international connectivity boosted international trade with Georgia, Iran, and the Russian Federation by 62% from $2.2 billion in 2006 to $3.5 billion in 2018.

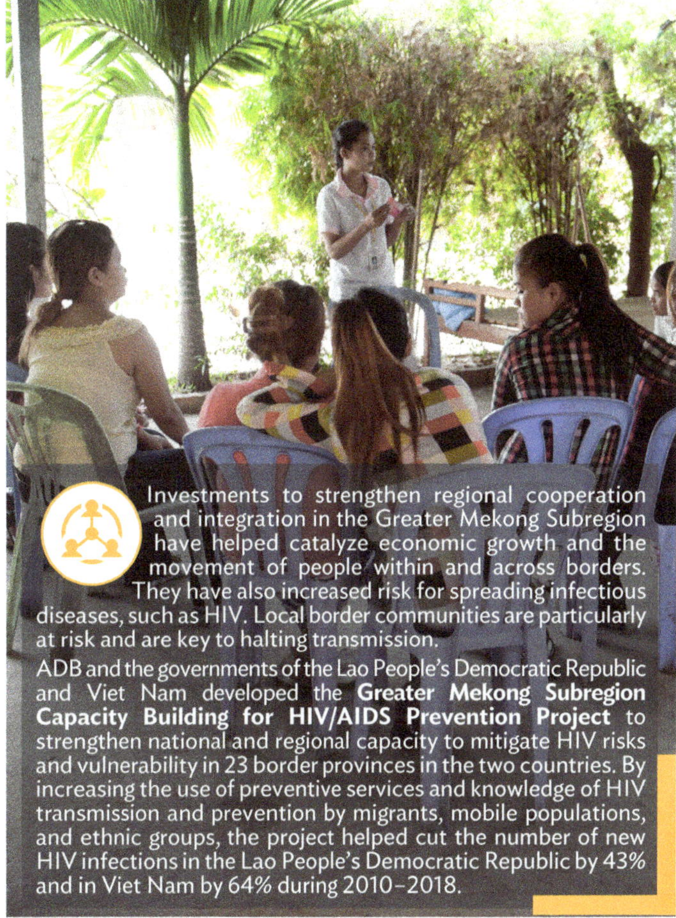

Investments to strengthen regional cooperation and integration in the Greater Mekong Subregion have helped catalyze economic growth and the movement of people within and across borders. They have also increased risk for spreading infectious diseases, such as HIV. Local border communities are particularly at risk and are key to halting transmission.

ADB and the governments of the Lao People's Democratic Republic and Viet Nam developed the **Greater Mekong Subregion Capacity Building for HIV/AIDS Prevention Project** to strengthen national and regional capacity to mitigate HIV risks and vulnerability in 23 border provinces in the two countries. By increasing the use of preventive services and knowledge of HIV transmission and prevention by migrants, mobile populations, and ethnic groups, the project helped cut the number of new HIV infections in the Lao People's Democratic Republic by 43% and in Viet Nam by 64% during 2010–2018.

ADB continued to support greater regional cooperation and integration by increasing physical connectivity, reducing barriers to global and regional trade and investments, and enhancing the provision of regional public goods. It also built a stronger sense of regional community, mobilized technical and financial resources from various development partners, supported policy dialogue and coordination among DMCs, and provided capacity building and knowledge products and services tailored to clients' needs. Completed projects in 2020 helped further transform transport corridors into trade and economic corridors in Central Asia Regional Economic Cooperation countries and address common challenges related to disease outbreaks in the Greater Mekong Subregion.

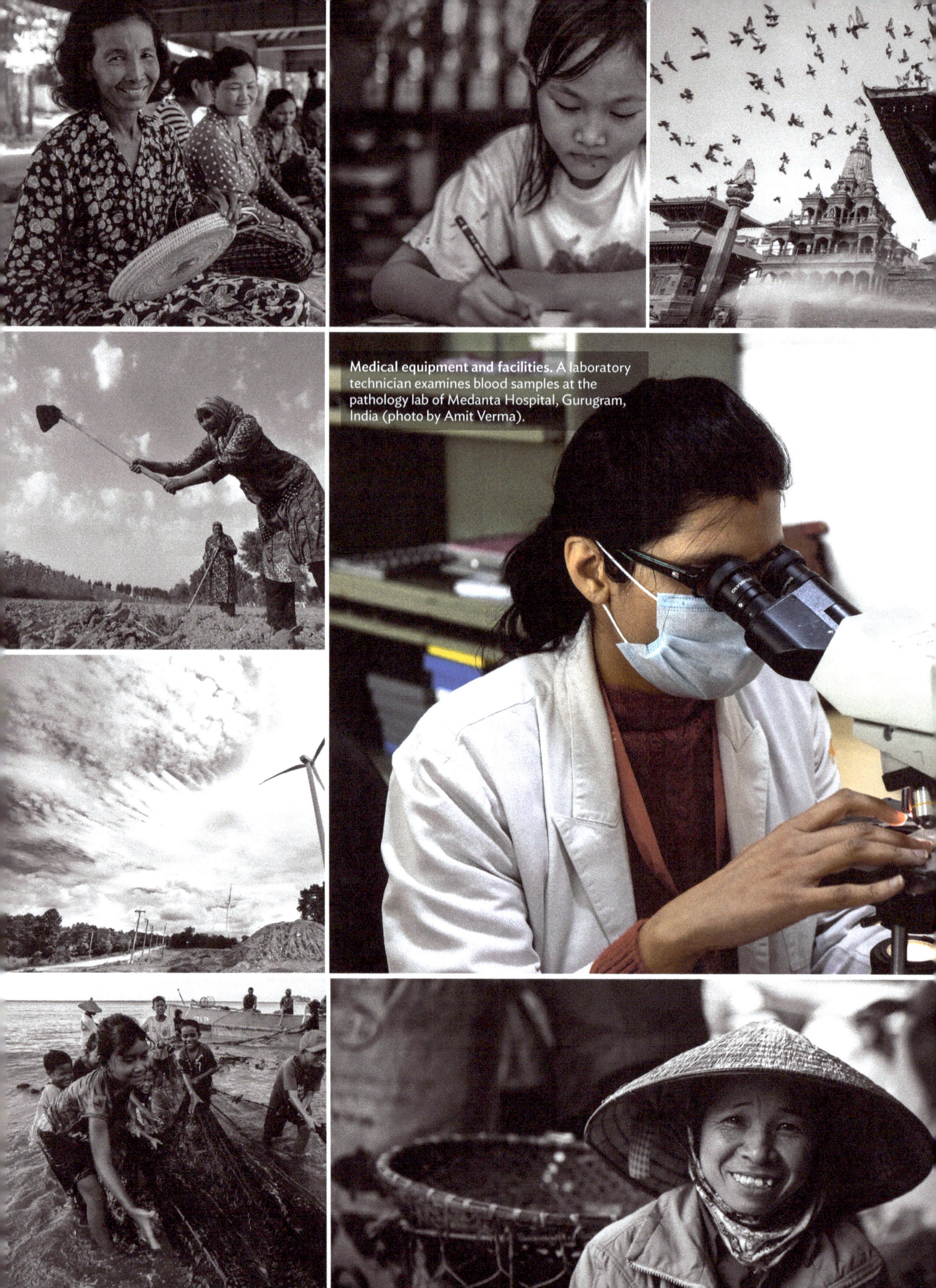

Medical equipment and facilities. A laboratory technician examines blood samples at the pathology lab of Medanta Hospital, Gurugram, India (photo by Amit Verma).

CHAPTER 2

ADB'S RESPONSE TO THE COVID-19 PANDEMIC

This special chapter examines how ADB responded to the challenge of supporting its developing member countries during the coronavirus disease (COVID-19) pandemic. It discusses seven key results areas of ADB's response: 1. Early and rapid response to the evolving regional health emergency, 2. Adaptability and agility ADB demonstrated in response to COVID-19, 3. Knowledge solutions applied in the COVID-19 response, 4. Developing member countries' programs supported by ADB in partnership, 5. Development effectiveness integrated in the project cycle, 6. Expected results of government programs supported by ADB, and 7. Post-pandemic recovery initiated.

ADB'S COVID-19 RESPONSE IN 2020

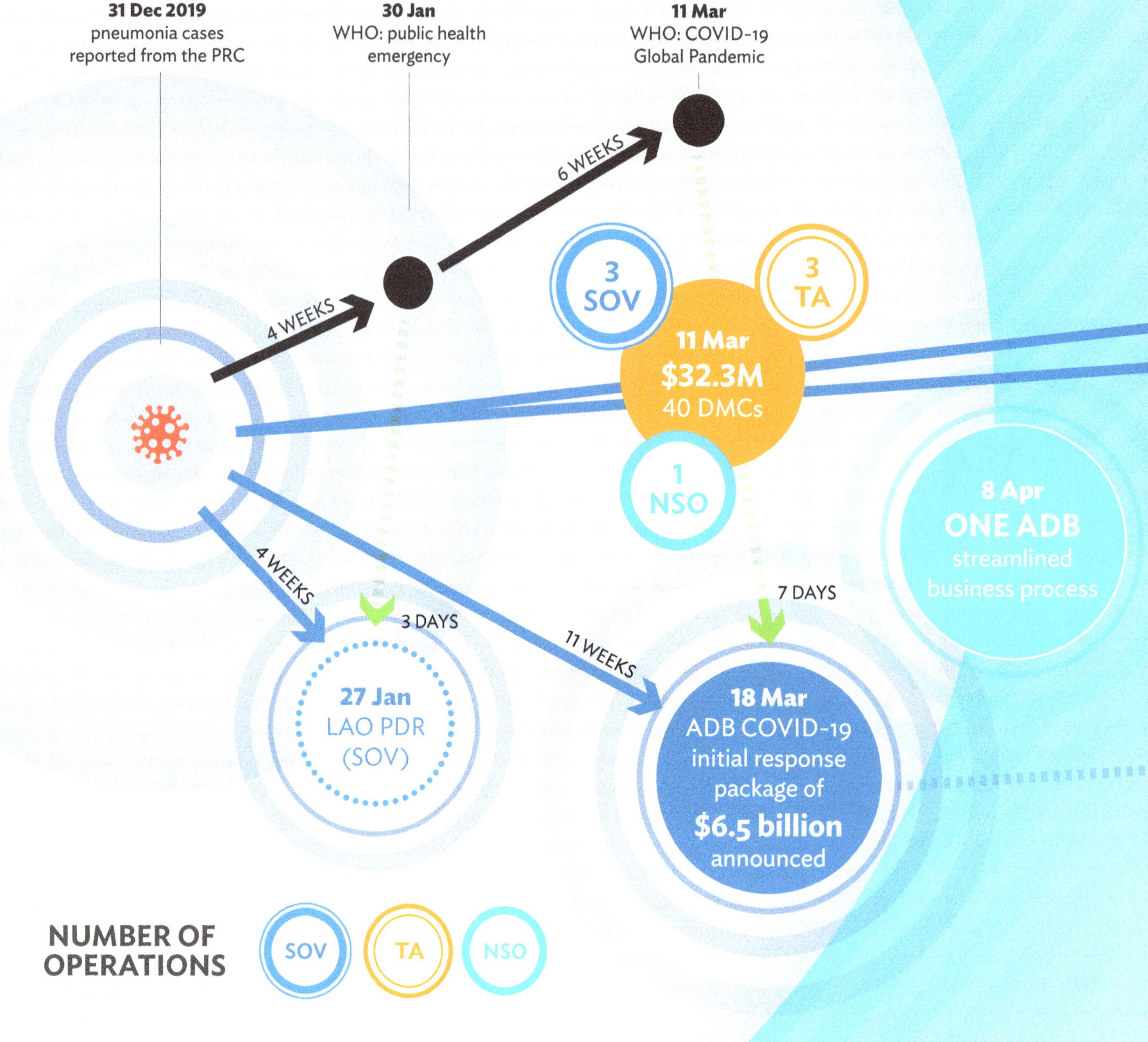

A. OVERVIEW OF COVID-19 RESPONSE

26. **Mystery virus emerges.** Since the end of December 2019, when the Government of the People's Republic of China (PRC) reported a cluster of unexplained pneumonia cases, coronavirus disease (COVID-19) has spread across the globe, disrupting lives and livelihoods on an unprecedented scale. More than 17 million positive cases have been recorded in Asia and the Pacific, causing more than 295,000 deaths as of December 2020. The region's gross domestic product is forecast to contract by 0.4% in 2020 in the first regional slump in 6 decades, erasing 3–4 years of progress in poverty reduction.

27. **Early, rapid actions.** As governments around the region enacted measures to contain COVID-19, ADB responded rapidly, initially drawing on its 2019 active portfolio of $102.6 billion. On 27 January 2020, 3 days before the World Health Organization (WHO) declared the COVID-19 outbreak a public health emergency of international concern, ADB refocused a health security project in the Lao People's Democratic Republic (Lao PDR) to respond to COVID-19; and on 25 February, ADB committed its first new nonsovereign COVID-19 project. By 11 March, the day WHO declared

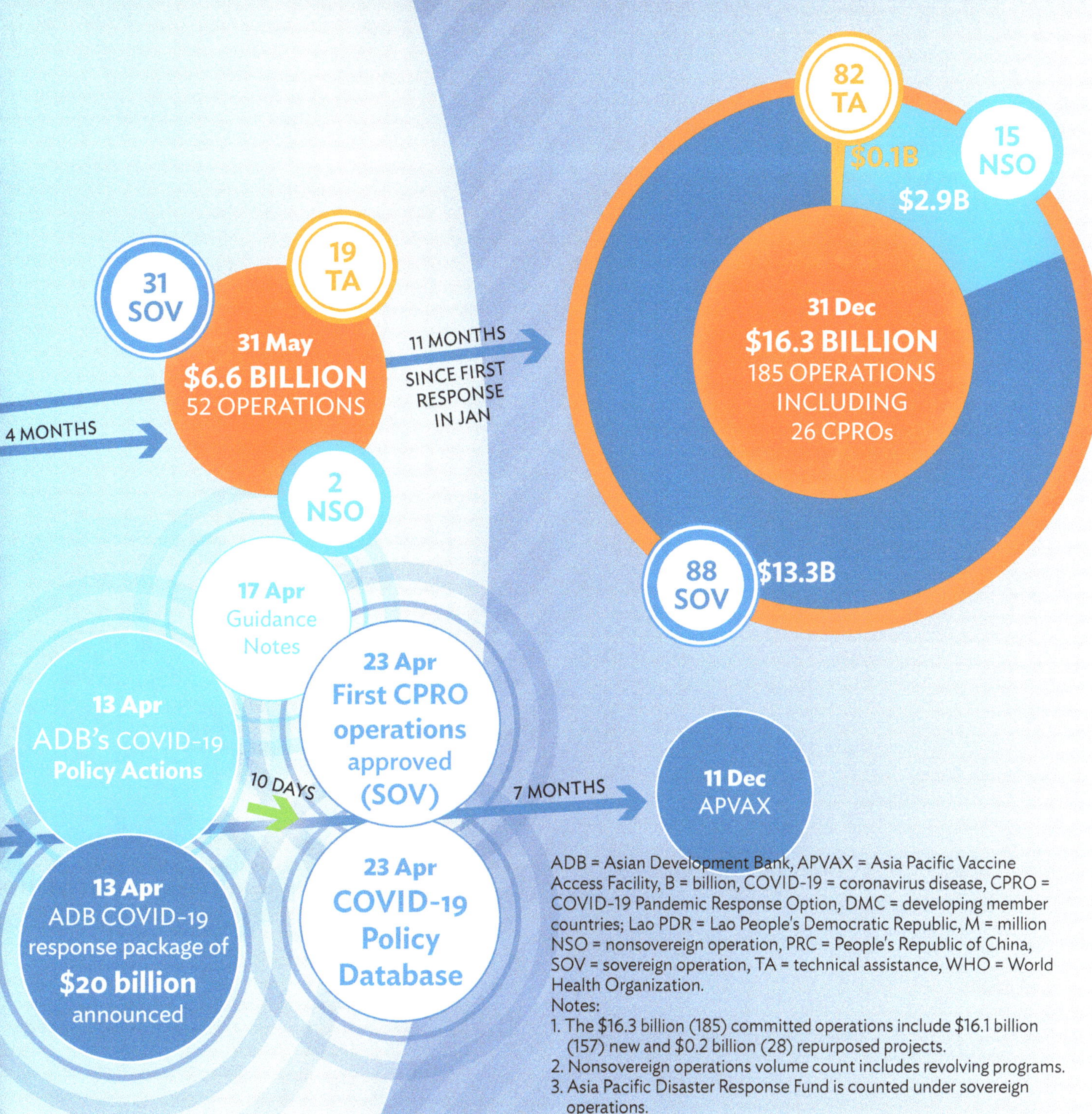

ADB = Asian Development Bank, APVAX = Asia Pacific Vaccine Access Facility, B = billion, COVID-19 = coronavirus disease, CPRO = COVID-19 Pandemic Response Option, DMC = developing member countries; Lao PDR = Lao People's Democratic Republic, M = million NSO = nonsovereign operation, PRC = People's Republic of China, SOV = sovereign operation, TA = technical assistance, WHO = World Health Organization.

Notes:

1. The $16.3 billion (185) committed operations include $16.1 billion (157) new and $0.2 billion (28) repurposed projects.
2. Nonsovereign operations volume count includes revolving programs.
3. Asia Pacific Disaster Response Fund is counted under sovereign operations.

COVID-19 a global pandemic, ADB had committed $32.3 million in seven refocused and new operations covering 40 of its developing member countries (DMCs).

28. **Agile, comprehensive response.** A week later, ADB announced a $6.5 billion initial package to address DMCs' immediate needs as they responded to the pandemic; and on 13 April, ADB increased the total size of its COVID-19 response package to $20 billion. Included in this comprehensive package were time-bound policy variations and Management actions to provide faster, more tailored responses befitting the urgency of the pandemic. As part of these new arrangements, "One ADB" teams could assume responsibility for ensuring due diligence.

29. **Knowledge solutions and partnerships.** To provide immediate and effective solutions for the COVID-19 response, ADB partnered with at least 113 multilateral and bilateral agencies, think tanks, civil society organizations (CSOs), and private companies in the areas of cofinancing, procurement, and knowledge. Cofinancing partnerships with a range of traditional and new partners increased the total development finance available to the DMCs.

30. **Development effectiveness ensured.** ADB ensured quality standards continued to be applied and sharpened throughout the project cycle. COVID-19 operations include clear targeting to mitigate the health and economic impacts of the pandemic. Five corporate reports on 2020 operations capture ADB's COVID-19 response.

31. **Expected results.** By the end of 2020, ADB had approved $16.5 billion for 185 COVID-19 response operations and committed $16.3 billion across the DMCs, of which $9.7 billion had been disbursed.[20] Nearly 1.1 billion people and more than 4.4 million businesses are expected to benefit. Expected results include 595 knowledge products to help individuals, governments, and businesses cope with the impacts of COVID-19.

32. **Road to recovery.** By mid-September 2020, ADB signaled a shift in focus toward a green, inclusive, and resilient recovery from the pandemic. On 11 December, ADB approved the $9 billion Asia Pacific Vaccine Access Facility (APVAX), bringing ADB's total COVID-19 response package to $29 billion.

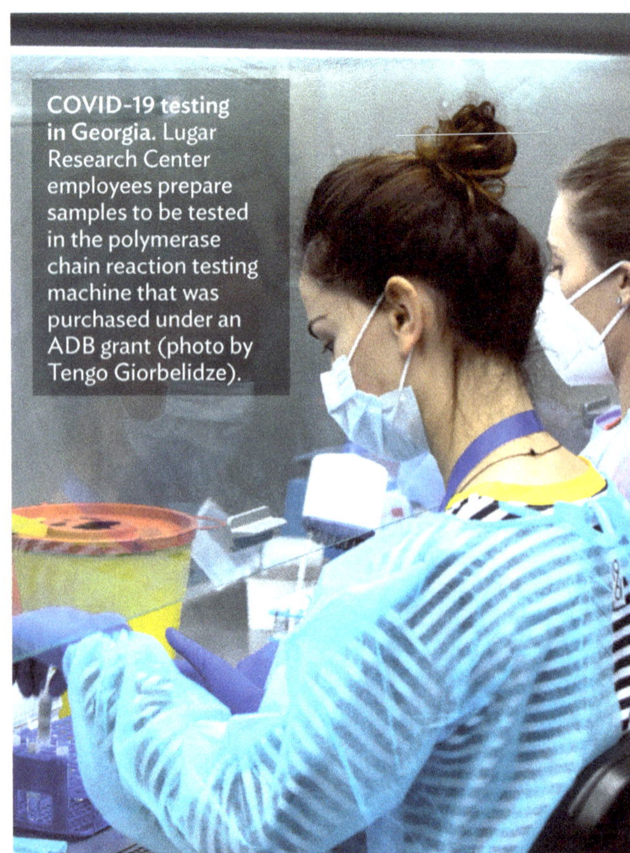

COVID-19 testing in Georgia. Lugar Research Center employees prepare samples to be tested in the polymerase chain reaction testing machine that was purchased under an ADB grant (photo by Tengo Giorbelidze).

ADB's COVID-19 Response before the WHO Declaration of the Global Pandemic

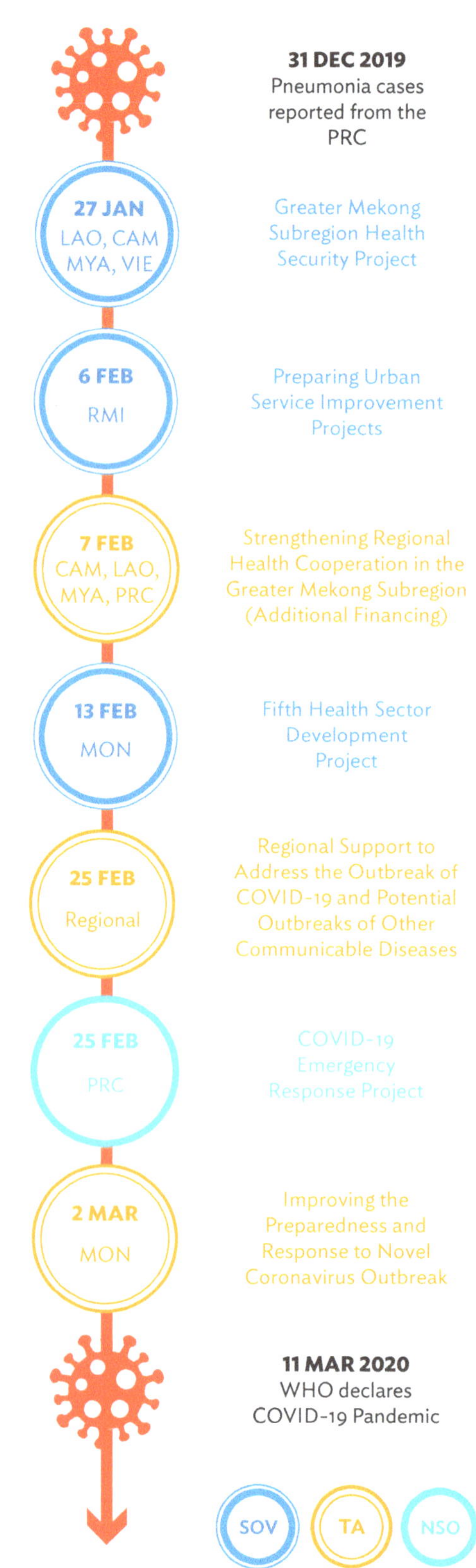

CAM = Cambodia, COVID-19 = coronavirus disease, LAO = Lao People's Democratic Republic, MON = Mongolia, NSO =nonsovereign operation, MYA = Myanmar, PRC = People's Republic of China, RMI = Marshall Islands, SOV = sovereign, TA = technical assistance,VIE = Viet Nam, WHO = World Health Organization.

B. RESULT 1: EARLY AND RAPID RESPONSE TO EVOLVING REGIONAL HEALTH EMERGENCY

33. **Early response to new virus reports.** Before many had begun to comprehend or acknowledge the enormous potential implications of the looming communicable disease emergency, ADB was already launching a response. By 27 January, 4 weeks after the initial reports of unexplained pneumonia cases in the PRC and 3 days before WHO declared COVID-19 a public health emergency of international concern, ADB had reorientated an ongoing disease surveillance and outbreak response project in the Lao PDR to quickly deploy funds to respond to COVID-19 and was starting to repurpose other projects. This was 6 weeks before WHO declared COVID-19 a global pandemic.

34. **First response package announced.** On 11 March, the day the pandemic was declared, ADB already had seven ongoing COVID-19 response operations providing $32.3 million in ADB assistance to 40 DMCs (Box 2.1). A week later, on 18 March, as staff at headquarters and in most resident missions were progressively shifting to remote working arrangements, ADB announced an initial response package of $6.5 billion and began preparing a COVID-19 facility. This milestone was reached just 11 weeks after the earliest reports of virus cases in the PRC.

Box 2.1: ADB's Initial Response Using New and Ongoing Projects

On 7 February 2020, the Asian Development Bank (ADB) committed its first regional technical assistance (TA) project dedicated to combating coronavirus disease (COVID-19). The assistance helped Cambodia, the Lao People's Democratic Republic, Myanmar, the People's Republic of China, Thailand, and Viet Nam improve outbreak investigation and surveillance and strengthen their health systems' resilience and epidemic response capacity. On 13 February, 2 days after the World Health Organization named the virus, ADB redirected savings from an ongoing health sector development project in Mongolia to procure essential medical equipment to detect cases and provide emergency care for COVID-19 patients.

The commitment on 25 February of a regional TA project made funds available to all ADB developing member countries for updating and implementing their pandemic response plans, including buying emergency supplies and equipment, and improving regional coordination to prevent, detect, and respond to disease outbreaks. On the same day, ADB committed its first nonsovereign COVID-19 response loan to help Wuhan-based Jointown Pharmaceutical Group Co. Ltd. ensure a continuous supply of essential medicines and personal protective equipment amid mobility restrictions and soaring demand at the disease's initial epicenter. On 2 March, ADB responded to an urgent request from the Government of Mongolia for TA to increase the country's COVID-19 preparedness.

35. **High client rating for ADB's speed.** An independent survey of ADB's primary clients conducted at the end of the year found high levels of satisfaction with the swiftness of ADB's response to development needs in the region, including the pandemic. About 80% of ADB's primary clients, including government officials and private companies involved in ADB-funded projects, rated the speed of ADB's COVID-19 response *good* (44%) or *excellent* (36%).

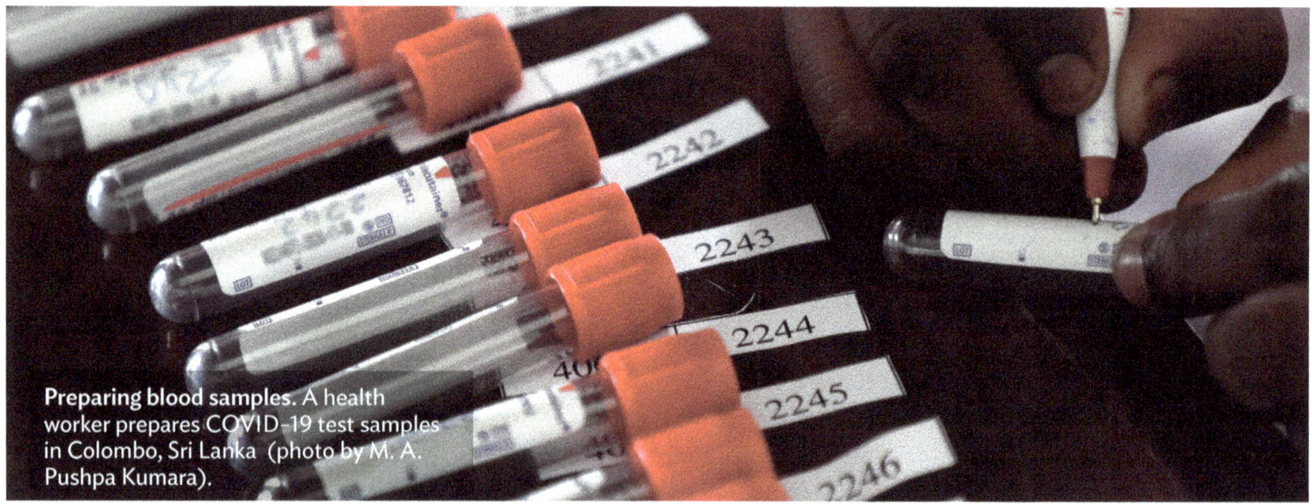

Preparing blood samples. A health worker prepares COVID-19 test samples in Colombo, Sri Lanka (photo by M. A. Pushpa Kumara).

C. RESULT 2: ADAPTABILITY AND AGILITY DEMONSTRATED IN RESPONSE TO COVID-19

36. **Enhanced package and policies to hasten and scale up response.** With the early response underway, ADB prepared and launched on 8 April a dedicated COVID-19 response package of financial and policy tools needed to respond to the pandemic with the necessary scale and speed. ADB's Comprehensive Response to the COVID-19 Pandemic policy paper announced nine Board-approved policy variations and five Management actions to fast-track business processes for COVID-19 response projects, together with a revised package of $20 billion. The first two sovereign operations were approved under the new COVID-19 Pandemic Response Option (CPRO) just 10 days later.

37. **Actions and policy variations for an agile response.** A major policy measure introduced under ADB's comprehensive pandemic response was the establishment of a dedicated new instrument—the CPRO—under the Countercyclical Support Facility to provide quick-disbursing budget support to help governments finance fiscal stimulus and COVID-19 response social protection programs. Other important measures included broadening the scope of ADB's Contingent Disaster Financing under policy-based lending and the Asian Development Fund 12 Disaster Response Facility to include health emergencies, and expanding nonsovereign support to provide working capital and short-term financing to rejuvenate supply chains and trade and to maintain employment. Management actions approved included fast-track processing of COVID-19 related sovereign, nonsovereign, and technical assistance (TA) projects and expanded use of ADB's substantial TA resources to help governments purchase urgently needed medical and personal protective equipment (PPE). Also, a procurement waiver introduced in the policy variation was critical for ADB to quickly establish more partnerships with the United Nations.

38. **Guidance notes, policy database, and dashboard launched.** In the second half of April, ADB released a series of guidance notes on topics such as design and monitoring frameworks (DMFs), safeguards, and financial due diligence to help ADB operations teams, DMC partners, and Management ensure the quality of the COVID-19 response operations. Late April also saw the launch of the COVID-19 Policy Database—a source of information on the key economic and green recovery measures that governments are taking to combat the COVID-19 pandemic—and the COVID-19 Dashboard to monitor funds flow and usage of COVID-19 response operations.

39. **Rapid scaling of assistance to all developing member countries.** These variations and innovations enabled ADB to quickly process new COVID-19 response operations. Four months after the Lao PDR project was reoriented to address the emerging virus, ADB had committed $6.6 billion for 52 COVID-19 response operations. By the end of the year, there were 185 such operations, 88 of them sovereign, 15 nonsovereign, and 82 TA, including 26 CPRO operations (Box 2.2) with a combined $16.3 billion in commitments.[21]

Box 2.2: Use of the COVID-19 Pandemic Response Option

The Asian Development Bank (ADB) committed 26 COVID-19 Pandemic Response Option (CPRO) operations in 2020 to rapidly deploy $10 billion to countries facing diverse impacts from the coronavirus disease (COVID-19) pandemic. In each case, ADB staff, working with government counterparts, tailored approaches that made the best use of ADB's resources to mitigate the impacts of the pandemic, focusing on women and the most vulnerable populations. In countries such as the Philippines, where community transmission was already widespread and strict lockdowns were in place, testing capacity needed to be ramped up, health systems strengthened, emergency food parcels and conditional cash transfers distributed to vulnerable households, and relief provided to severely affected sectors and small businesses. In many Pacific developing member countries, on the other hand, isolated locations and prompt preparedness measures had shielded them from the catastrophic health impacts of COVID-19, but their tourist-dependent economies had been plunged into crisis by global travel bans. In these countries, CPRO operations focused on strengthening disease surveillance and preparedness, implementing social assistance for the unemployed, and delivering economic relief to affected businesses.

40. **One ADB teams.** The Board-approved streamlined processes waived the requirement for concept papers and provided the option to exchange the formal interdepartmental review process for One ADB teams of technical experts and nominated staff who assumed responsibility for due diligence. This approach greatly increased the efficiency of delivery of ADB's COVID-19 response. Of the 185 COVID-19 response operations, 64 used One ADB teams (Figure 2.1). In total, $12.7 billion of COVID-19 response sovereign, TA, and Asia Pacific Disaster Response Fund projects—78% of 2020 COVID-19 response commitments—was processed using One ADB teams. Informal Board briefings were open to all CPRO processing teams, facilitating broader participation and exchange of ideas on the design of COVID-19 responses. Resident mission staff played a pivotal role in design and processing support, particularly given the absence of mission travel.

41. **Sovereign project processing times sharply reduced.** It took an average of only 2.3 months to process CPRO operations with a first disbursement in 2020 using One ADB teams versus 6.5 months for Countercyclical Support Facility operations in pre-COVID-19 years.[22] Other sovereign modalities also moved from fact-finding to first disbursement at record speeds (Figure 2.2). The swiftness of ADB's response to this unprecedented emergency was made possible by the dedication of ADB staff working closely with the Board of Directors, DMCs, and partner organizations as one team.

42. **High client rating on ADB's adaptive operations.** In a recent survey of ADB's primary clients, 81% of respondents described ADB's tailoring of its response to the country context as *excellent* (30%) or *good* (51%), and 76% viewed the size of ADB's response relative to the country's needs as *excellent* (30%) or *good* (47%).[23]

Figure 2.1: COVID-19 Related Sovereign Operations
(%)

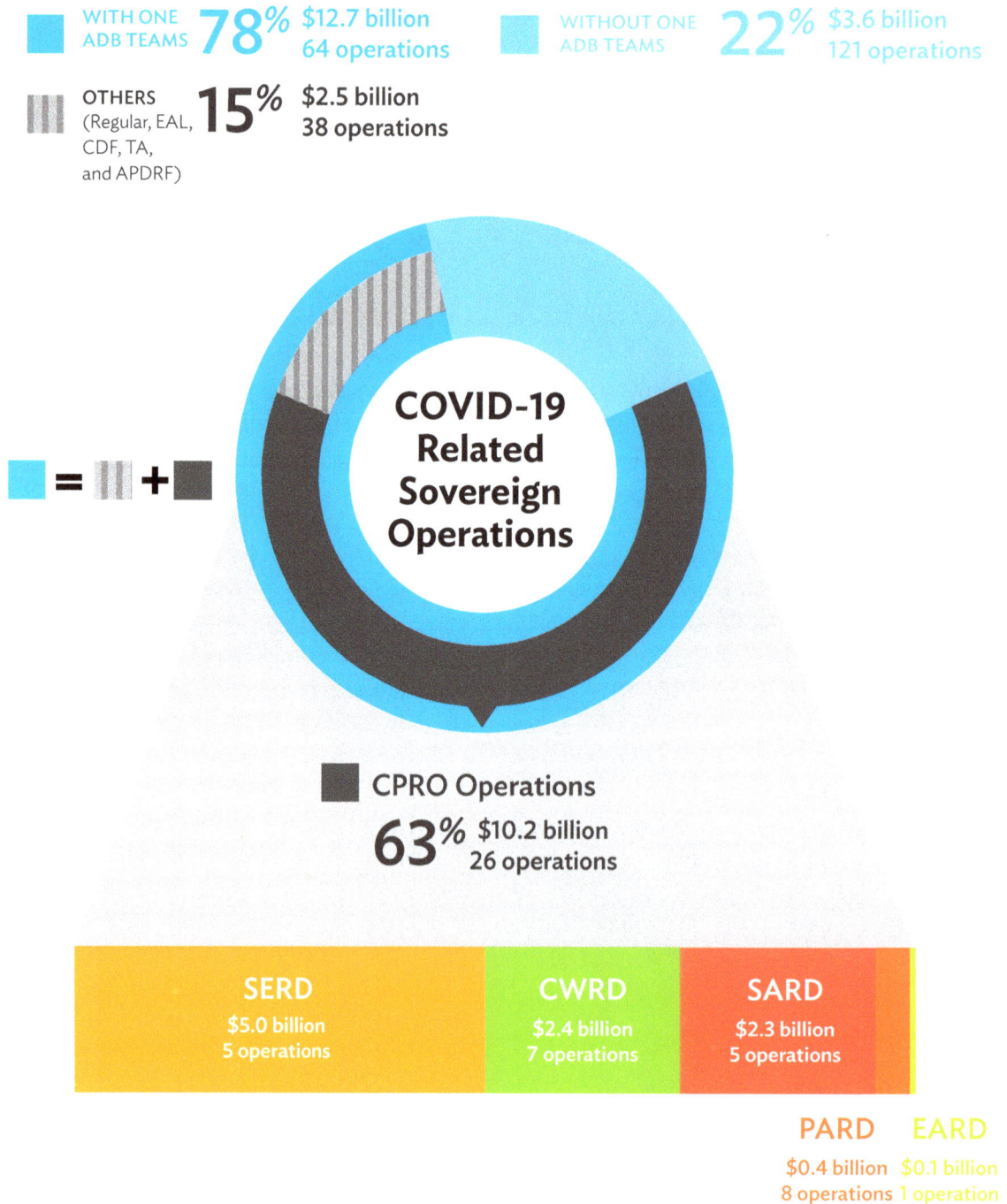

ADB = Asian Development Bank, APDRF = Asia Pacific Disaster Response Fund, CDF = contingent disaster financing, COVID-19 = coronavirus disease, CPRO = COVID-19 Pandemic Response Option, CWRD = Central and West Asia Department, EAL = emergency assistance loan, EARD = East Asia Department, PARD = Pacific Department, SARD = South Asia Department, SERD = Southeast Asia Department, SOV = sovereign operation, TA = technical assistance.

Figure 2.2: Comparison of Processing Time of COVID-19 Related and Pre-COVID-19 Sovereign Projects (months)

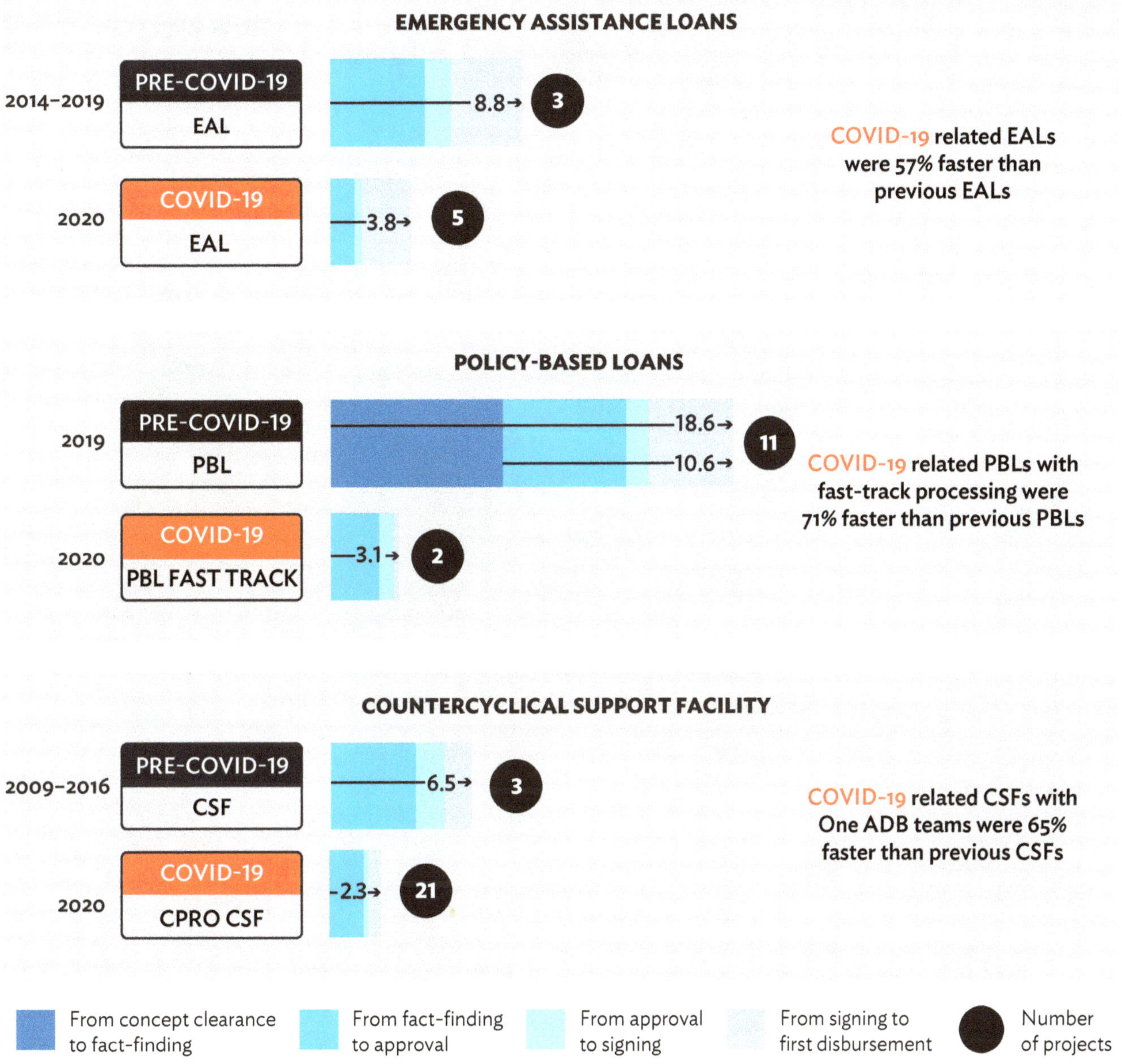

ADB = Asian Development Bank, COVID-19 = coronavirus disease, CPRO = COVID-19 Pandemic Response Option, CSF = Countercyclical Support Facility, EAL = emergency assistance loan, PBL = policy-based loan.

Note: The data set used to calculate the sovereign operations' processing time includes projects with complete milestones from concept clearance to first disbursement for regular project transations and from fact-finding to first disbursement for all COVID-19 related projects.

Sources: ADB Loan and Grant Financial Information Services as of 31 December 2020 and e-Operations for concept approval and fact-finding (end) dates.

SUMMARY OF ADB'S COVID-19 OPERATIONS IN 2020

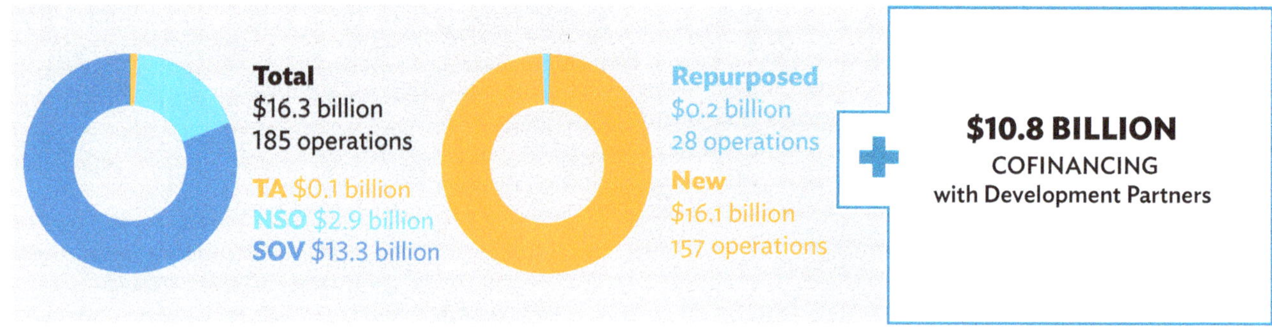

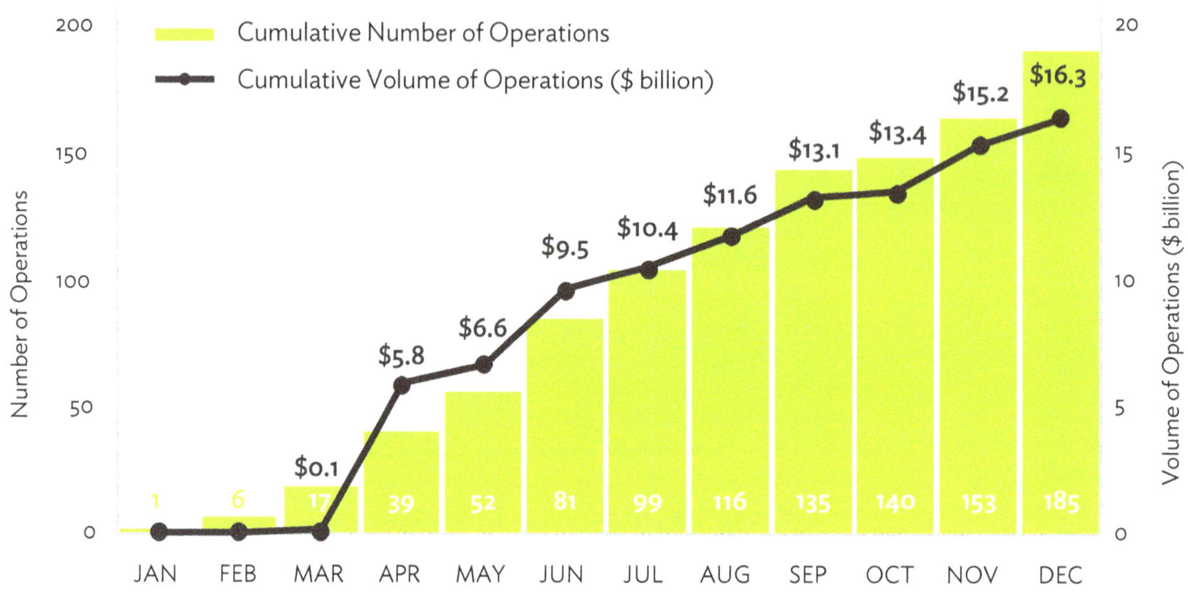

ADB = Asian Development Bank, APDRF = Asia Pacific Disaster Response Fund, CDF = contingent disaster financing, COVID-19 = coronavirus disease, CPRO = COVID-19 Pandemic Response Option, EAL = emergency assistance loan, PBL = policy-based loan, SOV = sovereign operation, TA = technical assistance.
Data on the number and volume of COVID-19 related 2020 commitments are as of 17 March 2021.

D. RESULT 3: KNOWLEDGE SOLUTIONS APPLIED IN RESPONSE TO COVID-19

43. Knowledge solutions have been a key part of ADB's assistance to help countries understand and address the complex and urgent challenges arising from the COVID-19 pandemic.

44. **COVID-19 hub site and policy database.** To provide a one-stop access point for ADB's knowledge solutions and publications, ADB launched a COVID-19 hub site in March 2020. Its 47 COVID-19 related publications were downloaded more than 120,000 times and generated more than 107,000 page views in 2020. Five knowledge products that examined the economic impacts of the pandemic were the most downloaded COVID-19 related publications of 2020. The open-access COVID-19 Policy Database, which holds details of ADB's COVID-19 operations and the policy measures implemented by its 68 member countries, also

79%
of ADB's primary clients found its COVID-19 knowledge solutions to be *excellent* (29%) or *good* (50%).

generated hundreds of thousands of page views and downloads. In a recent survey, 79% of ADB's primary clients found its COVID-19 knowledge solutions to be *excellent* (29%) or *good* (50%). Chapter 6 provides more details on ADB's performance as a knowledge organization.

45. **Regional knowledge products.** ADB's regional departments and the Private Sector Operations Department (PSOD) responded to the need for knowledge solutions tailored to the specific requirements of their DMCs. Boxes 2.3–2.5 and Appendix 2 provide illustrative examples.

Box 2.3: Knowledge Solution for the Kyrgyz Republic

The Asian Development Bank and the United Nations Development Programme conducted a joint assessment of coronavirus disease (COVID -19) in the Kyrgyz Republic. Their report, *COVID-19 in the Kyrgyz Republic: Socioeconomic and Vulnerability Impact Assessment and Policy Response*, informed the government's fiscal stimulus and health response packages and subsequent post-crisis planning.

Source: Asian Development Bank (Central and West Asia Department).

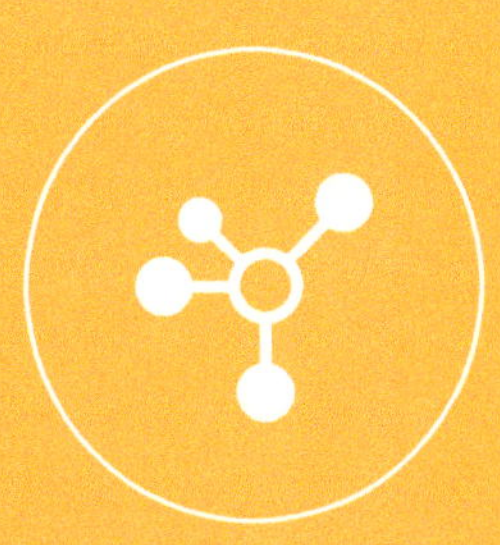

Box 2.4: Knowledge Solution for the Pacific

The Asian Development Bank brought together almost 100 country representatives and development partners in August 2020 to discuss advancements in vaccine development and supply chain innovations in the Pacific in the context of introducing a vaccine against coronavirus disease (COVID-19). Also discussed was how to leverage established regional cooperation channels to strengthen access and surveillance systems.

Source: Asian Development Bank (Pacific Department).

Box 2.5: Knowledge Solution to Map Global Supply Chains of Pandemic-Related Goods

The Asian Development Bank created a free interactive mapping tool for the supply chains of vital pandemic products to allow governments, banks, investors, health care professionals, and companies to trace every component used. About 13,000 visits have been made to the website, where users can search a database of more than 25,000 companies involved in supply chains around the world, including those for vaccines.

Source: Asian Development Bank (Private Sector Operations Department).

E. RESULT 4: COUNTRY PROGRAMS SUPPORTED BY ADB IN PARTNERSHIP

46. The scale, complexity, and speed of the COVID-19 response demanded deeper cooperation with and reliance on established and new partners. At least 91 partnerships with 113 or more development organizations, governments, civil society organizations (CSOs), and private sector entities improved the design and implementation of ADB-supported projects; leveraged knowledge, expertise, and additional resources; and enabled ADB to work more flexibly and responsively to bring solutions to the DMCs. ADB's CPRO facility, in particular, provided a platform for coordination with governments and bilateral and multilateral partners on COVID-19 response plans.

47. **Cofinancing partnerships.** ADB drew cofinancing resources from a wide range of partners, both traditional and new. By 31 December 2020, COVID-19 cofinancing commitments from multilateral and bilateral partners and from the private sector had reached $10.8 billion.[24] Most sovereign cofinancing ($8.2 billion) was for CPRO operations. Major cofinanciers include the Asian Infrastructure Investment Bank ($4.0 billion), the Japan International Cooperation Agency ($1.6 billion), and the Government of Australia ($1.1 billion). Partners also contributed to special funds and trust funds: Japan provided $75 million to the Asia Pacific Disaster Response Fund and $75 million for the Japan Fund for Poverty Reduction COVID-19 window; and the Republic of Korea contributed $1.8 million for a large regional TA COVID-19 response project through the e-Asia and Knowledge Partnership Fund. Some bilateral partners, such as Ireland and the People's Republic of China, also redirected earlier committed funds to COVID-19 related operations.

By 31 December 2020, COVID-19 cofinancing commitments had reached **$10.8 billion** from multilateral and bilateral partners and from the private sector.

48. New partnerships were entered into with Education Above All, a Qatari private foundation, (a $40 million grant commitment for primary education projects for children impacted by COVID-19); the Bill & Melinda Gates Foundation (vaccine development and deployment); the Bloomberg Philanthropies (sustainable and "blue" recovery from COVID-19); and the Rockefeller Foundation (sharing regional approaches to COVID-19 response). ADB-administered country- and region-specific trust funds were another important source of funding for the COVID-19 response.

49. **Procurement partnerships.** Soon after the declaration of the global pandemic, the United Nations Children's Fund (UNICEF)—the lead procurer of personal protective equipment (PPE) supplies for the United Nations and its partners—and ADB teamed up to strengthen the capacity of health systems in partner countries for the prevention of coronavirus transmission and the management of COVID-19 cases. Using each other's strengths, comparative advantages, and country teams, ADB and UNICEF quickly procured and delivered $18 million of critical supplies to 26 countries, playing an important role in limiting the pandemic's spread and impact in the region. The supplies included 44 million gloves, 39 million surgical masks, 4.6 million N95 respirator masks, 1 million gowns, 0.9 million face shields and goggles, and more than 9,400 oxygen concentrators.

50. Through pooled procurement, ADB's Procurement, Portfolio and Financial Management Department (PPFD) contracted the IDA Foundation, an independent social enterprise providing medicine and medical goods to health care organizations worldwide, and Medtechs Group, the world's largest supplier of PPE, to deliver $5.6 million items of PPE to 14 DMCs under regional TA, to address the outbreak of COVID-19 (Box 2.6). Working closely with IDA Foundation to perform due diligence, PPFD also registered about 250 supply partners for goods and services and created framework agreements for 10 health and vaccine specializations through a specially developed *response page to COVID-19*.

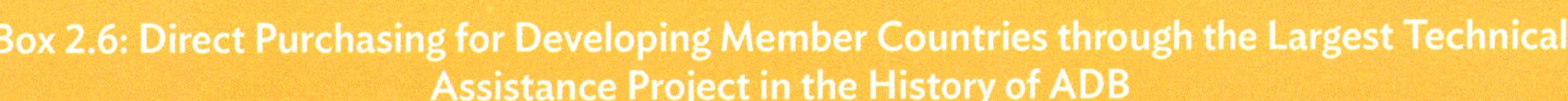

Box 2.6: Direct Purchasing for Developing Member Countries through the Largest Technical Assistance Project in the History of ADB

Procurement partnership. Half of the $41.6 million committed in 2020 to supply medical equipment and personal protective equipment and prepare for vaccine delivery was delivered through a procurement partnership with UNICEF.

One of the policy variations the Asian Development Bank (ADB) adopted in April 2020 that was instrumental in the speed and agility of ADB's response was to allow knowledge and support technical assistance to be used for the procurement of goods and equipment for coronavirus disease (COVID-19) response. For example, ADB's Regional Support to Address the Outbreak of Coronavirus Disease 2019 and Potential Outbreaks of Other Communicable Diseases Technical Assistance, committed on 25 February, quickly addressed market shortages of medical supplies to help developing member countries (DMCs) contain the outbreak of COVID-19. A total of $41.6 million was committed in 2020 to supply medical equipment and personal protective equipment (PPE) and prepare for effective vaccine delivery. Almost half of total assistance was delivered through a procurement partnership with the United Nations Children's Fund (UNICEF).

Notable results achieved under this project in 2020 include ADB's purchase and shipment of $12.63 million worth of PPE, medical equipment, and other supplies to 14 DMCs (of which 87% had been delivered by the end of 2020)[a]; and $1.3 million to Georgia and Turkmenistan (100% delivered). About $3.5 million was committed for consulting services to develop a communication strategy in the Philippines, prepare information and communication technology applications and solutions for a COVID-19 emergency medical response system in India, establish free online courses on COVID-19 to strengthen frontline workers' capacity, support vaccine-related assessments and strategies, and strengthen health systems in various DMCs.

[a] Afghanistan, Armenia, Azerbaijan, Cambodia, Kazakhstan, the Kyrgyz Republic, the Lao People's Democratic Republic, Mongolia, Myanmar, Pakistan, Papua New Guinea, Tajikistan, Uzbekistan, and Viet Nam.

Source: Asian Development Bank (Sustainable Development and Climate Change Department).

51. **Areas of partnership.** ADB entered into more than 91 COVID-19-focused knowledge-related partnerships. At least 18 of these were in the area of health, 9 focused on small and medium-sized enterprises (SMEs), 18 related to gender issues and social protection for the poor and vulnerable, and at least 46 related to the COVID-19 recovery. Box 2.7 illustrates ADB's knowledge partnership for health with the BMJ, a medical journal.

Box 2.7: Health Partnership with the BMJ to Create the COVID-19 ADB Information Center

The Asian Development Bank (ADB) formed a *partnership* with the BMJ, a weekly peer-reviewed medical research journal published by the British Medical Association, to help health professionals in ADB's regional member countries access the information they need quickly and efficiently so they can provide the best possible care for patients. The COVID-19 (coronavirus) ADB Information Centre provides free access to clinical decision support from BMJ Best Practice and online courses from BMJ Learning. Health care professionals can receive the latest guidance on diagnosis and treatment and essential skills on how to care for patients during an infectious disease pandemic, as well as information on prevention, diagnosis, epidemiology, prognosis, and complications.

Source: Asian Development Bank. 2020. *ADB Partners with BMJ on New COVID-19 Guidelines for Health Workers*. Manila.

52. **Partnerships in support of small and medium-sized enterprises.** ADB partnered with the United Nations Development Programme and other United Nations agencies, CSOs, and DMC government agencies to rapidly gather data and assess the socioeconomic impacts of COVID-19, especially on SMEs, trade, food security, livelihoods, and supply chains. Studies in Afghanistan, Cambodia, Indonesia, the Lao PDR, Mongolia, Myanmar, and the Philippines identified and recommended targeted policy measures to minimize the economic impact of COVID-19. ADB also partnered with the private sector to support SMEs (Box 2.8).

Enhanced health protocols. Members of the security staff check the temperature of anyone entering the Medanta Hospital in Gurugram, India (photo by Amit Verma).

Box 2.8: Joining Forces with HSBC to Support Trade in Critical Goods

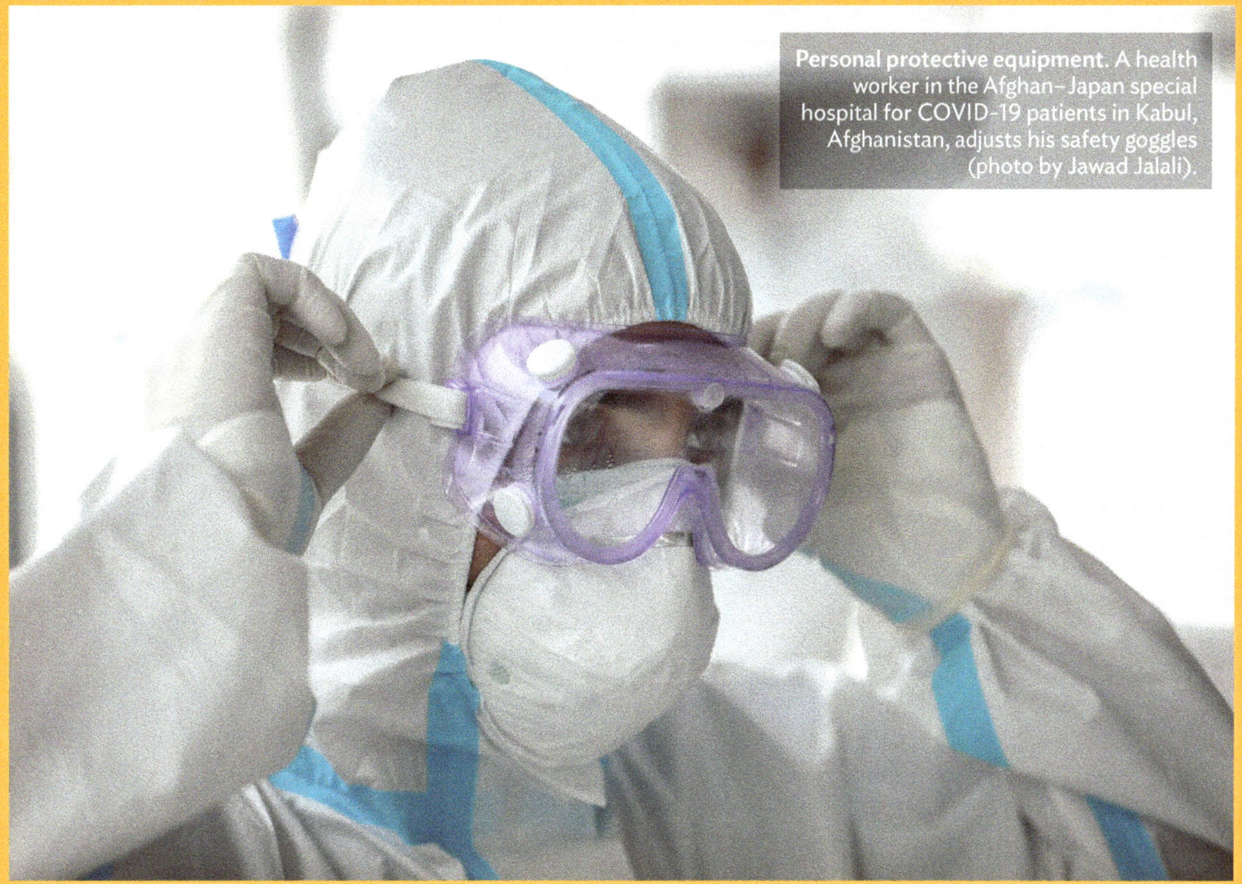

Personal protective equipment. A health worker in the Afghan–Japan special hospital for COVID-19 patients in Kabul, Afghanistan, adjusts his safety goggles (photo by Jawad Jalali).

On 29 July 2020, the Asian Development Bank (ADB) and HSBC launched a *program* to support up to $1.2 billion a year in trade by companies in Asia and the Pacific producing goods crucial to the fight against the coronavirus disease (COVID-19) pandemic. Targeted financing available through the new program will support trade in multiple sectors affected by the pandemic, including pharmaceuticals and apparel as well as critical medical supplies, providing much-needed support for small and medium-sized companies in the region. Partnerships like this one help close market gaps and fuel the necessary growth to build back the global economy and create jobs and prosperity.

Source: Asian Development Bank. 2020. *ADB, HSBC to Finance $1.2 Billion in Trade to Boost Supplies of Pandemic Products in Asia and the Pacific.* **Manila.**

53. **Partnerships for women and the poor and vulnerable.** Partnerships with women's organizations helped assess and counter some of the damaging impacts the pandemic had and continues to have on women. For example ADB worked with the Fiji Women's Rights Movement to publish an assessment of the impact of COVID-19 on women in Fiji. Collaboration with the National Center Against Violence, a CSO in Mongolia working to address and prevent domestic violence, is providing prevention awareness and virtual counseling support services to survivors of gender-based violence during the COVID-19 crisis. Partnerships with various organizations, such as the Cities Alliance, HelpAge International, Tsao Foundation, and the United Nations Development Programme, focused on social protection for the poor and vulnerable including the youth and the elderly. Box 2.9 describes social protection activities prioritizing women and the poor and vulnerable in Afghanistan.

Box 2.9: Social Protection in Afghanistan

Dealing with the pandemic. Doctors and health workers pose for a group photograph at the Afghan-Japan special hospital for COVID-19 patients in Kabul, Afghanistan (photo by Jawad Jalali).

The Asian Development Bank (ADB) supported Afghanistan's nationwide gender-sensitive public awareness campaign on coronavirus disease (COVID-19). The Ministry of Women Affairs and Ministry of Public Health partnered with mosques, educational institutions, and national print and broadcasting media to disseminate about 10 million informational documents related to COVID-19 across 34 provinces. In addition, the Ministry of Women Affairs collaborated with district governments in 26 provinces to distribute gender-sensitive information and sanitary kits and provide gender-sensitive services for women, particularly in hospitals with all women-only treatment facilities.

With the United Nations Children's Fund (UNICEF) and the World Health Organization, ADB provided and distributed essential medicines and medical equipment to all provinces in the second half of 2020 and strengthened the capacity of the national health system to respond to public health emergencies. A gender-sensitive resilience strategy is being developed that will include plans to improve women's access to sexual and reproductive health services and support mechanisms for victims of gender-based violence.

Source: Asian Development Bank (Central and West Asia Department).

54. **Partnerships for recovery.** ADB entered into partnerships with at least 40 organizations, including the Economic and Social Commission for Asia and the Pacific, the Institute for Fiscal Studies, the International Labour Organization, the Japan International Cooperation Agency, and WWF, covering the impact of COVID-19 on state-owned enterprises and related reforms, better governance for service delivery and policy making, strategies for building back better, financing options for long-term recovery, tax policies and tax administration in response to COVID-19, sustainable infrastructure for a green recovery, and the safe reopening of borders. ADB has also been working with other international organizations to facilitate vaccine procurement and distribution to its DMCs (Box 2.10).

Box 2.10: Collaboration on Vaccine Access and Distribution

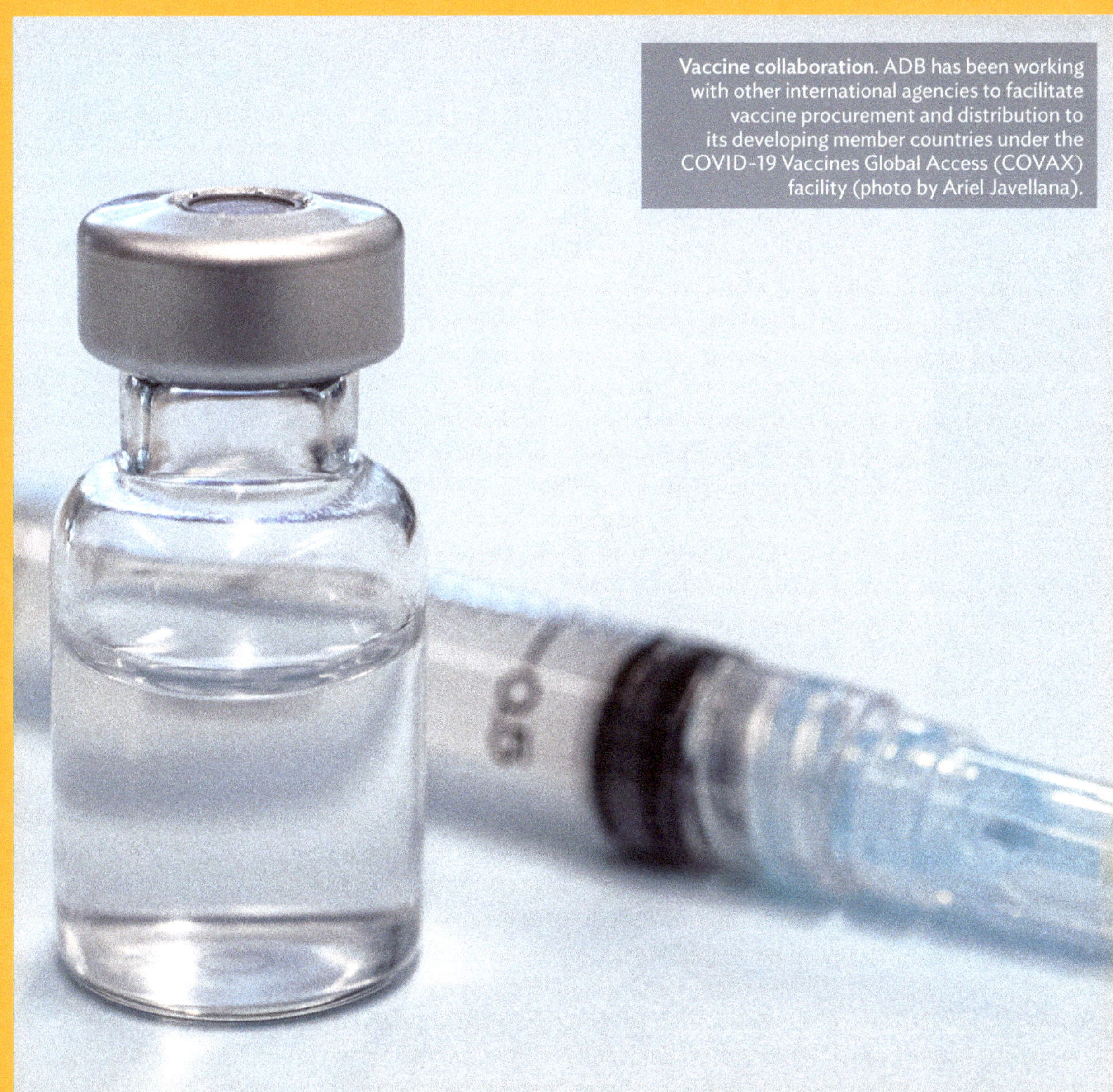

Vaccine collaboration. ADB has been working with other international agencies to facilitate vaccine procurement and distribution to its developing member countries under the COVID-19 Vaccines Global Access (COVAX) facility (photo by Ariel Javellana).

The Asian Development Bank (ADB) Asia Pacific Vaccine Access Facility (APVAX) relies on a regional framework of collaboration given the risks of cross-border outbreaks. ADB has been working with other international agencies to facilitate vaccine procurement and distribution to its developing member countries under the COVID-19 Vaccines Global Access (COVAX) facility. COVAX serves as the global platform for supporting the research and manufacturing of candidate vaccines, including negotiating their prices for access for both advanced and developing economies. It is coordinated by the World Health Organization; GAVI, the Vaccine Alliance; and the Coalition for Epidemic Preparedness Innovations (CEPI). ADB is also working with the United Nations Children's Fund (UNICEF), which is the lead global organization for freight, logistics, and storage of COVID-19 vaccines on behalf of the COVAX facility.

Source: Asian Development Bank. 2020. *ADB's Support to Enhance COVID-19 Vaccine Access*. Manila.

F. RESULT 5: DEVELOPMENT EFFECTIVENESS INTEGRATED IN PROJECT CYCLE

Identification, Design, and Preparation

55. **Identification, design, and preparation.** Ensuring development effectiveness throughout the project cycle for the record pandemic response operations implemented in 2020 was an integral part of ADB's day-to-day work. ADB's COVID-19 Pandemic Response Option (CPRO) operations adhered to stringent eligibility criteria, including requirements for DMCs to implement a COVID-19 pandemic response plan and to establish a dedicated CPRO results framework to clearly identify expenditure targeting to the poorest and most vulnerable groups. Consequently, almost 70% of the $16.3 billion in commitments targets the pandemic's health and economic impacts.[25]

56. CPRO operations provided a platform for dialogue with DMC government agencies on their COVID-19 response plans that resulted in stronger ownership and a high-quality response. For example, policy dialogue helped expand small business job-creation programs in Indonesia and design and implement a new small business employee wage subsidy in the Philippines. The CPRO also facilitated regular collaboration and timely discussions with key partners, such as the International Monetary Fund and the World Bank, maximizing synergies and avoiding overlap.

Approval

57. **At approval.** All COVID-19 response operations were approved with quality design following regular and enhanced standards in relation to design and monitoring frameworks (DMFs), poverty and social analysis, safeguards, procurement, and financial management. All have clear, quantifiable targets, measurement criteria, and monitoring and evaluation plans. Careful targeting meant that all CPRO operations were categorized *effective gender mainstreaming*. The number of social protection projects increased dramatically to 35 (30 for COVID-19 response) from 21 in 2017–2019.

Implementation and Monitoring

58. **Progress monitoring at the corporate level.** ADB enhanced corporate monitoring and evaluation of ongoing COVID-19 operations by providing weekly progress reports to the Board from March 2020. A dashboard to monitor the funds flow and usage of the $29 billion COVID-19 response package and *Asia Pacific Vaccine Access Facility (APVAX)* was also launched in May. Furthermore, ADB's Independent Evaluation Department (IED) introduced real-time evaluation of the design and implementation of COVID-19 operations to identify lessons on the relevance of ADB's support, the design and implementation of its operations, and ADB's preparedness.

59. **Monitoring and evaluation at the project level.** Social distancing and quarantine measures enacted by many DMCs made it extremely difficult for government staff and consultants to safely engage in monitoring and reporting activities in the field. Moreover, national and local government staff were often overwhelmed by competing demands. Consequently, ADB's operations departments had to innovate to optimize the implementation and monitoring of their ongoing projects and ensure accountable and effective use of resources. Box 2.11 describes the measures taken by the Southeast Asia Department and the South Asia Department, which together account for 72% ($7.3 billion) of the CPRO operations.

Post-completion Evaluation

60. **Completion and post-completion evaluation.** COVID-19 operations are reported on in five corporate reports planned for 2021, each of which has a different focus. The Annual Report offers a comprehensive overview of 2020 operations. The Annual Portfolio Performance Review gives a strategic overview and analysis of the performance trends, size, composition, and quality of ADB's active portfolio. The Development Effectiveness Review measures ADB's development effectiveness against indicators in the CRF. The Review of ADB's Comprehensive Response to the COVID-19 Pandemic Policy will provide lessons from implementing special policy variations launched in April. Finally, the IED's ongoing real-time formative evaluation report will focus on ADB's support for implementation to inform future COVID-19 support and post-completion evaluation of ADB's COVID-19 response policy variations upon completion of the initial 15-month period since their launch on 13 April 2020.

Box 2.11: Implementation Challenges and Responses by ADB Regional Departments

Remote working arrangements. Like many organizations, ADB utilized remote tools to ensure continued operations in support of its developing member countries (photo by Eric Sales).

The Southeast Asia Department made effective use of remote tools for review and due diligence missions. It enhanced headquarters–resident mission collaboration to support operations processing and administration while in-person review missions by headquarters-based staff were suspended, and processed disbursement using e-mail submission of withdrawal applications where the client portal for disbursement had not yet been rolled out. National policy committees, supported by subcommittees or technical working groups, received and reviewed quarterly progress reports and provided guidance.

Monitoring of progress toward design and monitoring framework indicators, conducted every 2 weeks, was a feature of the South Asia Department's COVID-19 Pandemic Response Option operations. All 11 planned reports for the 5 such operations committed in 2020 were completed within the year. Monthly, quarterly, and semiannual reports tracked progress toward health care interventions, socioeconomic measures for poor and vulnerable groups, and rebuilding the economy including through support to small and medium-sized enterprises.

Source: Asian Development Bank (South Asia Department and Southeast Asia Department).

G. RESULT 6: EXPECTED RESULTS OF GOVERNMENT PROGRAMS SUPPORTED BY ADB

61. Early in the pandemic, ADB's Strategy, Policy and Partnerships Department reviewed 16 COVID-19 response operations to derive a list of the most frequently used indicators of expected results as a basis for gauging the effectiveness of ADB's response. The DMFs and narrative of the project documents were found to contain 11 key types of indicators in 6 main categories: (i) beneficiaries of emergency social protection programs that alleviate the social and economic impact of COVID-19 and other public health emergencies; (ii) beneficiaries of improved health services related to the prevention, treatment, or control of COVID-19; (iii) infrastructure and related equipment and supplies to combat COVID-19; (iv) small and medium-sized enterprises (SMEs), including those owned and led by women, benefiting from COVID-19 related socioeconomic support; (v) improved capacities of health systems and communities to effectively control and manage COVID-19; and (vi) knowledge products to address the impacts of COVID-19.[26] The infographic shows aggregate expected results from six expected results categories, based on estimates in the reports and recommendations of the President, and actual project results as of 31 December from the e-Operations database. ADB's 2020 client perception survey also polled clients on the effectiveness of ADB's COVID-19 response. Eighty percent of clients knowledgeable of ADB's COVID-19 response rated the results achieved by ADB to address COVID-19 *excellent* (28%) or *good* (52%).

1.1 BILLION
PEOPLE BENEFITING FROM SHORT-TERM CASH OR IN-KIND COVID-19 RELATED SUPPORT

OF WHOM
528 MILLION ARE WOMEN

ADB-supported projects are helping mitigate income shocks caused by the pandemic through short-term cash transfers, wage subsidies, food rations, provision of essential commodities, and other social safety nets for affected households and individuals. ADB's COVID-19 support in this area targets women and the poor and other vulnerable groups, such as the elderly, people with disabilities, and people who have lost livelihoods or suffered significant income loss.

ADB committed a loan of $300 million to help the Government of Pakistan provide quick financial support to vulnerable and poor segments of society at the height of the pandemic. Through the **Pakistan Emergency Assistance for Fighting the COVID-19 Pandemic, 3.3 million** households (nearly 21 million people) benefited from at least one form of cash or in-kind support under emergency social protection schemes.

Source: Asian Development Bank (Central and West Asia Department).

8.4 MILLION
PEOPLE BENEFITING FROM IMPROVED HEALTH SERVICES INCLUDING TESTING OF 7.6 MILLION

AND

32 IMPROVED TESTING SERVICES

10 QUARANTINING SERVICES

38 TREATMENT SERVICES

ADB is supporting improved testing services through the procurement of **79** PCR (polymerase chain reaction) machines and **2,020,418** testing kits, and upgrading and construction of **132** laboratories; and improving quarantining services by helping construct or upgrade **586** isolation units and **9,095** quarantine centers and screening facilities. Treatment services are also expected to be improved with ADB support through the construction or upgrading **1,606** hospitals and **3,551** critical care units equipped with **192,021** hospital beds and procurement of emergency medical equipment and supplies including **15,019** ventilators, **84 million** items of personal protective equipment, **303 million** units of antiviral medication, and **320 million** basic hygiene products.

The **Bangladesh COVID-19 Response Emergency Assistance Project**, committed in April 2020, supports the procurement of equipment and supplies; upgrading of health and testing facilities; and strengthening of systems and community capacities for COVID-19 surveillance, prevention, and response. More than **2.1 million** patients have benefited from improved COVID-19 related health services.

Source: Asian Development Bank (South Asia Department).

4.4 MILLION
BUSINESSES, INCLUDING SMES BENEFITING FROM COVID-19 RELATED SUPPORT

OF WHICH

1.4 MILLION
ARE WOMEN-OWNED OR -LED SMEs

ADB is supporting the provision of credit to boost the working capital of businesses including small and medium-sized enterprises (SMEs) and microenterprises. ADB's nonsovereign COVID-19 related operations have also expanded their scope to provide working capital to businesses in the health; energy; and agriculture, natural resources, and rural development sectors during the pandemic. Besides on-lending to businesses, ADB is supporting the provision of tax breaks and incentives, rent subsidies, reductions in import tariffs and tariffs on utilities and other goods and services, tax payment deferrals, and loans for businesses.

To help the Government of the Kyrgyz Republic cope with the pandemic, ADB committed $500 million in loan and grant financing to supply health sector needs, ensure social protection for vulnerable people, support SMEs and the economy, and build resilience to shocks. The **Kyrgyz Republic COVID-19 Active Response and Expenditure Support Program** provided support to **416,947** businesses, of which **125,084** are led by women.

Source: Asian Development Bank (Central and West Asia Department).

2.6 MILLION HEALTH WORKERS WITH IMPROVED ABILITY TO MANAGE COVID-19

OF WHOM **1.6 MILLION** ARE WOMEN

ADB support is being used to train **28,573** health workers (of whom **10,915** are women) in infection prevention and control, including the testing and treatment of COVID-19 patients; help ensure **29,502** health workers (of whom **24,487** are women) have access to fully functioning medical equipment and facilities for infection prevention; and provide **2,509,773** health workers (of whom **1,536,230** are women) with financial incentives such as higher pay, bonuses, honoraria, and insurance coverage.

The **Tajikistan COVID-19 Active Response and Expenditure Support Program**, supported by a $50 million grant from ADB, helped pay for a 100% salary increase for **8,617** frontline medical staff directly managing COVID-19 cases, of whom **6,894** were women.

Source: Asian Development Bank (Central and West Asia Department).

595 DMC-RESPONSIVE KNOWLEDGE PRODUCTS AND SERVICES

SUPPORTING **COVID-19** RESPONSE

Knowledge solutions form an integral part of the pandemic response. ADB is developing knowledge products to help understand and devise strategies to address the impacts of the pandemic on the health of people, businesses, and economies and to help developing member countries recover from the crisis.

The $100 million **Georgia COVID-19 Active Response and Expenditure Support Program** supports the government's efforts to set up a web page dedicated to COVID-19 (www.StopCoV.ge) that includes non-pharmaceutical interventions and health standards protocols. The website provides government institutions and the general population with information on COVID-19, including risk communication, epidemiology, and outbreak-control mechanisms for different groups. It is available in the Abkhaz, Armenian, Azeri, English, and Georgian languages.

Source: Asian Development Bank (Central and West Asia Department).

H. RESULT 7: POST-PANDEMIC RECOVERY INITIATED DURING PANDEMIC RESPONSE

62. **Shift to recovery begins.** The initial focus on emergency projects gradually gave way to an emphasis on building back smartly and sustainably to support a longer-term vision for a green, inclusive, and resilient recovery. At ADB's Fifty-Third Annual Meeting, held virtually on 17–18 September, President Asakawa signaled the shift to post-pandemic recovery, vowing that ADB would be developing Asia's steadfast *partner for recovery* from COVID-19. He outlined a plan to ensure societies are resilient, sustainable, and climate-smart. The five-point recovery plan emphasizes deepening regional cooperation and integration, addressing inequality, building a green and resilient recovery, harnessing digitalization, and strengthening domestic resource mobilization.

63. **Project pipeline refocused toward recovery.** As governments began to recalibrate their priorities, operations departments revisited most ongoing and pipeline projects to build in a recovery focus. In Sri Lanka, for example, ADB doubled the size of two projects—one that will extend loans to revive liquidity-starved small and medium-sized enterprises (SMEs), and another to refurbish secondary school information and communication technology (ICT) labs and support remedial learning. ADB's agriculture and natural resources operations in Southeast Asia are developing new businesses to meet the DMCs' pandemic recovery and economic development demands, such as community-based tourism for COVID-19 recovery in Cambodia and agro-enterprise development in the Philippines. Policy-based lending is seeking to contribute to climate finance, and urban and water projects are building in marine life and biodiversity conservation components. Chapter 9 discusses how ADB plans to address ongoing and new challenges in 2021 to reinvigorate progress toward the Sustainable Development Goals (SDGs) agenda.

64. **Guidance notes developed to support recovery.** ADB's sector and thematic teams also worked together to discuss lessons learned from COVID-19 operations and consider how to build on successes for a post-pandemic recovery. They condensed these ideas into a series of *guidance and technical notes* to help countries grasp the opportunities the unprecedented disruption of COVID-19 provides to address deep-seated problems and support recovery in sectors such as finance, education, and transport. *Accelerating Climate and Disaster Resilience and Low-Carbon Development through the COVID-19 Recovery*, for example,

The five-point recovery plan emphasizes deepening regional cooperation and integration, addressing inequality, building a green and resilient recovery, harnessing digitalization, and strengthening domestic resource mobilization.

presents a framework to help decision-makers prioritize a package of recovery interventions that will collectively achieve recovery, climate, and resilience objectives; and *COVID-19 Recovery: A Pathway to a Low-Carbon and Resilient Future* presents a step-wise approach to designing a low-carbon and resilient recovery that addresses vulnerabilities and mainstreams resilience to help manage future shocks.

65. **Vaccine facility launched.** Promoting safe, equitable, and effective access to vaccines is a top priority for ADB's COVID-19 recovery efforts. ADB has been working closely with development partners to bring safe, effective, and affordable COVID-19 vaccines to its DMCs and strengthen their vaccine delivery systems. On 11 December, this effort received a $9 billion boost with the establishment of ADB's *Asia Pacific Vaccine Access Facility (APVAX)*, an unambiguous signal that the recovery phase has begun.

On 11 December, this effort received a $9 billion boost with the establishment of ADB's Asia Pacific Vaccine Access Facility (APVAX), an unambiguous signal that the recovery phase has begun.

66. APVAX provides a comprehensive framework and resource envelope for supporting developing Asia's vaccine access, using two complementary components. The rapid response component will support critical vaccine diagnostics, procurement of vaccines, and transporting vaccines from the place of purchase to ADB's DMCs, while the project investment component will support investments in systems for successful distribution, delivery, and administration of vaccines along with associated investments in building capacity, community outreach, and surveillance. This financing will be provided in close coordination with other development partners including the COVID-19 Vaccines Global Access (COVAX) facility; GAVI, the Vaccine Alliance; the World Bank Group; and WHO.

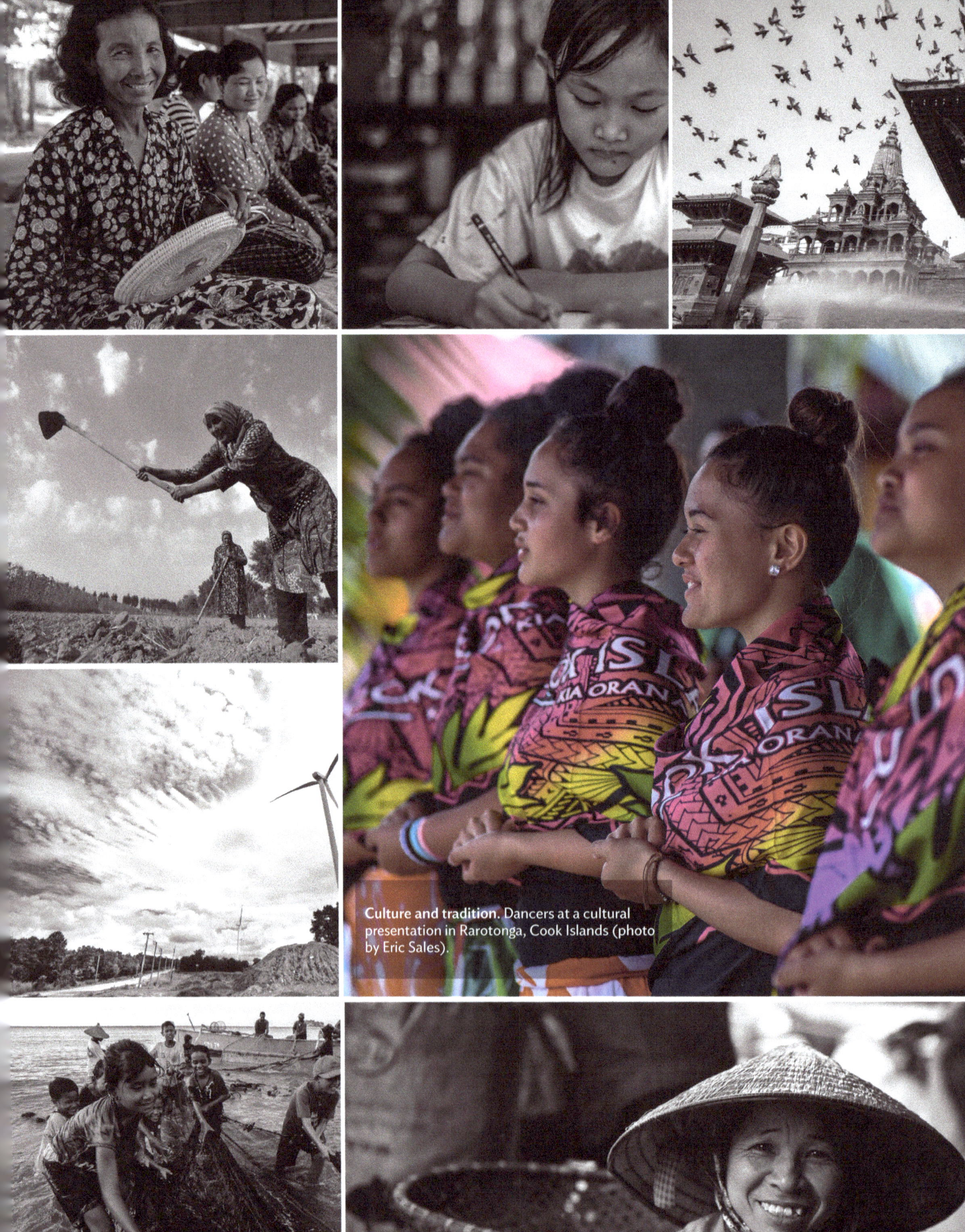

Culture and tradition. Dancers at a cultural presentation in Rarotonga, Cook Islands (photo by Eric Sales).

CHAPTER 3

DEVELOPMENT FINANCE AND STRATEGIC ALIGNMENT

As a development bank, ADB provides needed finance to its developing member countries in line with its vision of a prosperous, inclusive, resilient, and sustainable Asia and the Pacific free of extreme poverty. Strong and diverse partnerships with private and public financing institutions and traditional and new development partners help catalyze and mobilize financial resources for this development.

ADB is focusing its investments on Strategy 2030's seven operational priorities in alignment with the Sustainable Development Goals and is working to efficiently disburse financing to its developing member countries.

DEVELOPMENT FINANCE

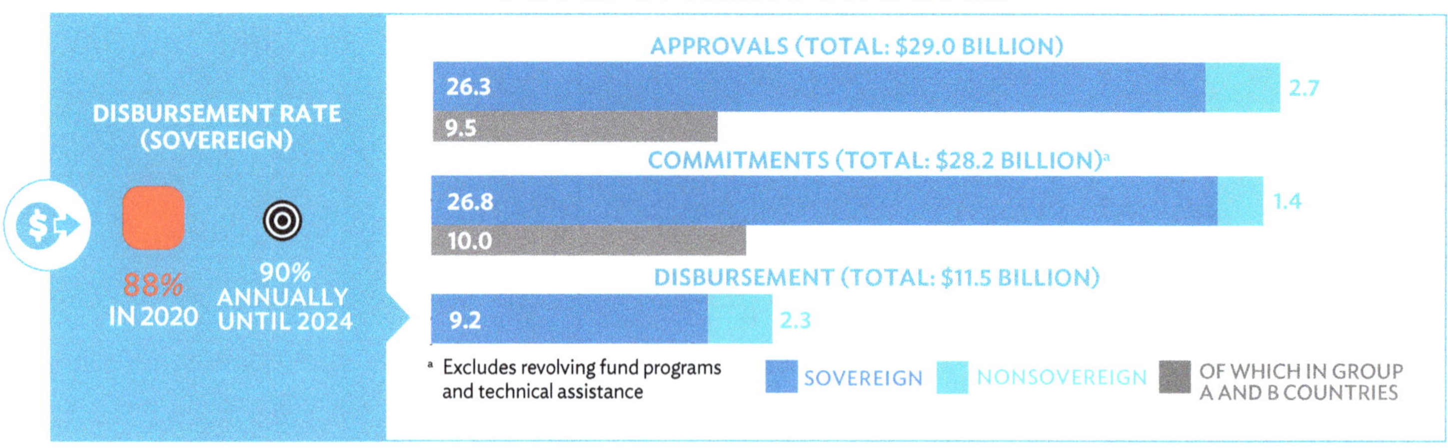
DISBURSEMENT RATE (SOVEREIGN)
88% IN 2020
90% ANNUALLY UNTIL 2024
APPROVALS (TOTAL: $29.0 BILLION)
26.3
2.7
9.5
COMMITMENTS (TOTAL: $28.2 BILLION)[a]
26.8
1.4
10.0
DISBURSEMENT (TOTAL: $11.5 BILLION)
9.2
2.3
[a] Excludes revolving fund programs and technical assistance
SOVEREIGN
NONSOVEREIGN
OF WHICH IN GROUP A AND B COUNTRIES

PROGRESS ON STRATEGY 2030 TARGETS AND PRIORITIES

2020 PROGRESS ON STRATEGY 2030 TARGETS

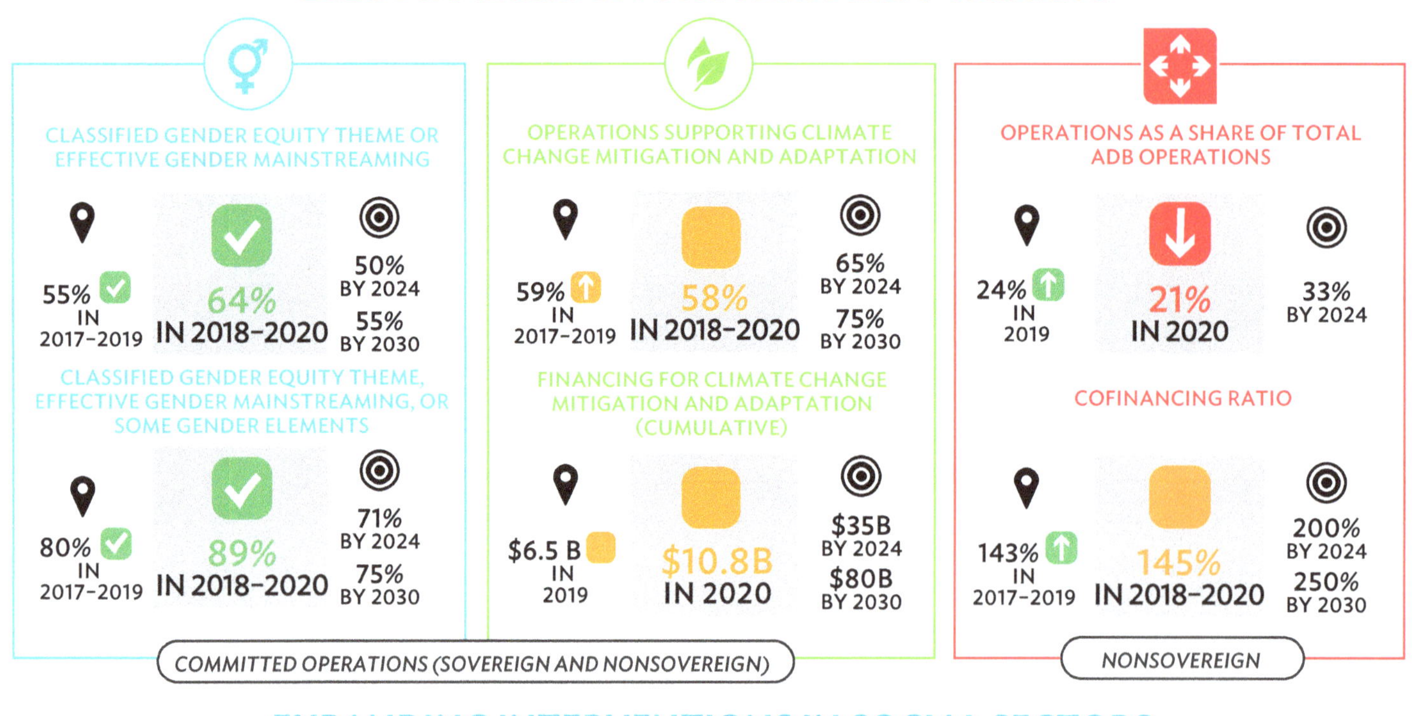
CLASSIFIED GENDER EQUITY THEME OR EFFECTIVE GENDER MAINSTREAMING
55% IN 2017–2019
64% IN 2018–2020
50% BY 2024
55% BY 2030
CLASSIFIED GENDER EQUITY THEME, EFFECTIVE GENDER MAINSTREAMING, OR SOME GENDER ELEMENTS
80% IN 2017–2019
89% IN 2018–2020
71% BY 2024
75% BY 2030
OPERATIONS SUPPORTING CLIMATE CHANGE MITIGATION AND ADAPTATION
59% IN 2017–2019
58% IN 2018–2020
65% BY 2024
75% BY 2030
FINANCING FOR CLIMATE CHANGE MITIGATION AND ADAPTATION (CUMULATIVE)
$6.5 B IN 2019
$10.8B IN 2020
$35B BY 2024
$80B BY 2030
COMMITTED OPERATIONS (SOVEREIGN AND NONSOVEREIGN)
OPERATIONS AS A SHARE OF TOTAL ADB OPERATIONS
24% IN 2019
21% IN 2020
33% BY 2024
COFINANCING RATIO
143% IN 2017–2019
145% IN 2018–2020
200% BY 2024
250% BY 2030
NONSOVEREIGN

EXPANDING INTERVENTIONS IN SOCIAL SECTORS

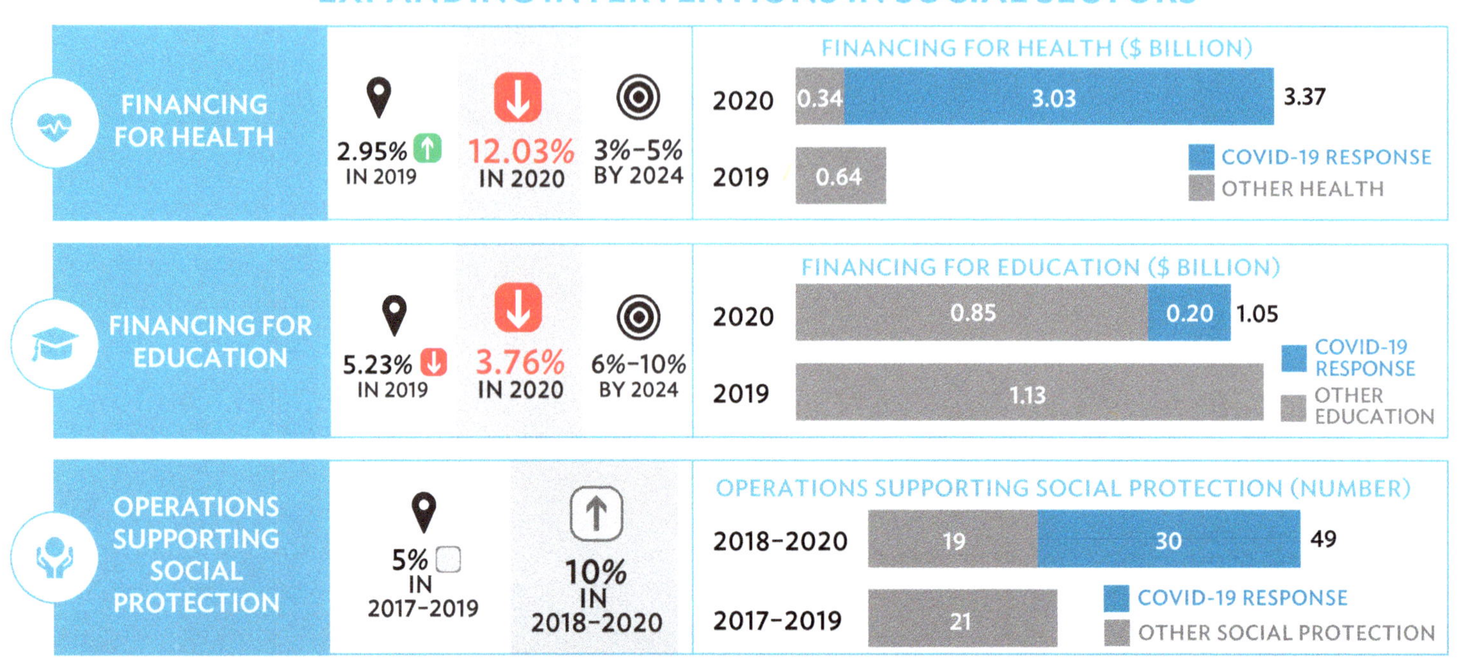
FINANCING FOR HEALTH
2.95% IN 2019
12.03% IN 2020
3%–5% BY 2024
FINANCING FOR HEALTH ($ BILLION)
2020
0.34
3.03
3.37
2019
0.64
COVID-19 RESPONSE
OTHER HEALTH
FINANCING FOR EDUCATION
5.23% IN 2019
3.76% IN 2020
6%–10% BY 2024
FINANCING FOR EDUCATION ($ BILLION)
2020
0.85
0.20
1.05
2019
1.13
COVID-19 RESPONSE
OTHER EDUCATION
OPERATIONS SUPPORTING SOCIAL PROTECTION
5% IN 2017–2019
10% IN 2018–2020
OPERATIONS SUPPORTING SOCIAL PROTECTION (NUMBER)
2018–2020
19
30
49
2017–2019
21
COVID-19 RESPONSE
OTHER SOCIAL PROTECTION

A. DEVELOPMENT FINANCE MOBILIZED AND TRANSFERRED

67. ADB approved $29.0 billion and committed $28.2 billion for operations financed by regular and concessional ordinary capital resources and Asian Development Fund grants in 2020, both new highs.[27] The urgent need to respond to the COVID-19 pandemic (Chapter 2) changed plans and patterns in both finance mobilization and transfers. Pandemic-related support drove an increase in the volume of sovereign commitments that more than compensated for the decline on the nonsovereign side. Almost half of 2020's total commitments ($13.5 billion) went to 66 operations to help DMCs deal with the disease and its socioeconomic effects. Almost one-third of the total ($10.0 billion) financed 105 operations in concessional assistance countries, 4 percentage points less than in 2019. Of the 183 ADB operations committed overall, 136 were sovereign, 38 nonsovereign, and 9 project-readiness financing facilities.

68. ADB suspended its disbursement volume targets for 2020 because of this critical shift from regular pipeline investment projects and programs to respond to the pandemic. The year's $9.2 billion in disbursements for sovereign projects and results-based lending were nonetheless 88% of the original $10.5 billion target and only 2 percentage points short of the 90% target rate.

B. PROGRESS ON STRATEGY 2030 TARGETS AND PRIORITIES

69. ADB found opportunities within rapid pandemic response operations to pursue Strategy 2030 priorities. These operations prioritized safeguarding and furthering gender equality, and helped push gender mainstreaming indicators to another record level during 2018–2020. To meet critical DMC pandemic crisis needs, ADB reoriented and swiftly approved and committed operations focused on health and social protection, including extensive support for DMCs' pro-poor countercyclical expenditure programs. Despite efforts to integrate climate actions into pandemic response operations where appropriate, progress toward the Strategy 2030 climate targets slowed. The share of climate change mitigation and/or adaptation operations was roughly unchanged from 2019, and the climate financing committed dropped by one-third. Both remain *on track but watch.*

70. The DMC government requirements of direct financial support during the crisis also affected other Strategy 2030 objectives. The higher number of sovereign operations that resulted (a 23% increase from 2019) left ADB *off track* on its target for increasing the nonsovereign share of its overall operations committed, even though the number of nonsovereign operations remained constant at 38. ADB mobilized a high share of long-term cofinancing for its nonsovereign operations relative to its own lending in 2020, achieving a cofinancing ratio of 212%. However, this did little to move the 3-year rolling ratio on which targeting is based because of the year's comparatively small absolute ADB nonsovereign and catalyzed financing amounts.

71. ADB's agile and appropriate reply to an unprecedented health emergency in its DMCs, many with already challenged health care capacity, led to a fivefold increase in financing for health operations during the year. This overshot the 3%–5% range targeted for more normal times, and performance on this indicator is therefore considered to have declined and fallen *off track*. ADB committed 35 social protection operations in 2020, exceeding the 21 commitments in the previous 3 years combined, of which 30 directly addressed the effects of the pandemic. On the other hand, some education projects planned for the year were postponed in favor of other COVID-19 response operations.

C. IN FOCUS

1. Accelerating Gender Equality and Tackling Climate Change

Gender mainstreaming

72. ADB raised gender mainstreaming in its operations to new historic highs for the fifth consecutive year (Figure 3.1). The share of operations committed in 2018–2020 and classified *gender equity as a theme* (GEN) or *effective gender mainstreaming* (EGM) grew by 9 percentage points, as did those classified GEN, EGM, or *some gender elements.* This focus on gender equality intensified in both sovereign and nonsovereign operations (Figure 3.2). The 65% share for GEN and EGM operations in overall financing in 2018–2020 was also a new record, although the share of this financing allocated to concessional assistance operations declined by 4 percentage points to 67%.

Figure 3.1: Gender Mainstreamed ADB Operations, 2016–2020

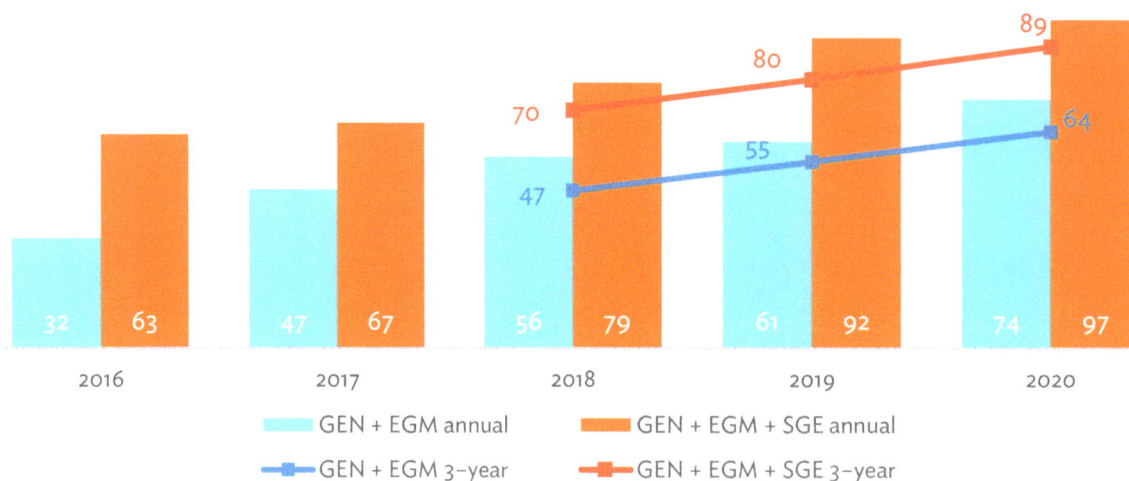

(%)

	2016	2017	2018	2019	2020
GEN + EGM annual	32	47	56	61	74
GEN + EGM + SGE annual	63	67	79	92	97
GEN + EGM 3-year			47	55	64
GEN + EGM + SGE 3-year			70	80	89

Figure 3.2: ADB Operations Supporting Gender Equality by Classification, 2016–2020

(%)

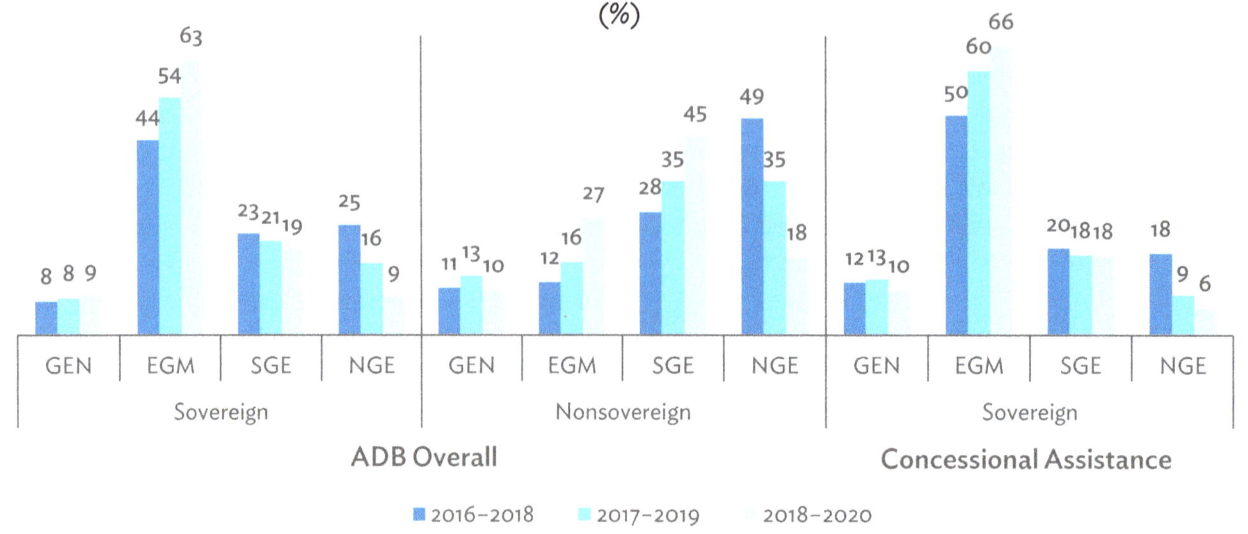

ADB = Asian Development Bank, EGM = effective gender mainstreaming, GEN = gender equity as a theme, NGE = no gender elements, SGE = some gender elements.

Source: Asian Development Bank (Sustainable Development and Climate Change Department).

73. **Strong gender focus of COVID-19 response.** ADB's COVID-19 response operations powered its latest gender mainstreaming performance in multiple ways. Health operations, which tripled during the year and 89% of which were gender mainstreamed, included support such as female-size PPE and gender-sensitive treatment areas. All 26 COVID-19 Pandemic Response Option (CPRO) Countercyclical Support Facility operations were also rated EGM.

74. **Social and health support for women.** The CPRO operations helped DMCs implement effective programs to expand access by women to social assistance. This included cash and in-kind transfers to households and individuals and concessional loans and wage subsidies for micro, small, and medium-sized enterprises owned or led by women. Measures also included insurance, transport, and cash incentives for health care workers, the majority of whom are usually women. Intersecting inequalities because of the age, disabilities, ethnicity, or social status of women were also addressed, as were the needs to support women affected by violence and keep reproductive health services available throughout the pandemic. Several DMC governments will improve the collection of sex-disaggregated data on program beneficiaries under the operations, which they can use to inform gender-based budgeting in their regular programs once the pandemic has ended.

75. **Helping women's businesses survive and rebound.** Gender mainstreamed operations that played a part in ADB's COVID-19 response in the private sector extended working and operating capital to help women-owned and -led micro, small, medium-sized enterprises—including businesses providing critical goods and services—to sustain operations, rebound from the crisis, and grow. A few projects took steps to create more opportunities for women to find quality jobs. These included an operation to support dairy farmers and improve food security in Indonesia. That will provide 250 positions for women as dairy sales agents, jobs traditionally dominated by men. In addition, 1,000 female smallholder farmers will receive technical and financial literacy training.[28]

76. **Good returns on internal ADB mainstreaming push.** The concerted efforts by ADB Management and staff continued to mainstream gender equality considerations across all sectors. The gains were particularly notable in industry and trade, finance, and energy operations. Guidance by ADB's gender specialists has helped project teams halve the share of operations with no gender elements, leaving only 3% of all those committed by ADB in 2020 still in that category. Details on gender equality results are in Chapter 1.

Supporting climate change mitigation and adaptation

77. **Steady share of climate operations.** Despite prioritization of urgent pandemic response needs, the proportion of committed ADB operations during 2018–2020 that supported climate change adaptation and/or mitigation was roughly unchanged from the previous period at 58% (Figure 3.3). ADB's performance on climate is thus rated *on track but watch.* The climate operation share of concessional assistance held steady at 63%. The number of committed climate change operations grew from 83 in 2019 to 93 in 2020 but formed a smaller proportion of a portfolio enlarged by the many health and public sector management (PSM) interventions required to address the COVID-19 crisis. Only about 17% of the pandemic response projects had climate change as a focus, although climate operations constituted 75% of the rest of those committed during the year. More operations (44) supported both climate change mitigation and adaptation in 2020 than in the 4 prior years.

Figure 3.3: ADB Operations Supporting Climate Change Mitigation and Adaptation, 2016–2020 (%)

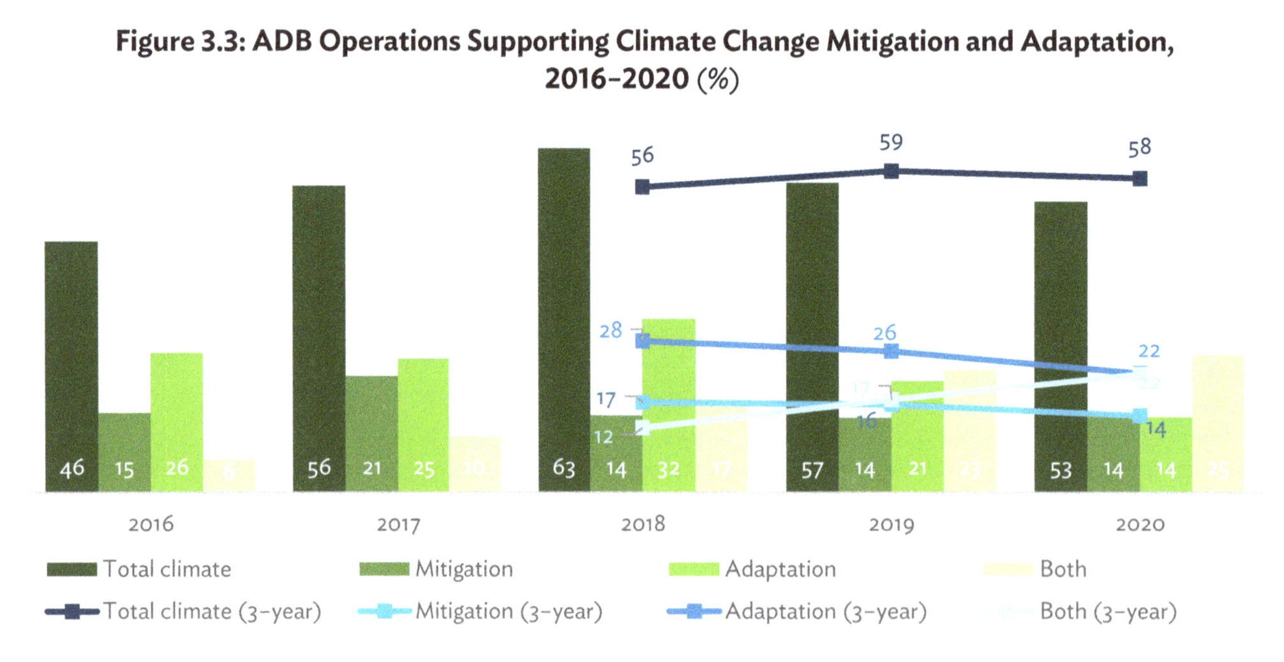

Source: Asian Development Bank (Sustainable Development and Climate Change Department).

78. **Climate financing progress slows.** After reaching its 2015 commitment to double annual climate investments from $3 billion in 2014 to $6 billion by 2020 a year early in 2019, ADB's climate financing commitments dipped to $4.3 billion in 2020 as resources were diverted from scheduled operations to help DMCs deal with the pandemic crisis.[29] The 2019 financing level was almost sustained for interventions tackling mitigation and adaptation together (Figure 3.4). The $3.1 billion committed to these operations in 2020 accounted for the largest share of overall climate financing (73%) in 5 years. The largest commitment in this category was $500 million in mitigation and adaptation financing for a regional rapid transit rail system to be built in India's National Capital Region.[30] Financing was lower by 66% for operations addressing mitigation alone, and by 59% for those targeting only adaptation. In 2019, two large commuter rail transport projects, one in the Philippines ($1.3 billion) and one in India ($926 million), contributed almost half (43%) of ADB's total mitigation financing committed, but no such large infrastructure projects were committed in 2020. In 2020, the largest commitment of financing focused specifically on climate mitigation was $123 million for a project that will build a system of elevated walkways in Metro Manila, Philippines.[31]

Figure 3.4: ADB Financing for Climate Change Mitigation and Adaptation, 2019–2020
($ billion)

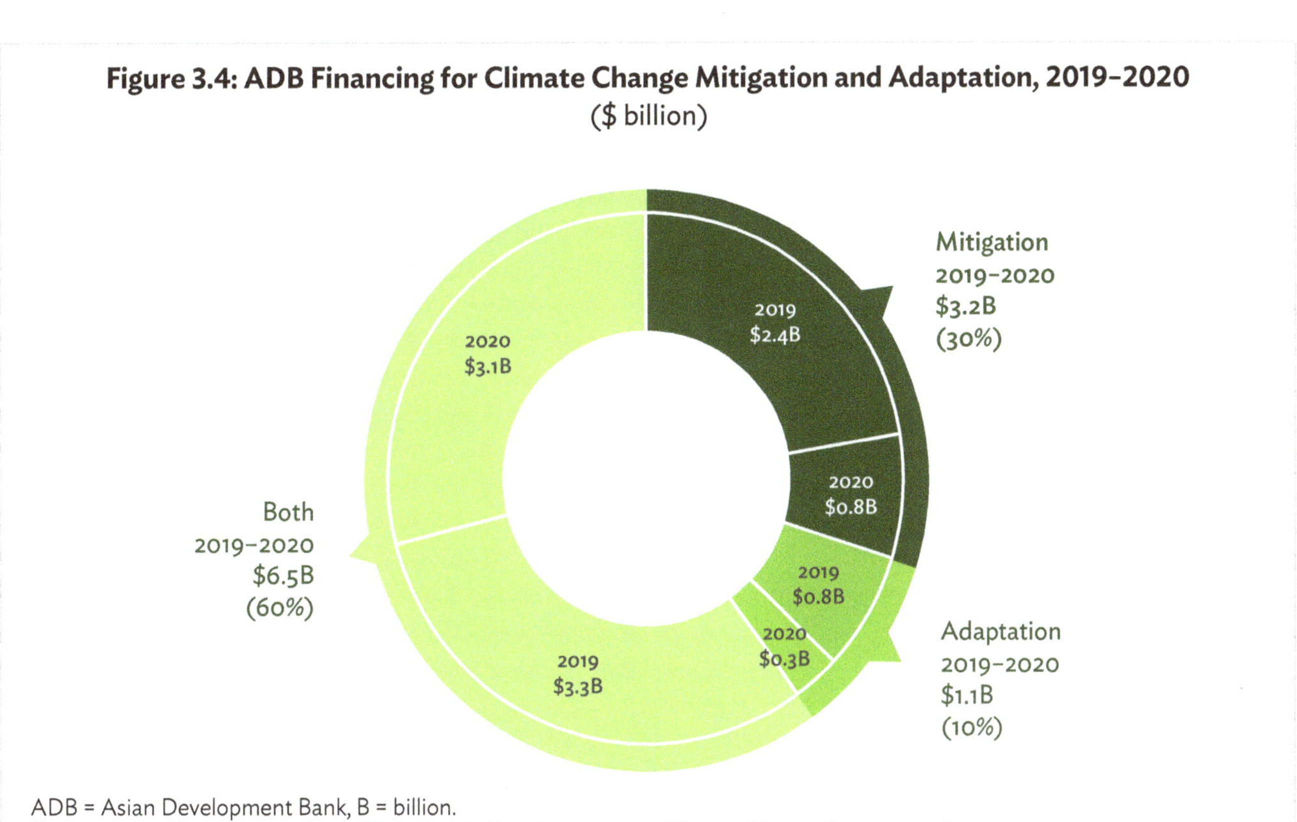

ADB = Asian Development Bank, B = billion.
Source: Asian Development Bank (Sustainable Development and Climate Change Department).

79. **Climate change features integrated into pandemic response**. Where possible and practical, ADB integrated climate change mitigation and/or adaptation into its emergency pandemic operations. Examples include projects in Afghanistan and Pakistan that will build energy-efficient hospitals and medical facilities that make use of solar panels. These operations also feature components to provide off-grid renewable energy systems in remote areas.[32] The Pakistan project will invest at least $10 million to reduce emissions and provide $1 million in climate change adaptation financing for climate-resilient features in 1,000 new WHO-standard public water, sanitation, and hygiene facilities in remote rural communities and informal urban settlements.

80. **Innovations in climate mitigation projects.** ADB will help finance Uzbekistan's first public–private partnership renewable energy project.[33] The 100-megawatt solar power plant will be built with Canadian Climate Fund cofinancing by the Nur Navoi Solar Foreign Enterprise Limited Liability Company and give the country's rural areas better access to a reliable source of affordable renewable energy through a 25-year power purchase agreement. In another ADB climate change-related intervention, a 26.6-kilometer bus rapid transit corridor in Karachi will employ an innovative waste-to-fuel scheme to reduce carbon emissions and air pollution in Pakistan's largest city.[34] The operation, committed in 2020 with Green Climate Fund cofinancing, is also expected to cut commuting time and vehicle operating costs.

81. **Investing in ocean health and sustainable blue economies.** The ocean and coasts provide essential ecosystem services including carbon storage and oxygen generation. In 2019, ADB announced its Action Plan for Healthy Oceans and Sustainable Blue Economies, which targets expanding financing and technical assistance (TA) for ocean health and marine economy projects to $5 billion between 2019 and 2024, including cofinancing from partners.[35] In 2019–2020, ADB committed a cumulative total of $863 million toward this target.

2. Mobilizing Private Sector Resources for Development

82. ADB was *on track but watch* to meet the Strategy 2030 nonsovereign cofinancing ratio target of 200% by 2024. The ratio held roughly steady at 145% during 2018–2020. A total of $9.1 billion in long-term financing was mobilized during this 3-year period against $6.3 billion in net ordinary capital resources (less risk transfers). At 212%, catalyzation by ADB's nonsovereign operations, particularly for COVID-19 response, was far higher in 2020. However, the pandemic-related falloff in the absolute amount dedicated to nonsovereign operations meant 2020's greater leverage did little to increase the rolling 3-year average performance (Figure 3.5).

Figure 3.5: Long-Term Cofinancing for Nonsovereign Operations, 2017–2020

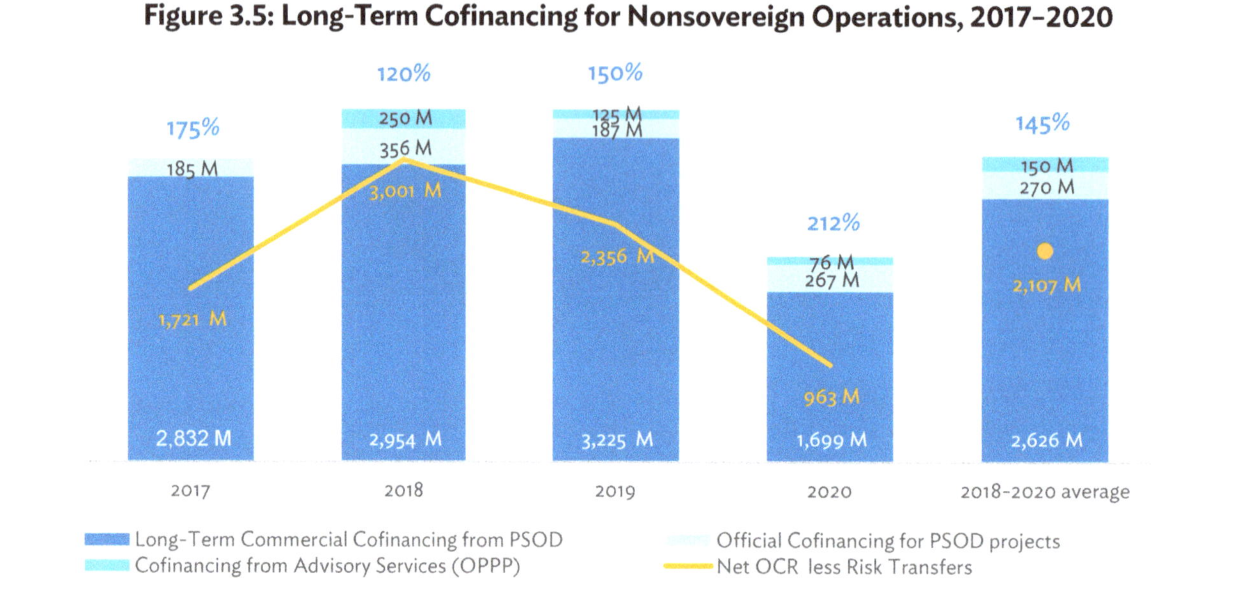

ADB = Asian Development Bank, M = million, OCR = ordinary capital resources, OPPP = Office of Public-Private Partnership, PSOD = Private Sector Operations Department.
Note: The corporate results framework indicator excludes financing for nonsovereign revolving funds.
Source: ADB (Private Sector Operations Department and Office of Public–Private Partnership).

3. Expanding Interventions in Social Sectors

83. Financing rose in two of the three social sectors and areas in which Strategy 2030 commits ADB to expanding its investments. Education, health, and social protection are important pathways toward achieving operational priority 1: addressing remaining poverty and reducing inequalities. ADB's COVID-19 response demonstrated its ability to swiftly ramp up support in the social sectors when needed.

84. **Health financing share quadrupled.** Of the $3.37 billion ADB committed for 44 health sector operations in 2020, 90% ($3.03 billion) was for 41 operations that support DMCs' COVID-19 response (Figure 3.6). More than half of the total health financing ($2.02 billion) and about half of the health operations (24) were countercyclical financing support provided through ADB's CPRO. For 11 COVID-19 response operations ($528 million) health was the primary sector of focus. Chapter 2 provides further details on ADB's COVID-19 response operations.

85. Health plays a secondary part in three non-COVID-response (other health) multisector operations that ADB committed during the year. One project will finance a portion of conditional health and education cash transfers that the national Philippines' Pantawid Pamilyang Pilipino Program (4Ps) is to extend to poor households.[36] Two ADB investments went to private equity funds that are in turn expected to provide growth capital to companies that can meet the demand for higher-quality and more affordable health care in DMCs including India, the People's Republic of China (PRC), and Viet Nam.[37]

Figure 3.6: Financing for and Number of Health Operations, 2016–2020

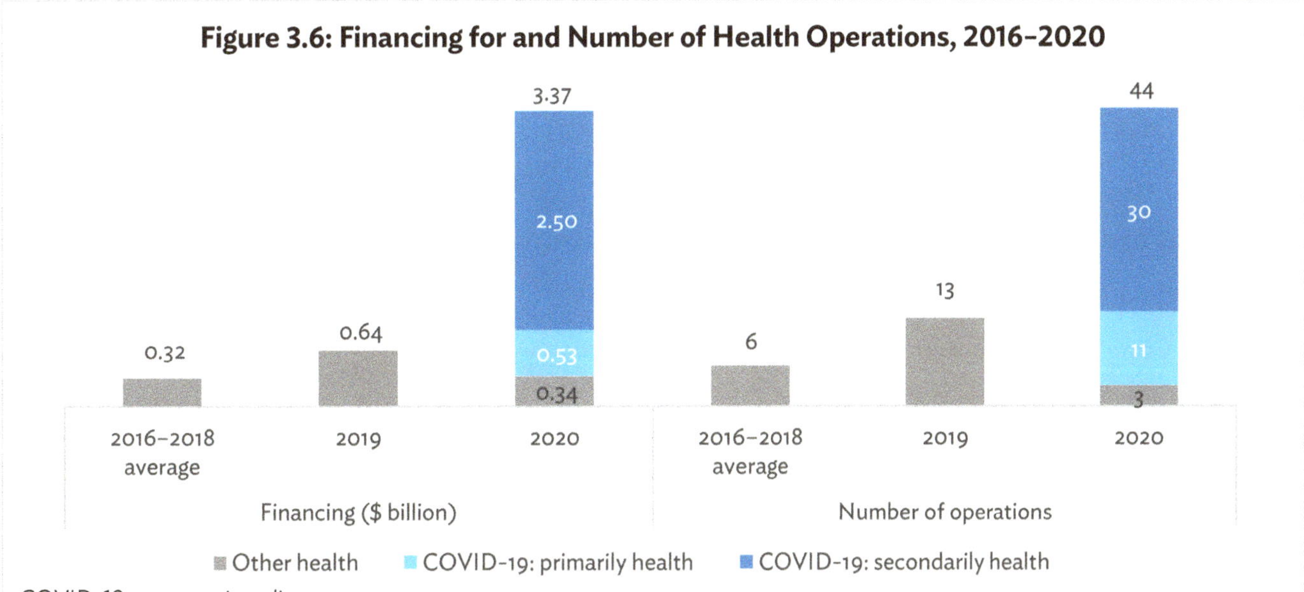

COVID-19 = coronavirus disease.
Note: Financing for health is computed based on financing allocated to health subsectors. COVID-19 operations that are "primarily health" are those whose subsectors are exclusively health subsectors. COVID-19 operations that are "secondarily health" are those that had health subsectors among other sectors. "Other health" are the remaining health operations that did not support COVID-19 response.

86. **Increase and shift in focus of social protection operations.** The COVID-19 crisis reemphasized the importance of social protection. Unlike in previous years, where education (particularly technical and vocational education and training) dominated, most social protection operations in 2020 supported countercyclical expenditure programs that expanded targeted social protection measures to mitigate the pandemic's impacts on the poor and other vulnerable groups (Chapter 2). Social protection was the primary focus of 10 of the 35 operations committed during the year. The rest combined social protection aims with inclusive access to economic opportunities (24) or with the creation and expansion of these opportunities (1). One operation, for example, will develop the innovation and entrepreneurial skills needed for untrained workers, returning migrants, farmers, women, and other socially vulnerable groups to find employment in emerging industries in the large PRC municipality of Chongqing.[38]

87. **Pandemic-driven change in operational planning.** An implementation assessment of ADB's 2014–2020 social protection operational plan concluded that the new plan must add a focus on inclusive post-pandemic recovery in the wake of massive socioeconomic setbacks to the existing Strategy 2030 operational priority of addressing the remaining poverty and inequality in the DMCs.[39] This will require special attention to the new poor and the growth in vulnerability the crisis has created.[40] Economic activities must be restarted, employment and livelihoods restored, disruptions in sectors overcome, and opportunities provided by digital technology to improve service delivery and raise efficiencies.

88. **Education operations postponed.** DMCs' requests for urgent support to address the COVID-19 emergency's health, economic, and social protection challenges led to postponement of several education operations in the pandemic's early stages. The $1.05 billion in education commitments during 2020 were nonetheless down only slightly from $1.13 billion in 2019. They dropped further, however, as a percentage of the significantly higher total ADB financing committed. Lending was highest for secondary education (48%), followed by broader education sector development (24%). The project pipeline indicates an increase in education lending in 2021. This will include financing in the strategically crucial areas of distance learning and the building of digital skills.

89. **Supporting continuity of quality education during the pandemic and beyond.** In Sri Lanka, the shift to e-learning and televised classes forced by COVID-19 caused access challenges, particularly in rural areas where internet connectivity, digital devices and platforms, and the training required to deliver and participate in distance education are lacking. To help the government ensure the continuity of upper secondary education during the pandemic, ADB reoriented the $400 million results-based lending program it had under preparation for secondary education system reforms. This program includes blended learning (a combination of online learning, educational television and radio programs, remote learning, and classroom-based face-to-face approaches); multimodal learning; and remedial education to help fill learning gaps from school closures.

90. **Matching skills to labor market needs.** Two other operations committed during 2020 aim to develop skills to match emerging labor market needs in Central Asia Regional Economic Cooperation Program countries. ADB's first education operation in Georgia combines policy reforms with investments in systems and infrastructure, such as establishing sector skills organizations and upgrading vocational education and training (VET) institutes, to build a more responsive VET network that promotes job creation in high-value sectors.[41] The program also focuses on increasing the participation of women in nontraditional fields of VET and in the labor market, and encouraging stronger private sector involvement in VET. In Tajikistan, ADB committed a project to help returning migrants and unemployed workers acquire skills and find jobs at home and overseas during and after the COVID-19 pandemic.[42]

4. Alignment with the Seven Operational Priorities

91. **Increased alignment.** A larger share of the operations committed in 2020 aligned with four of the seven operational priorities of Strategy 2030. These were operational priority (OP) 1: addressing remaining poverty and reducing inequalities, OP2: accelerating progress in gender equality, OP6: strengthening governance and institutional capacity, and OP7: fostering regional cooperation and integration (Figure 3.7). An equal share of operations aligned with OP4: making cities more livable; and a lower share with OP3: tackling climate change, building climate and disaster resilience, and enhancing environmental sustainability; and OP5: promoting rural development and food security. Fluctuation in alignment is expected year on year. Results for 2020 were calculated using an interim methodology to be replaced in 2021 based on enhanced methodologies for identifying the alignment with each operational priority. Chapter 1 highlights results by ADB operations under each priority.

92. **Focus on poverty reduction and inclusiveness to combat pandemic's effects.** The proportion of committed ADB operations supporting poverty reduction and inclusiveness was up by 5 percentage points to 79% in 2018–2020 from the preceding 3-year period. ADB's pandemic response program in 2020 was primarily responsible. Operations during the year were more heavily concentrated than previously on social protection and gender equality. The share of operations committed in fragile and conflict-affected situations (FCAS) and small island developing states (SIDS) was greater than in previous years. An enhanced methodology for measuring this indicator will be completed in 2021.

Figure 3.7: ADB Operations Aligned with Each Strategy 2030 Operational Priority, 2020
(%)

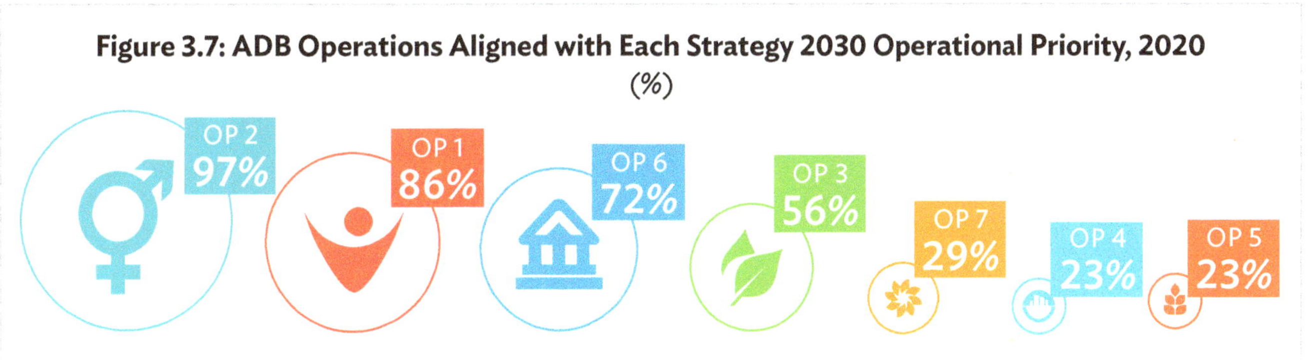

93. **More projects supporting disability inclusion.** The share of committed operations in 2020 supporting disability inclusion was 32% (55 of 173) (Figure 3.8), up from 22% in 2019.[43] Three operations (2% of 2020 commitments) were rated *principally or significantly disability inclusive.* One, a project in the Philippines, will build a new system of elevated walkways with elevators and ramps to address the needs of the older persons, pregnant women, people with disabilities, and people traveling with small children (endnote 31). The other two, a regional rapid transit rail system to be built in India's National Capital Region and a bus rapid transit system to be built in the city of Karachi, Pakistan, are designed to improve mobility and economic opportunities for differently abled people, which in India will include providing them with hearing, visual, and/or mobility aids (endnotes 30 and 34). Eleven operations (6% of 2020 commitments) have *some disability inclusion elements* and involve the differently abled in project planning, monitoring, or providing feedback. Six of these are COVID-19 response projects that explicitly identify people with disabilities as target beneficiaries or considered their needs during the planning of the project. Most operations (41 of 55, or 24% of 2020 commitments overall) have enabling conditions for disability inclusion without setting specific disability inclusiveness indicators or explicitly including people with disabilities in their design, monitoring, or implementation.

Figure 3.8: ADB Operations that Support Disability Inclusion, 2020
(%)

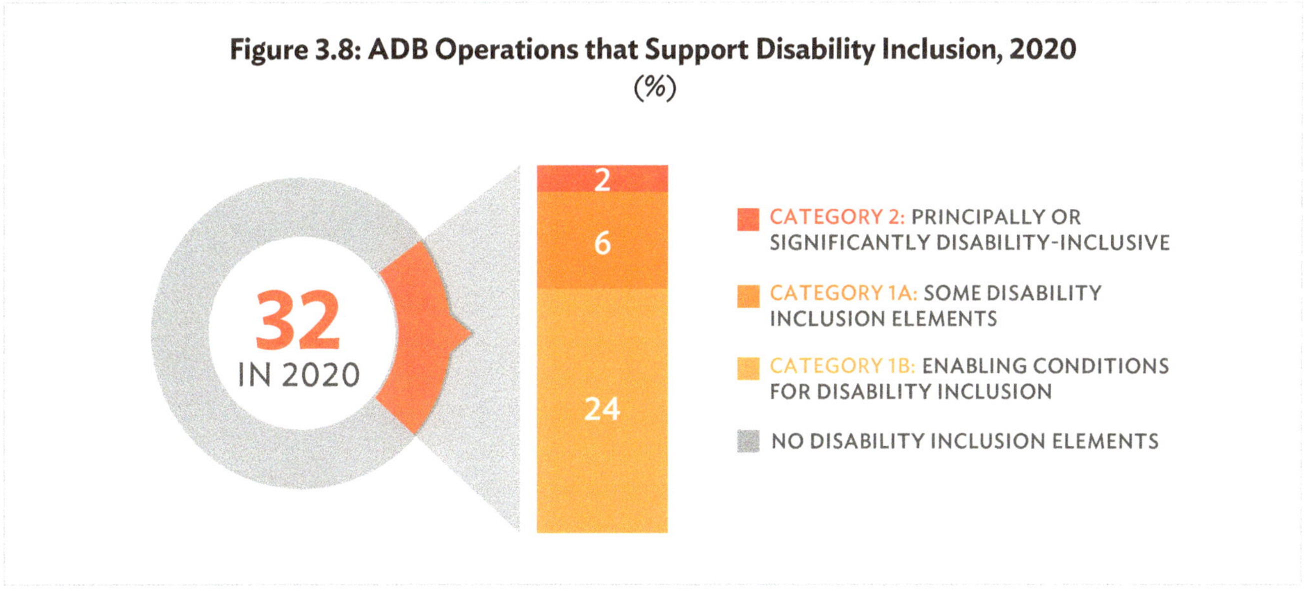

5. Quality Infrastructure: Green, Resilient, Inclusive, and Sustainable

94. Under Strategy 2030, ADB supports quality infrastructure that is green, resilient, inclusive, and sustainable. In 2019, ADB developed a new methodology to assess the quality of infrastructure sector projects based on 16 criteria organized around these four principles, and highlight good practices. The indicator was piloted on projects approved in 2019 and 2020. In 2020, all committed infrastructure projects reviewed met minimum quality standards, and 98% included at least one good practice related to the criteria for the green, resilient, inclusive, and sustainable principles. More than 70% included at least two good practices for each principle.

6. Supporting the Sustainable Development Goals

95. ADB's pandemic response measures in 2020 enlarged the share of its operations linked to Sustainable Development Goal (SDG) 8 for decent work and economic growth (Figure 3.9). Building resilient infrastructure as captured under SDG 9 continued to be prominently represented in the year's commitments. The percentage of operations linked to SDG 3 for good health and well-being rose from 12% in 2019 to 27% in 2020 as ADB helped DMCs respond to the COVID-19 crisis. The pandemic's influence was also evident in the rising share of programs with links to eradicating poverty (SDG 1) and reducing inequality (SDG 10). An emphasis on gender dimensions in the CPRO operations, including those with health and social protection elements, led to a higher number of links to SDG 5 (gender equality). ADB also provided resources to help eliminate violence against women and girls (SDG target 5.2), particularly given the spikes in domestic violence brought on by the pandemic lockdowns.

Figure 3.9: Alignment of ADB Commitments with the Sustainable Development Goals, 2020
(%)

SECTOR-BASED GOALS

CROSS-CUTTING THEMATIC GOALS

ADB = Asian Development Bank.
Based on enhanced project classification tagging system rolled out on 1 April 2019.

Rail connectivity. Families enjoy a comfortable train ride on the ADB-supported railway connecting the cities of Dali and Lijiang in the People's Republic of China (photo by Deng Jia).

Water supply and sanitation. The Community-Based Infrastructure Service Sector Project in the Kyrgyz Republic aims to improve the living and health conditions of the poor by providing an adequate safe water supply and proper sanitation (photo by Vyacheslav Oseledko).

CHAPTER 4
SOVEREIGN OPERATIONS

ADB is pursuing sustainable development and quality growth with its developing member countries. Success in this effort demands high-level performance throughout the project cycle. This chapter assesses the quality of the design and implementation of ADB's sovereign operations in 2020 and examines whether those recently completed performed as planned. The main factors affecting the relevance, efficiency, effectiveness, and likely sustainability of these completed operations are analyzed.

PROJECTS APPROVED IN 2020

DESIGN QUALITY OPERATIONS THAT ARE IMPLEMENTATION-READY

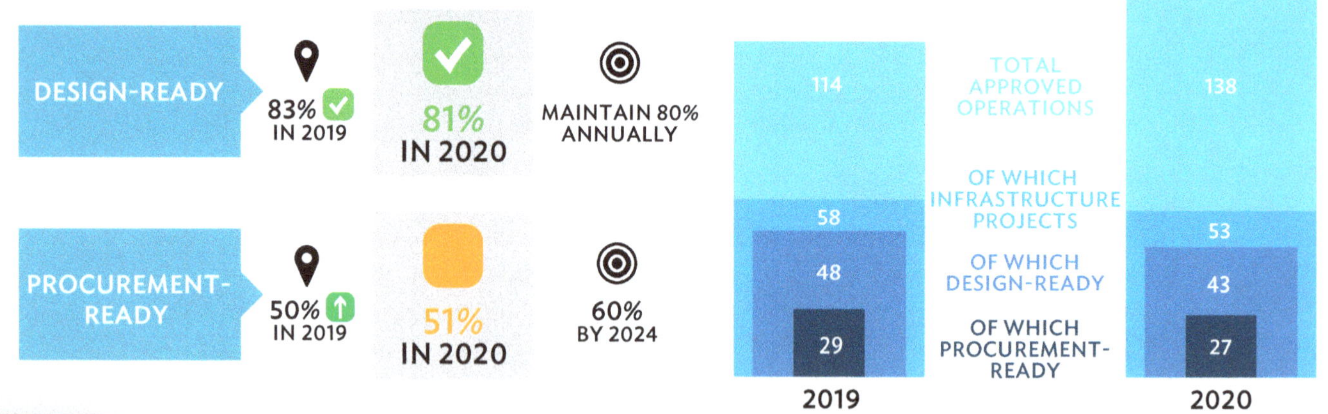

PROJECTS UNDER IMPLEMENTATION IN 2020

ENSURE SATISFACTORY IMPLEMENTATION OF PROJECTS

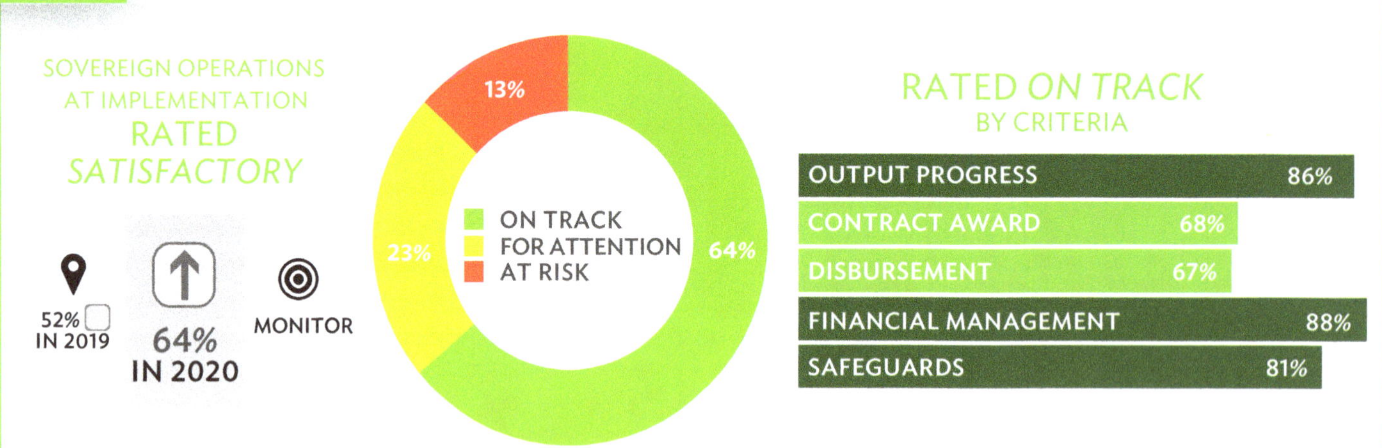

COMPLETED OPERATIONS VALIDATED 2018-2020

DEVELOPMENT RESULTS DELIVERED TO CLIENTS AND BENEFICIARIES

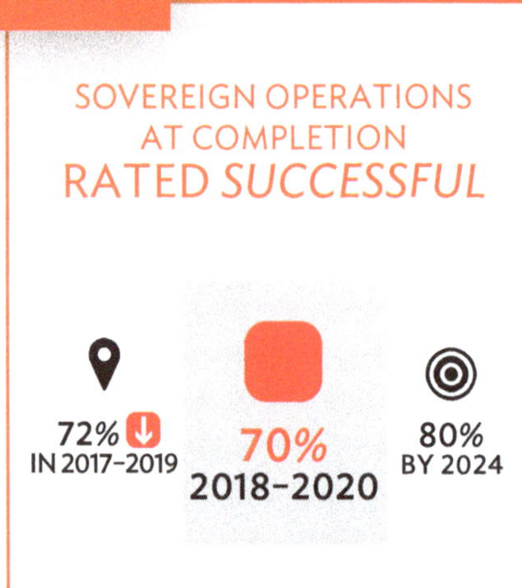

SOVEREIGN OPERATIONS AT COMPLETION RATED SUCCESSFUL
72% IN 2017–2019
70% 2018–2020
80% BY 2024

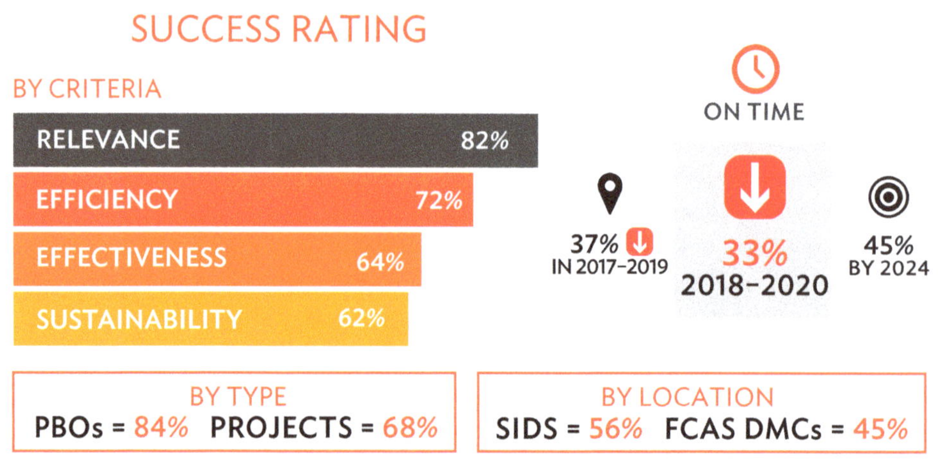

DMC = developing member country, FCAS = fragile and conflict-affected situations, PBO = policy-based operation, SIDS = small island developing state.

A. READINESS AT DESIGN STAGE

96. Sovereign infrastructure project readiness remained steady in 2020. Design readiness was on target. Of the 43 design-ready projects, 65% had detailed engineering designs when approved and all had completed preliminary designs and specifications. The share of procurement-ready projects was *on track but watch* because at 51%, it advanced only 1 percentage point toward the 2024 target of 60%.

97. ADB's regional departments continued to use project-readiness financing facilities to support DMCs with project preparation. Nine were committed in 2020 versus 10 in 2019. Project pandemic-related travel restrictions in some countries prevented the preparation of detailed designs for infrastructure projects, especially for those in the Pacific and Southeast Asia. In some DMCs, it is not possible to achieve project readiness because national regulations prohibit investment in detailed designs or issuance of bidding documents before a project is committed. The *2020 Annual Portfolio Performance Report* provides further details on implementation readiness.

B. IMPLEMENTATION PROGRESS

98. The purpose of ADB's project performance rating system is to identify risks and issues early in project implementation so that corrective actions can be taken to address them. To be able to do this more effectively, ADB improved the rating methodology in 2019, strengthening the assessment requirements for three of the five criteria: output progress, financial management, and safeguards compliance. In 2020, the share of operations rated *satisfactory* (on track) increased to 64% from 52% in 2019 when the new methodology was piloted and introduced. Performance on the three strengthened criteria improved because project teams addressed performance issues that the more rigorous and precise methodology had flagged. Project teams updated project design and monitoring frameworks (DMFs) to reflect approved changes to project scope, ensured more timely and complete submission of financial reporting, and addressed safeguards compliance issues. However, delays in project implementation brought about by the COVID-19 crisis caused the contract awards and disbursements of many projects to fall behind schedule. Ratings for these two criteria declined, especially for disbursement, which dropped from 75% in 2019 to 67% in 2020.

C. PERFORMANCE OF COMPLETED OPERATIONS

99. The share of the completed sovereign operations rated *successful* in reporting years (RY) 2018–2020 remained relatively constant and was 10 points short of the 2024 target of 80%. The main factor keeping success rates low was a 10-percentage-point drop in the effectiveness criterion to 64% in RY2018–2020 from the baseline in RY2016–2018. This general decline was widespread and affected the infrastructure and public sector management (PSM) sectors and both standalone investment projects and policy-based operations. Of the three other equally weighted criteria used to determine a project or program's overall success, completed sovereign operations performed best on relevance (82%) and efficiency (72%). However, efficiency ratings declined by 3 percentage points and the share of projects that closed within 1 year of the targeted date or earlier was *off track*. The 33% average for on-time completion was a historic low. Sustainability was nearly unchanged at 62% compared with 61% in the previous period.

100. Policy-based operations, including sector development programs, continued to outperform the overall sovereign success rate, but their share has become steadily smaller. Investment projects, on the other hand, maintained the largest share (more than 80% over the 3 reporting periods) while continuing to return a weakening average success rate, which reached 68% in RY2018–2020.

101. For results stories, performance summaries, and details on gender equality results, refer to Chapter 1. For the performance in fragile and conflict-affected situations (FCAS) and small island developing states (SIDS), refer to Chapter 8.

D. IN FOCUS

1. Main Factors Affecting Sovereign Success Rates

102. **Overall drop in effectiveness ratings.** The main factor responsible for lower success rates was a continuing decline in the effectiveness of completed operations. The share of operations rated *effective* dropped a further 4 percentage points from RY2017–2019 to 64%, reaching a cumulative 10-percentage-point drop from the baseline in RY2016–2018. Effectiveness has trended downward since 2014–2016. Although policy-based operations continued to outperform the average, overall effectiveness ratings declined for the third consecutive reporting period to 72% in RY2018–2020 from 76% in RY2017–2019 and 77% in RY2016–2018. Throughout the three reporting periods, the education sector contributed a disproportionate share to *less than effective* policy-based operations. Noteworthy factors reported to have influenced performance on this criterion included overly ambitious objectives, underestimated project costs, insufficient safeguards management, inadequate implementation capacity, poor performance of contractors, and reduced scope or loan cancellation because of loss of client commitment. The decline in effectiveness ratings was widespread and affected infrastructure and PSM operations, which together account for 69% of completed sovereign operations.

103. **Lower effectiveness of infrastructure projects.** For infrastructure projects, effectiveness ratings continued to weaken (to 68% from 71% in RY2017–2019). Of the 18 infrastructure projects rated *less than successful* and *unsuccessful*, 16 fell short on effectiveness, including 6 in the transport sector, 5 in water and other urban infrastructure and services, 4 in energy, and 1 in information and communication technology (ICT). For these operations, reported factors included the partial delivery of targeted outputs and outcomes was attributed to design deficiencies, institutional capacity constraints, and cost overruns. Figure 4.1 provides a breakdown by criterion of the success rates of sovereign operations.

104. **Public sector management operations also less effective on average.** About 71% of PSM operations were rated *effective*, down from 81% in the preceding reporting period. Factors reported to be affecting this criterion included lack of appropriate risk mitigation measures, performance indicators that did not adequately measure intended development results, lower participation of implementing agencies, long delays in completing the financed tranches, and reduced government commitment. Among the 25 PSM operations, 20 were policy-based operations. Effectiveness ratings for this subset of PSM operations declined for the third consecutive reporting period to 72% in RY2018–2020 (from 76% in RY2017-2019), contributing to the overall decline.

105. Two of the 10 PSM operations that fell short of success in RY2020 were rated *less than effective*. Both were policy-based operations. In one case, despite assessments of *relevant* and *efficient*, the program was rated *less than effective* and *less than likely sustainable* after waning government commitment stalled planned reforms and caused the program to miss its target of increasing public sector enterprises' profitability and dividends. The other operation met none of the four success criteria after the government decided to prioritize other issues instead of proceeding with the follow-up subprogram necessary to complete the reform program.

Figure 4.1: Satisfactory Ratings of Sector Groupings by Criterion, Reporting Years 2014–2020
(%)

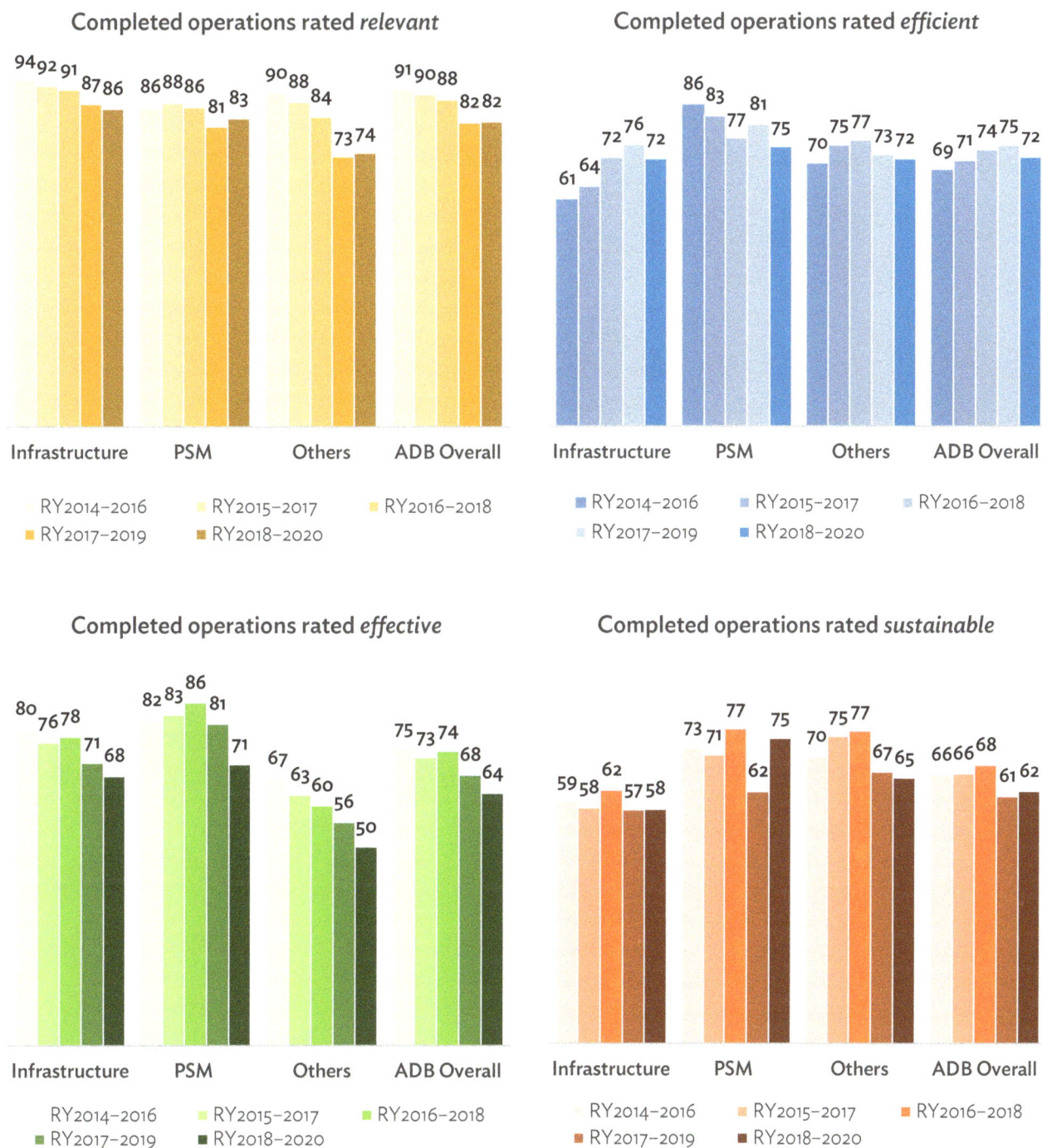

Completed operations rated *relevant*

	Infrastructure	PSM	Others	ADB Overall
RY2014–2016	94	86	90	91
RY2015–2017	92	88	88	90
RY2016–2018	91	86	84	88
RY2017–2019	87	81	73	82
RY2018–2020	86	83	74	82

Completed operations rated *efficient*

	Infrastructure	PSM	Others	ADB Overall
RY2014–2016	61	86	70	69
RY2015–2017	64	83	75	71
RY2016–2018	72	77	77	74
RY2017–2019	76	81	73	75
RY2018–2020	72	75	72	72

Completed operations rated *effective*

	Infrastructure	PSM	Others	ADB Overall
RY2014–2016	80	82	67	75
RY2015–2017	76	83	63	73
RY2016–2018	78	86	60	74
RY2017–2019	71	81	56	68
RY2018–2020	68	71	50	64

Completed operations rated *sustainable*

	Infrastructure	PSM	Others	ADB Overall
RY2014–2016	59	73	70	66
RY2015–2017	58	71	75	66
RY2016–2018	62	77	77	68
RY2017–2019	57	62	67	61
RY2018–2020	58	75	65	62

ADB = Asian Development Bank, PSM = public sector management, RY = reporting year.
Note: Groupings are based on primary sector classification of operations. "Others" includes operations in agriculture and natural resource management, education, finance, health, and industry and trade sectors.
Source: ADB (Independent Evaluation Department).

106. **Sustainability a perennial challenge for infrastructure but up for policy-based operations.** Low ratings for the sustainability of infrastructure operations continued to weigh down the overall success rating. Only 58% of completed infrastructure operations were rated *likely sustainable*. Weak sustainability was attributed to a lack of government ownership, poorly developed institutional and legal arrangements, and insufficient budget support for effective maintenance regimes. In a few projects, the financial internal rate of return was inadequate to cover operational costs after project completion. On the other hand, 75% of PSM operations were rated *sustainable* (up from 62%). The average for policy-based operations improved to 72% in RY2018–2020 from 65% in RY2017–2019 but was still lower than the 77% achieved in RY2016–2018.

107. **Efficiency of infrastructure projects hampered by delayed completion.** The average efficiency rating for policy-based operations reached a new high of 88%, but for infrastructure projects it decreased from 76% to 72%, mainly because of delayed government engagement and procurement.

108. **Less than one-third of projects closed on time.** On-time completion is among the measures of a project's efficiency. Of the projects closed financially during calendar years (CY) 2018–2020, 33% did so within 1 year of the closing date indicated in the loan agreement. This was down from 37% in CY2017–2019 and far short of the 45% 2024 target. The average delay lengthened by a month. Issues related to safeguards, procurement, and the performance of contractors and consultants continued to cause delays. Education and ICT operations experienced the longest delays (6 years). Overall, for investment projects in CY2018–2020, delayed projects were generally older and had shorter planned implementation periods. For projects approved during 2001–2008, 74% were delayed and 26% were on time. However, for projects approved during 2009–2017, 65% were delayed and 35% were on time. Delayed projects had shorter planned implementation periods on average (5.5 years) than those that closed on time (6.0 years).

109. **Overall success rates lower across major sectors.** Infrastructure and PSM operations comprised 69% of all completed sovereign operations and therefore had an outsized effect on the overall sovereign success rating. The infrastructure sectors in particular pulled down the overall sovereign operations success rate. Success rates declined for transport (lower by 4 percentage points to 64%), energy (down by 8 percentage points to 88%), water and other urban infrastructure and services (down by 10 percentage points to 59%), and ICT (down by 17 percentage points to 33%) (Figure 4.2). The success rate of PSM operations also dipped slightly, to 85% in RY2018–2020 from 88% in RY2017–2019.

Figure 4.2: Success Rates of Completed ADB Sovereign Operations by Sector and Shares of Operations, Reporting Years 2017–2020
(%)

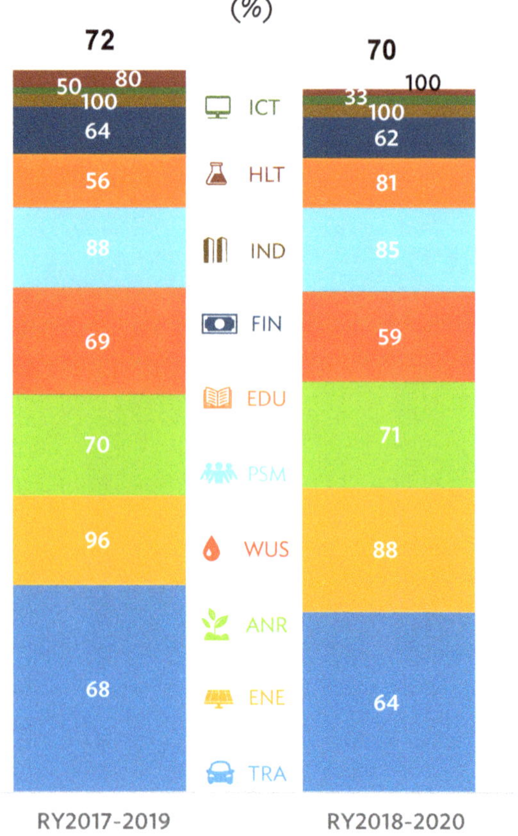

ADB = Asian Development Bank; ANR = agriculture, natural resources, and rural development; EDU = education; ENE = energy; FIN = finance; HLT = health; ICT = information and communication technology; IND = industry and trade; PSM = public sector management; RY = reporting year; TRA = transport; WUS = water and other urban infrastructure and services.
Source: ADB (Independent Evaluation Department).

110. **Education improved the most.** The average success rate of education operations increased by 25 percentage points to 81% in RY2018–2020, making it the most improved sector. Ratings for efficiency rose by 18 percentage points (to 88%), relevance by 19 (to 81%), and sustainability by 7 (to 88%), but the average rating for effectiveness remained unchanged at 56%. The strong performance was attributed to sound project designs, synergy between ADB and other development partners and the private sector, enhanced institutional capacity in sector management, and stronger government commitment.

2. Performance of Completed Concessional Assistance Operations

111. Of the completed concessional assistance operations evaluated in RY2018–2020, 65% were rated *successful*. This *off track* performance was 5 percentage points lower than in the previous period for the same reasons that ADB sovereign operations performed more poorly overall. Ratings for relevance, efficiency, effectiveness, and sustainability were similar as well. On-time performance also worsened, although less so (2 percentage points) than it did for the overall sovereign category (4). Only 31% of concessional assistance operations closed on time. This left ADB *off track* on the target. Timely implementation is more difficult to achieve in concessional assistance countries, given the heightened institutional capacity challenges and other operational issues projects must overcome to finish on schedule.

Smallholder agriculture. Storage facilities built with ADB support help farmers in Bamyan, Afghanistan, keep their potatoes fresh for up to 6 months (photo by Jawad Jalali).

Renewable energy. ADB helped install floating solar photovoltaic panels on the reservoir of the Da Mi hydropower plant in Viet Nam (photo by Gerhard Joren).

CHAPTER 5
PRIVATE SECTOR OPERATIONS

Strategy 2030 sets ambitious goals for its private sector operations in recognition of their importance to development results in Asia and the Pacific. These nonsovereign operations should account for one-third of all ADB operations by number in 2024, help further all seven Strategy 2030 operational priorities, and deliver the intended results in a financially sustainable way without compromising portfolio quality. The indicators in the corporate results framework reflect these aims.

NONSOVEREIGN OPERATIONS COMMITTED IN 2020

SCALE UP NONSOVEREIGN OPERATIONS AND ENSURE THEIR STRATEGIC RELEVANCE

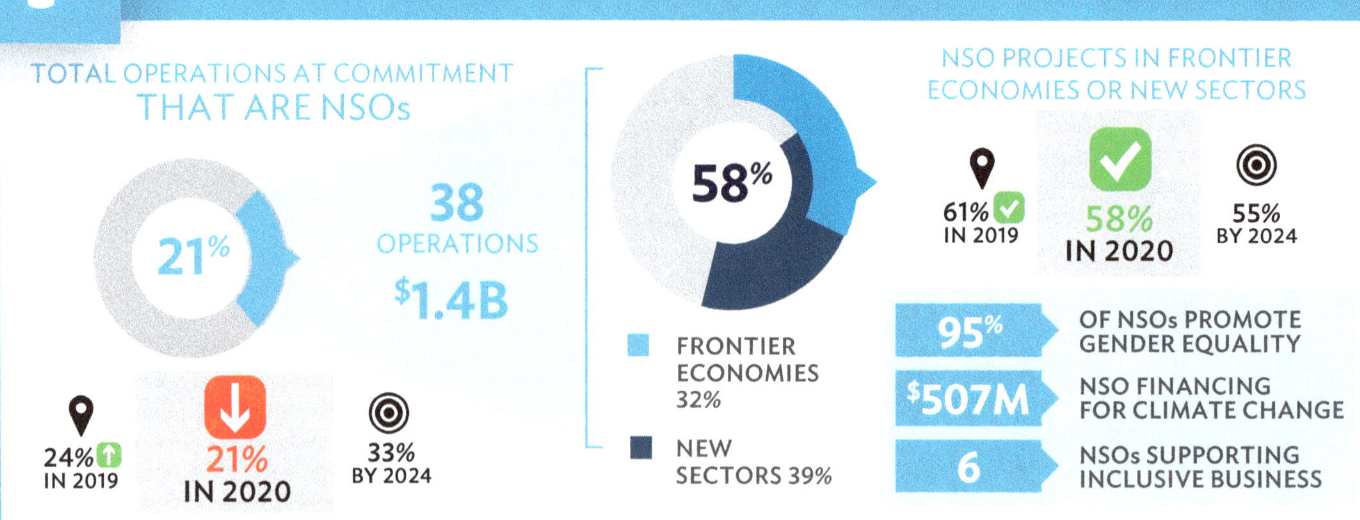

OPERATIONS UNDER IMPLEMENTATION IN 2020

ENSURE PORTFOLIO IS HEALTHY AND DELIVERING RESULTS

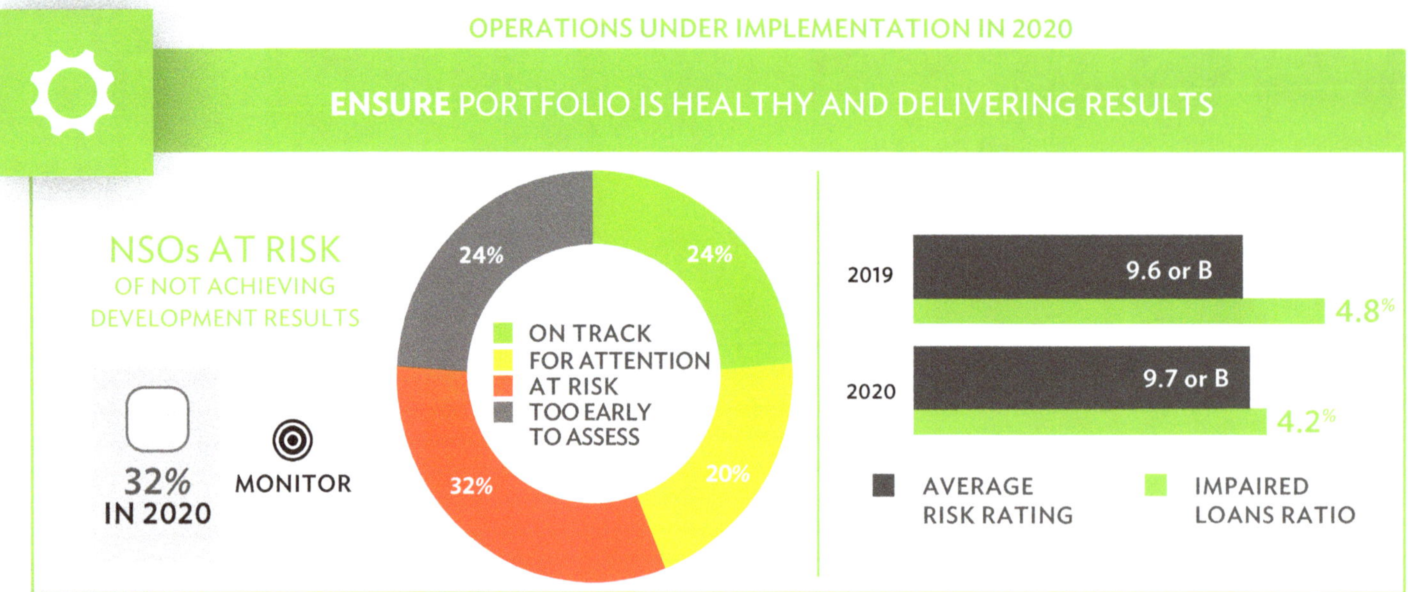

COMPLETED OPERATIONS VALIDATED 2018–2020

DEVELOPMENT RESULTS DELIVERED TO CLIENTS AND BENEFICIARIES

ADB = Asian Development Bank, B = billion, M = million, NSO = nonsovereign operation.

A. SCALING UP AND STRATEGIC FIT

112. The number of nonsovereign operations committed remained constant in 2020 as ADB scaled up sovereign support by 23% to help developing member country (DMC) governments respond urgently to the coronavirus disease (COVID-19) crisis. The nonsovereign share in the total number of operations fell *off track* as a result. Overall commitment of nonsovereign operation financing declined by $1.6 billion as ADB's Private Sector Operations Department (PSOD) shifted priorities and supplied shorter-term, smaller-scale liquidity and working capital to private entities that were responding to the pandemic with much-needed goods and services.

113. About 58% of the nonsovereign projects committed in 2020 were in frontier economies or in new sectors. This was a slightly smaller share than that achieved through ADB's above-target performance in 2019 but still above the 2024 target of 55%. Operations in support of ADB's inclusive business promotion agenda declined in number, and overall financing for climate change mitigation and/or adaptation was lower by $215 million. The share of nonsovereign operations supporting gender equality increased by 13 percentage points, with 36 of the 38 committed in 2020 rated *gender equity as a theme, effective gender mainstreaming*, or *some gender elements*.

114. ADB is rated *on track but watch* for meeting its nonsovereign cofinancing target of 200% by 2024. A total of $9.1 billion in cofinancing was mobilized during 2018–2020 against the $6.3 billion in net ordinary capital resources (less risk transfers) ADB committed to nonsovereign operations. This equates to $1.45 in cofinancing for every $1.00 of ADB commitment—a ratio similar to that of the previous rolling 3-year period.

B. PERFORMANCE AT IMPLEMENTATION

115. ADB completed its full rollout of a new indicator in 2020 to measure the risk that ongoing nonsovereign operations will not achieve their targeted development results and flag issues so that they can be addressed early. The indicator showed almost one-third of the active nonsovereign portfolio to be "at risk." About half of these operations were making insufficient progress toward their design and monitoring framework (DMF) targets. About 40% featured incomplete or overdue development effectiveness monitoring reports. A few were flagged on both counts.

116. The weighted average risk rating of nonsovereign operations weakened slightly under the credit and macroeconomic stresses imposed by the pandemic, although the financial performance of ongoing projects remained sound. The impaired loan ratio declined slightly because of some successful recoveries from impaired transactions, and credit portfolio growth partly driven by ADB COVID-19 support for clients.

C. PERFORMANCE AT COMPLETION

117. The share of completed nonsovereign operations rated *successful* increased by 2 percentage points to 53% during reporting years (RY) 2018–2020, but it remained below the baseline year performance of 54% and left ADB *off track* to meet the 2024 target of 70%. The recent improvement in performance is mainly the result of the larger share contributed by infrastructure in overall nonsovereign operations. It has been the best-performing nonsovereign sector and accounted for 33% of the portfolio in RY2018–2020, compared with 17% during RY2017–2019. This shift offset a 7 percentage-point decline to 76% in the infrastructure operations success rate and a drop to 10% from 14% for the private equity fund operations that comprised 20% of all nonsovereign operations in RY2018–2020.

118. The rating for the ADB work quality criterion increased the most compared to the last reporting period, by 13 percentage points to 53%, driven primarily by significantly higher ratings among infrastructure operations (82%). Performance on this criterion remains weakest, however, alongside that for development results, which improved slightly and mirrors the overall success rate. Private sector operations performed the best on investment profitability during this reporting period. Chapter 1 highlights results achieved by completed nonsovereign operations.

D. IN FOCUS

3. Newly Committed Nonsovereign Operations

119. **Smaller deals for pandemic response.** Strategy 2030 and ADB's operational plan for private sector operations during 2019–2024 prioritize smaller transactions with high development impact potential spread over a larger number of countries.[44] The COVID-19 pandemic accelerated this repositioning. ADB responded to client needs as uncertain economic conditions diminished the risk appetite of project sponsors and led to the delay or cancellation of major capital undertakings. The provision of small amounts of working capital and liquidity support was preferred to traditional large-scale financing for infrastructure. Although ADB committed the same number of nonsovereign operations as in 2019, average deal size fell by more than half—from $79 million to $37 million (Figure 5.1). These operations covered 11 DMCs and included 5 regional operations versus 16 DMCs and 7 regional operations the year before. Among them was a regional equity investment that covers all DMCs and aims to scale up investments in sustainable infrastructure. This was accomplished alongside a higher ratio of commercial cofinancing in 2020 than in the 2 years prior. (See Chapter 3 for details on nonsovereign cofinancing.)

Figure 5.1: Nonsovereign Operation Commitments in Number and Financing Relative to Number of Sovereign Operation Commitments, 2016–2020

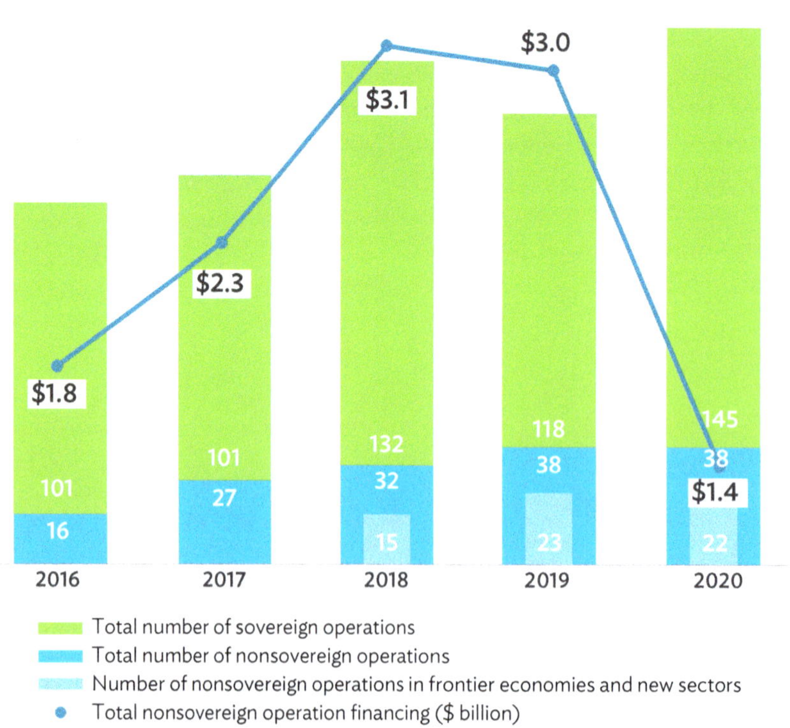

Note: Nonsovereign operation financing excludes commitments through revolving funds, which totaled $3.1 billion in 2020.

120. **More than half of new transactions in frontier economies or new sectors.** The private sector operational plan seeks to intensify development impact by redirecting more of ADB's nonsovereign operations into frontier economies in the group A and B countries (Appendix 4) and to new sectors such as health, education, and agribusiness, outside of the traditional focus on the energy sector. The pandemic context made it challenging to identify suitable new clients, and ADB focused instead on addressing the urgent pandemic-related needs of existing clients. Of the 22 projects committed in frontier economies or new sectors in 2020, fewer were in frontier economies (7 compared with 9 in 2019), more were in new sectors (10 compared with 8 in 2019), and 5 operations were in both a frontier economy and a new sector (versus 6 in 2019).

121. Health care and agribusiness played a major part in ADB's COVID-19 response. In one example, ADB provided working capital needed by a pharmaceutical company to continue manufacturing and ensuring the availability of generic pharmaceutical drugs in Viet Nam amid the pandemic's supply chain disruptions.[45] It also financed a project in the country's water and urban services sector (Box 5.1). COVID-19 response deals in the agriculture sector provided liquidity to stabilize the supply of wheat flour during the pandemic in Mongolia; procure milk from smallholder dairy farmers and other farmers who would otherwise lose income in Bangladesh; and support the livelihoods of smallholder farmers in Indonesia, Papua New Guinea, and Viet Nam.[46]

Box 5.1: Investments in New Sectors and Frontier Economies

In 2020, the Asian Development Bank (ADB) committed four deals in the new sector of water and other urban infrastructure and services. Engaging private sector operators to run infrastructure services is still at a nascent stage even in the more advanced developing member countries. ADB's nonsovereign lending demonstrates the viability of such investments to other private players.

ADB and Indorama Ventures Global Services Limited signed a $100 million financing package to reduce the environmental impact of plastics and contribute to the creation of a circular economy. The project will boost the capacity of Indorama Ventures' plastic recycling plants in India, Indonesia, the Philippines, and Thailand and allow the collection and treatment of plastic waste that would otherwise end up in oceans and landfills. The new and expanded plants, once fully operational in 2022, are expected to divert almost 5 billion additional plastic bottles from polluting the environment every year. The transaction involved ADB's first independently verified nonsovereign blue loan under its $5 billion 2019–2024 investment and technical assistance Action Plan for Healthy Oceans and Sustainable Blue Economies.[a]

ADB's 2020 nonsovereign investment in frontier economies includes an $8 million loan to expand the Tan Hiep Water Treatment Plant in Viet Nam. The operation, also in the water and other urban infrastructure services sector, aims to increase the volume and reliable delivery of potable water for residents of Binh Duong, one of the country's fastest developing provinces. The Japan International Cooperation Agency is providing parallel cofinancing of $8 million to introduce gender-inclusive and equitable human resources policies at the company.

[a] ADB. 2019. *Action Plan for Healthy Oceans: Investing in Sustainable Blue Economies for Poverty Alleviation in Asia and the Pacific.* Manila.

Sources: ADB. 2020. *Report and Recommendation of the President to the Board of Directors: Proposed Loan and Administration of Loan to the Indorama Ventures Global Services Limited for the Indorama Ventures Regional Blue Loan Project in India, Indonesia, the Philippines, and Thailand.* Manila; and ADB. 2020. *FAST Report: Proposed Loan and Administration of Technical Assistance Grant to the Binh Duong Water Environment Joint Stock Company for the Binh Duong Water Treatment Expansion Project in Viet Nam.* Manila.

122. **Inclusive business operations focused largely on agribusiness.** Six nonsovereign operations committed in 2020 will support inclusive business, two fewer than in 2019. Five are agribusiness projects that aim to integrate farmers into the value chain and create better livelihood opportunities and jobs for low-income people. The sixth transaction will help finance low-cost housing and enable low-income people to own their own homes.

123. In 2020, ADB established a new platform to support and invest in technology solutions that will further the Strategy 2030 priorities of tackling climate change and increasing gender equality. The ADB Ventures Financing Partnership Facility focuses on early-stage technology companies that are taking on both challenges.

4. Main Factors Influencing Success Rates

124. **Performance better overall, but lower in each main investment type.** A bigger role for the portfolio's relatively strongly performing infrastructure projects pushed the overall nonsovereign operation successful rating average up to 53% (27 of 51 projects) in RY2018–2020 (Figure 5.2). Infrastructure, historically the highest rated among the three main nonsovereign sectors, accounted for two-thirds of the operations completed in RY2018–2020, almost double its share of 17% in the preceding period. The success rate averages were nonetheless lower in all three sectors individually. Infrastructure slipped to 76%. Of the 10 private equity fund investments completed in RY2018–2020, all but one was rated *unsuccessful*. The finance sector retained a relatively stable *successful* rating average of 54%, down a point from the RY2017–2019 period.

125. **Factors affecting poorly performing projects.** The average success rates of operations completed in RY2020 were down in the infrastructure sector (75%) and finance (50%). The rate for private equity funds remained 0%. Two of the four *unsuccessful* infrastructure investments became commercially unviable during implementation and were closed. Of the other two, an information and communication technology (ICT) operation failed because of corporate governance issues, and an urban sewerage improvement project lacked the data needed for assessment of its results. Three finance sector operations fell short of their intended outcomes. One involved a financial institution in Azerbaijan forced by capital inadequacy to default and liquidate. A second had supported a leasing company in Mongolia that was badly hurt by an economic downturn in 2015–2016. The third case was a clean-bus leasing project in the People's Republic of China (PRC). Its economic and private sector development benefits were found to be most directly attributable to government actions rather than ADB's investment.

Figure 5.2: Performance at Completion by Type of Investment, and Share of Investment to Total Completion Reports, 2016–2020
(%)

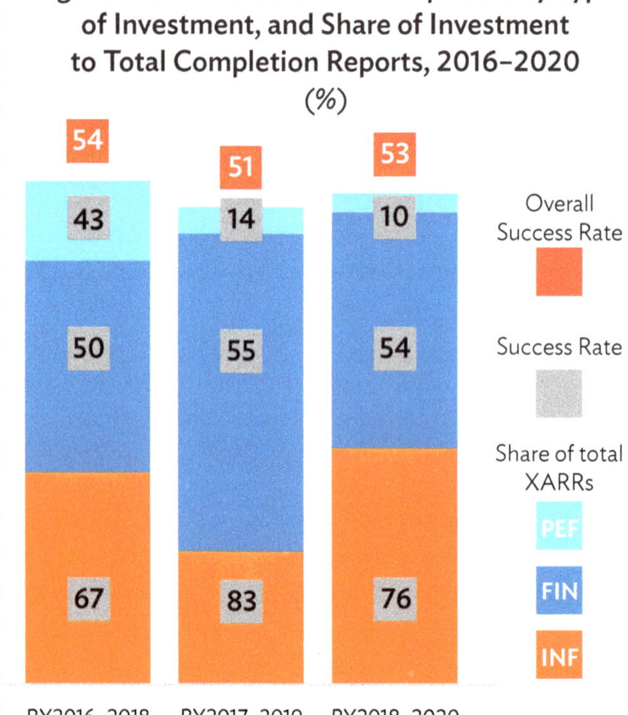

FIN = direct equity and loans to financial institutions, INF = direct equity and loans in infrastructure, PEF = private equity fund, RY = reporting year, XARR = extended annual review report.
Source: Asian Development Bank (Independent Evaluation Department).

126. **Challenging private equity fund operations.** Weaknesses in investee companies led to the failure of all four private equity investments completed in RY2020 to demonstrate economic and business success. Investments were high risk because they were mostly in companies that were start-ups or at an early stage, small and family-owned, or that lacked the business models needed to attract further investments. The results were negative or very low financial returns, and a high likelihood that ADB's nonsovereign support was not in these cases achieving the intended private sector expansion, job creation, and catalyzation of additional investments.

127. **Improved ADB work quality.** *Satisfactory* ratings were up for three of the four criteria used to assess a nonsovereign operation's performance—development results, additionality, and work quality. Work quality posted the biggest improvement, jumping from 40% to 53% (Figure 5.3). Improved screening, appraisal, and structuring, as well as monitoring and supervision contributed to this improvement. More timely and complete monitoring and reporting are notable given that projects are sometimes rated *unsuccessful* because they lack data and evidence to show whether their intended development results were achieved. ADB work quality was weaker in the areas of finance (42%) and private equity funds (30%) than in infrastructure projects (82%).

128. **Weaker investment profitability.** Operations did best overall on the fourth criterion—investment profitability. Even so, the average for satisfactory profitability was down 6 percentage points. Investment profitability and additionality suffered alongside weak development results in 8 of 11 completed projects that underperformed in RY2020. These included all four private equity fund investments as well as three finance sector investments.

Figure 5.3: Performance at Completion by Criteria, 2016-2020
(%)

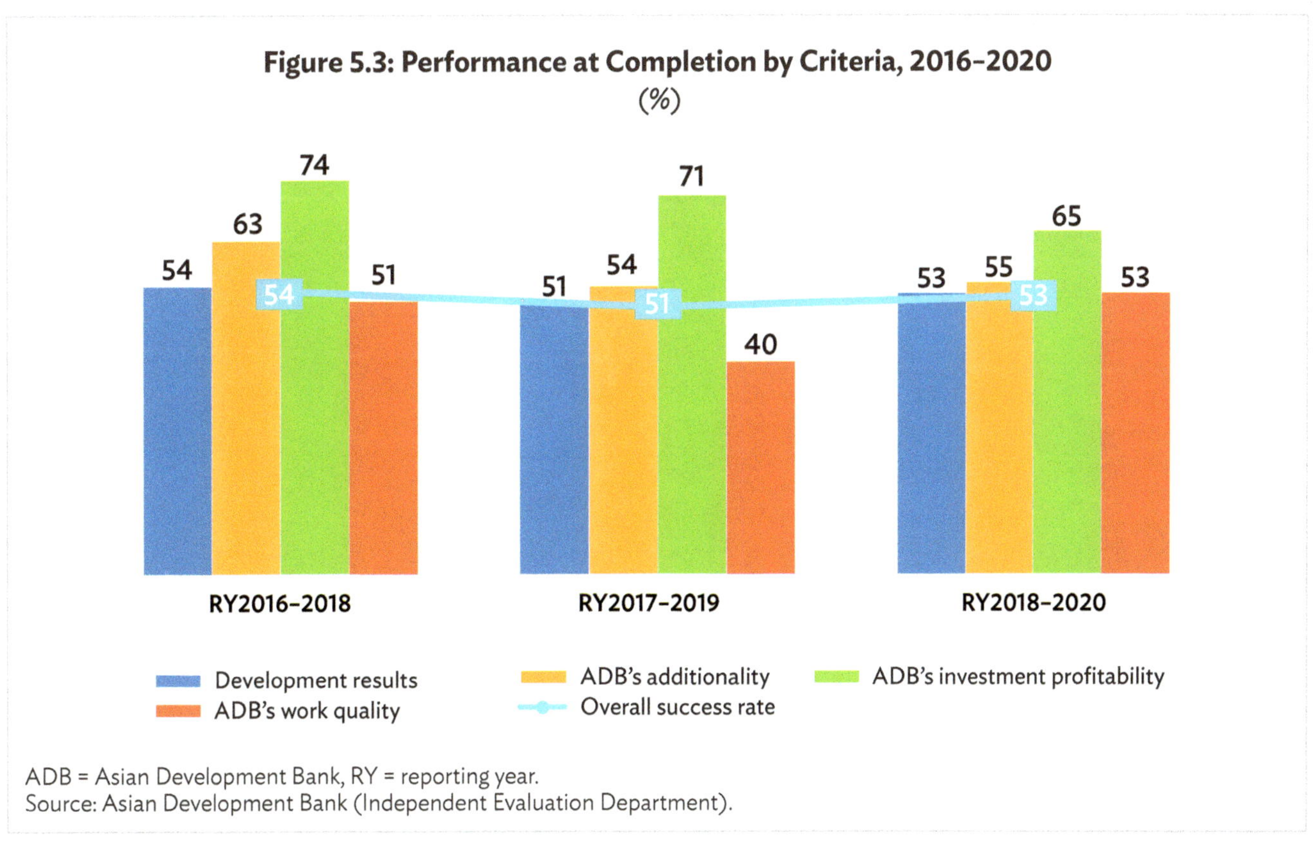

ADB = Asian Development Bank, RY = reporting year.
Source: Asian Development Bank (Independent Evaluation Department).

Tertiary education in the Pacific. The University of the South Pacific is an intergovernmental organization with regional campuses throughout the Pacific (photo by Eric Sales).

CHAPTER 6

ADB AS A KNOWLEDGE ORGANIZATION

Strategy 2030 recognizes that ADB's continued relevance will increasingly depend on its role as a knowledge institution. As countries address complex and urgent challenges, such as climate change and coronavirus disease (COVID-19), delivering on Strategy 2030's knowledge ambitions is more important than ever. Based on the performance indicators in ADB's corporate results framework, this chapter assesses how well ADB is performing in this area and how well others perceived it to be doing. The report examines factors that affected performance in 2020 and considers how successful ADB has been in pushing forward its agenda to become a stronger knowledge and learning organization.

A. BENEFITS

Clients' Feedback to Deliver Quality Knowledge Solutions

129. **Client satisfaction rate above baseline at 79% but shy of target.** ADB conducted a survey in 2020 to gauge the reach, quality, use, and benefits to its developing member country (DMC) clients of the knowledge products and services (KPS) it delivers. Of the 1,153 clients who responded to the survey, 79% rated ADB's KPS *very useful*, a result just short of the 80% satisfaction rate targeted.[47] Among primary clients (562 respondents), 80% gave a rating of *very useful*. The survey is conducted every 2 years.

130. **Substantially higher ratings for three components.** Much of the increase in 2020 was driven by a growing perception among ADB's primary clients that KPS are useful for designing and implementing policies, programs, or projects; and developing learning materials.

Stakeholders Satisfied with ADB's Knowledge Solutions

131. **First feedback on events participation.** ADB holds many knowledge-related events each year on a variety of topics and projects across all its sectors and themes.[48] The corporate results framework (CRF) includes a tracking indicator to measure annually the number of participants who report gaining knowledge and/or skills from such events. Of 3,951 event participants in 2020, 3,421, or 87%, strongly agreed or agreed with the statement "My knowledge of/skills in the subject matter increased as a result of this event."

132. **Plan to introduce standard post-event surveys delayed.** Only 37 of 265 reported events and training courses conducted in 2020 measured improvement in knowledge or skills as part of post-event surveys. The onset of coronavirus disease (COVID-19) disrupted plans to pilot and disseminate a standard form for post-event surveys. The detailed content and use of the form, especially for online events, will be revisited in 2021 to provide fuller information for this indicator.

133. **Technical assistance success rates steady.** Technical assistance (TA) supports the development of knowledge solutions that are tailored to the needs of individual DMCs. Of the 471 sovereign and nonsovereign TA projects completed in reporting years (RY) 2018–2020, 83% were self-rated *successful* in the completion reports of the departments, a decrease of 3 percentage points from the ratio for RY2017–2019. Of 167 TA projects with completion reports submitted in RY2020, 78% were rated *successful*.

134. **Validation guidelines issued.** ADB's Independent Evaluation Department (IED) launched a TA completion report validation system in January 2020, becoming only the second multilateral development bank after the International Finance Corporation to systematically assess and validate the performance of TA projects. In February 2020, IED issued *Technical Assistance Completion Report Validation Guidelines*, which provide a robust process for assessing the quality and outcomes of TA operations and an opportunity for capturing knowledge generated. The guidelines specify the framework for validating TA completion reports to capture lessons learned from completed TA operations and improve accountability for achieving results, the quality of the reports, and the independence of project ratings. Project teams have adopted these guidelines. Of the 167 TA completion reports circulated in RY2020, IED validated a sample of 27. IED validations downgraded to *successful* 8 of 9 TA completion reports with *highly successful* ratings. These projects had design flaws that affected the achievement of outputs and outcome, implementation delays that led to prolonged project closing necessitating additional funding support, and major changes in scope.

Learning How to Deliver Successful Technical Assistance Projects

135. **Evaluating the success of technical assistance projects.** TA is one of ADB's most important instruments for financing knowledge solutions at the country and regional levels, and is one of ADB's comparative advantages, so it is important to know what drives or prevents these projects' success. Box 6.1 gives a synopsis of the major strengths and weaknesses of selected TA projects with completion reports in RY2020.

Box 6.1: Lessons from Technical Assistance

All 24 technical assistance (TA) projects that achieved *highly successful* ratings were closely aligned with the strategies and priorities of both the Asian Development Bank and the government and had strong political buy-in. Both of these aspects contributed to the sustainability of their outputs and outcomes. Strong stakeholder support was a crucial factor in the success of capacity development TA projects. Partnership with civil society organizations and the presence of cofinancing support were sometimes instrumental in success. *Highly successful* TA projects were typically managed by the same team throughout their implementation or had few staffing changes. They also disseminated knowledge in innovative ways that were tailored to the client context and had planned to do so from the outset.

Of the five TA projects with *unsuccessful* ratings, two suffered design flaws and three lacked government or client buy-in. In one project, communication among stakeholders was insufficient to address issues and ensure commitment; and in another, deterioration in the macroeconomic outlook led to the eventual cancellation of the TA.

B. USED

136. **Downloads of knowledge products and services continued to grow.** The volume of client interaction with ADB websites and social media is a leading indicator of the use of ADB KPS. Knowledge solution downloads through ADB.org increased by 17% from 834,900 to 978,229, surpassing the year-on-year increase of 15% in 2019. Reader-relevant content, improved presentation and navigation, and campaigns to attract readers were behind this trend. There were significantly more downloads across ADB's knowledge dissemination platforms, most notably the ADB Data Library (up 76%), while pageviews of the Asian Development Blog rose by 70%.

137. **COVID-19 hub site generates interest.** A COVID-19 hub site, launched in March 2020, drew a large readership, particularly to its datasets on the economic impact of COVID-19 and the ADB COVID-19 Policy Database. Downloads of 47 COVID-19 related publications surpassed 120,000. The COVID-19 related publications with the most downloads are shown below.

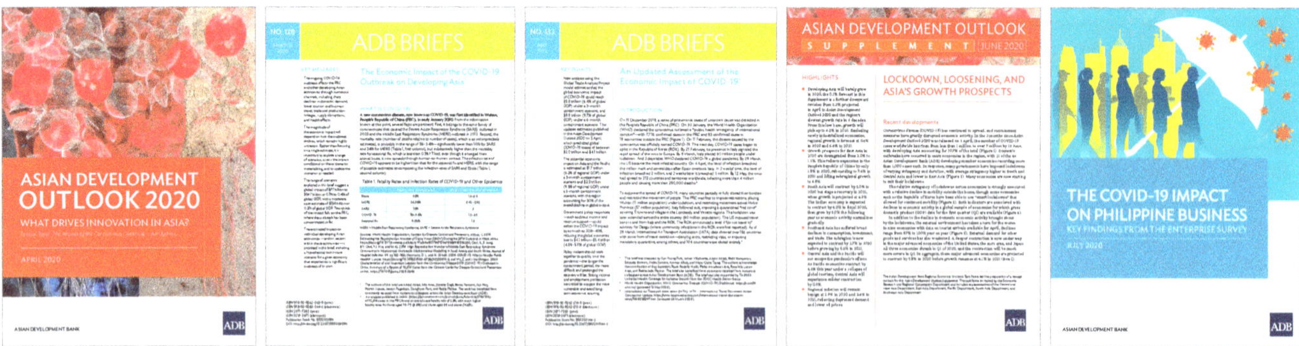

Note: ADB recognizes "South Korea" as Republic of Korea.

138. **Broader social media audience and higher engagement.** Social media enables ADB to reach and disseminate KPS to a broader audience. The overall number of followers and subscribers to the social media platforms ADB uses increased by 19% year on year to 921,414 in 2020.[49] This was accompanied by a sharp increase in audience interaction with and commitment to content (shares and comments on posts) to 1,090,184 shares and likes from 391,830 in 2019.

139. **Effects of new social media approach and COVID-19 interest.** The substantial increase in engagement can be attributed to a new social media approach, which prioritized timely and engaging curated posts that appealed to different audiences, and enormous public interest in ADB's response to the COVID-19 crisis. ADB's resident missions and other affiliated social media accounts also played an increasingly important role in promoting ADB initiatives to a global audience and driving traffic to ADB.org.

KNOWLEDGE PRODUCTS AND SERVICES DRAWN FROM K-NEXUS
424 IN 2020
KNOWLEDGE PRODUCTS AND SERVICES DELIVERED
102% IN 2020
IMPACT EVALUATIONS COMPLETED
2 IN 2020

More ADB Knowledge Products and Services Delivered

140. **Use of k-Nexus increased.** ADB developed an online platform, k-Nexus, to better manage and share its knowledge internally, along with data and information on what KPS are currently in or planned for operations pipelines. A tracking indicator measures the use of this database through the number of KPS drawn from k-Nexus to support the development of ADB's country operations business plans. Of the planned titles in the 24 country operations business plans approved in 2020, 424 (44%) were taken from k-Nexus. This is higher than the previous year's 301 titles. The inclusion of the LINK report builder, a user-friendly new feature in k-Nexus that automatically generates the tables showing the list of indicative KPS, encouraged users to input more KPS into the database.

141. **More knowledge products and services delivered than planned.** In line with Strategy 2030's vision for ADB as a knowledge bank, explicit knowledge is shared through KPS, making it important to know how effectively this is being done. Slightly more ADB KPS were delivered during the year than planned (352 versus 344) in the annual work program and budget framework. The rate of delivery has steadied from 84% in 2018, to 106% in 2019, and to 102% in 2020. About 26% of KPS delivered were related to COVID-19. They include flagship publications, such as *Asian Development Outlook 2020 Update: Wellness in Worrying Times*; technical studies, such as *Green Finance Strategies for Post-COVID-19 Economic Recovery in Southeast Asia—Greening Recoveries for Planet and People*; working papers; policy briefs; and op-eds.

142. **Two impact studies completed.** ADB conducts impact studies to gather empirical evidence for planning future operations on what has worked well in previous interventions and what has not. Of the eight impact evaluations scheduled for completion in 2020, only one, on Enhancing Rooftop Solar Power Supply, was completed. A special study of the Impact of COVID-19 on Lao Tourism Enterprises, which was not part of the planned eight studies, was also completed. Pandemic-related movement restrictions resulted in the suspension of most field activities and training, which delayed progress on most of the planned studies.

System, Process, and Capacity Promoting Innovation at ADB

143. **Innovation indicator and framework development still in process.** ADB will increase its sharing of experience, best practices, and innovation with its DMCs under Strategy 2030. As an initial step, ADB established a bank-wide 150-member innovation task force to discuss how it can best enhance innovation. Members of this task force are preparing an innovation framework that will provide a structured road map to enhancing innovation. Because of the disruption caused by COVID-19, the framework and indicator are scheduled to be finalized in 2021.

D. KNOWLEDGE ORGANIZATION

ADB AS KNOWLEDGE ORGANIZATION

STAFF RATING ADB AS AN EFFECTIVE KNOWLEDGE AND LEARNING ORGANIZATION

65% IN 2019

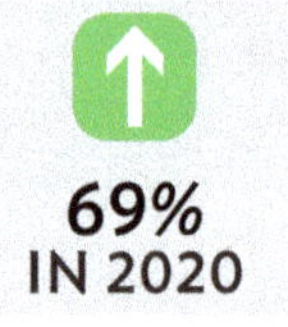

69% IN 2020

75% BY 2024

Transformation into a Knowledge and Learning Institution

144. **Further transformation into a knowledge and learning institution taking place.** ADB's transformation into a knowledge and learning institution requires the right culture, processes, and capacity. ADB's performance on the eight drivers of a knowledge-driven enterprise, based on its latest globally benchmarked Most Admired Knowledge Enterprise (MAKE) survey of all staff, rose by 4 percentage points from 2019 to 69% (55.42 out of 80 points). This puts ADB *on track* on the CRF indicator. The 2020 survey received substantially more responses than the previous year's survey (1,568 versus 1,115).

145. **Notable dimension scores.** The scores of all eight dimensions improved. The three dimensions in which ADB achieved its highest score were "creating a learning organization," "delivering knowledge-based products/services/solutions," and "creating an enterprise knowledge-driven culture." For the third year in a row, ADB scored lowest on "maximizing enterprise intellectual capital." This dimension also showed the biggest improvement in 2020. Figure 6.1 provides the dimension scores from the 2019 and 2020 surveys.

146. **Independent evaluation of knowledge solutions released.** In 2020, IED released *Knowledge Solutions for Development: An Evaluation of ADB's Readiness for Strategy 2030*. The evaluation report provided Management with timely and useful inputs for the preparation of the Knowledge Management Action Plan and other complementary corporate initiatives.

Figure 6.1: Dimensions of the Most Admired Knowledge Enterprise Survey Scores
(point score)

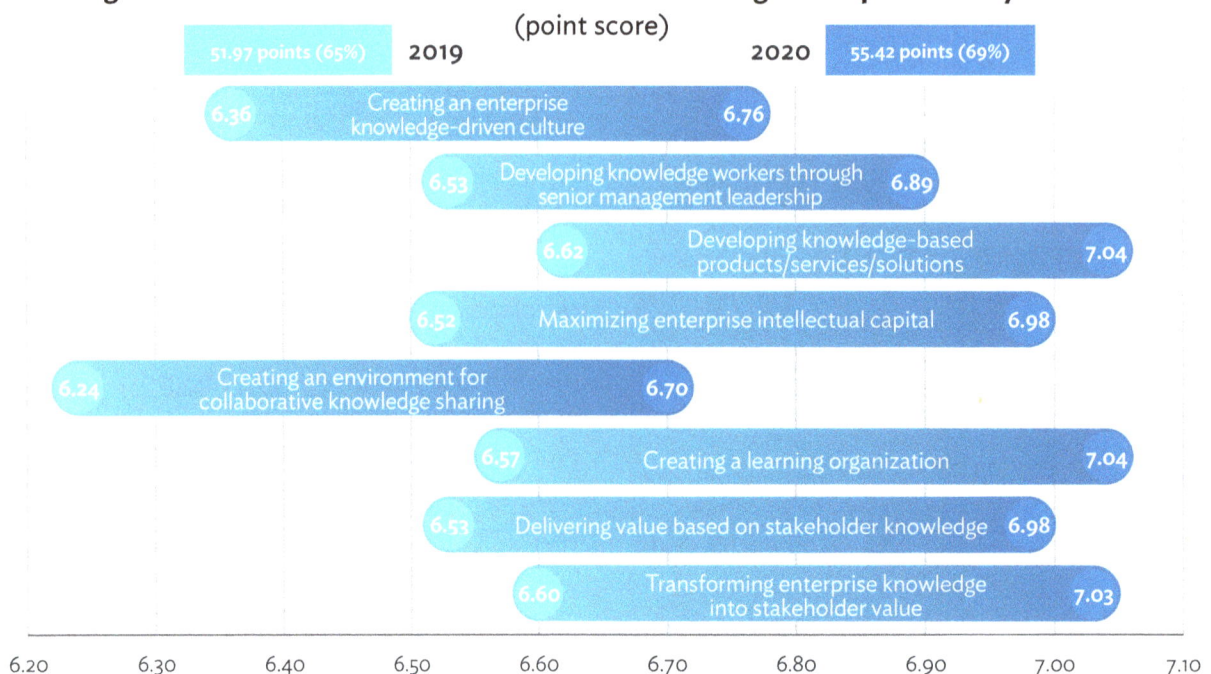

Dimension	2019 (51.97 points (65%))	2020 (55.42 points (69%))
Creating an enterprise knowledge-driven culture	6.36	6.76
Developing knowledge workers through senior management leadership	6.53	6.89
Developing knowledge-based products/services/solutions	6.62	7.04
Maximizing enterprise intellectual capital	6.52	6.98
Creating an environment for collaborative knowledge sharing	6.24	6.70
Creating a learning organization	6.57	7.04
Delivering value based on stakeholder knowledge	6.53	6.98
Transforming enterprise knowledge into stakeholder value	6.60	7.03

Each dimension has a 10-point score and the total is 80.
Source: Asian Development Bank (Sustainable Development and Climate Change Department).

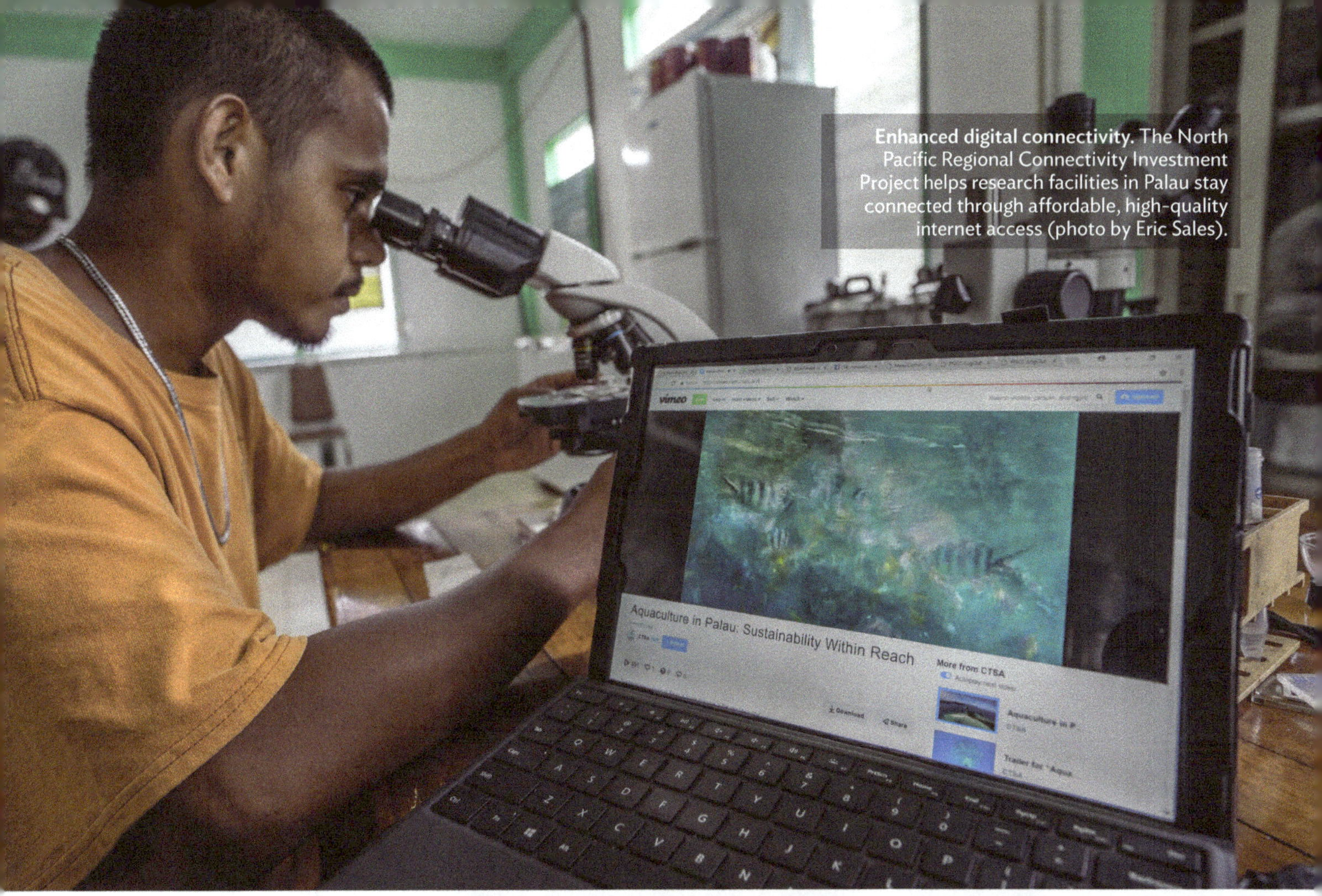

Enhanced digital connectivity. The North Pacific Regional Connectivity Investment Project helps research facilities in Palau stay connected through affordable, high-quality internet access (photo by Eric Sales).

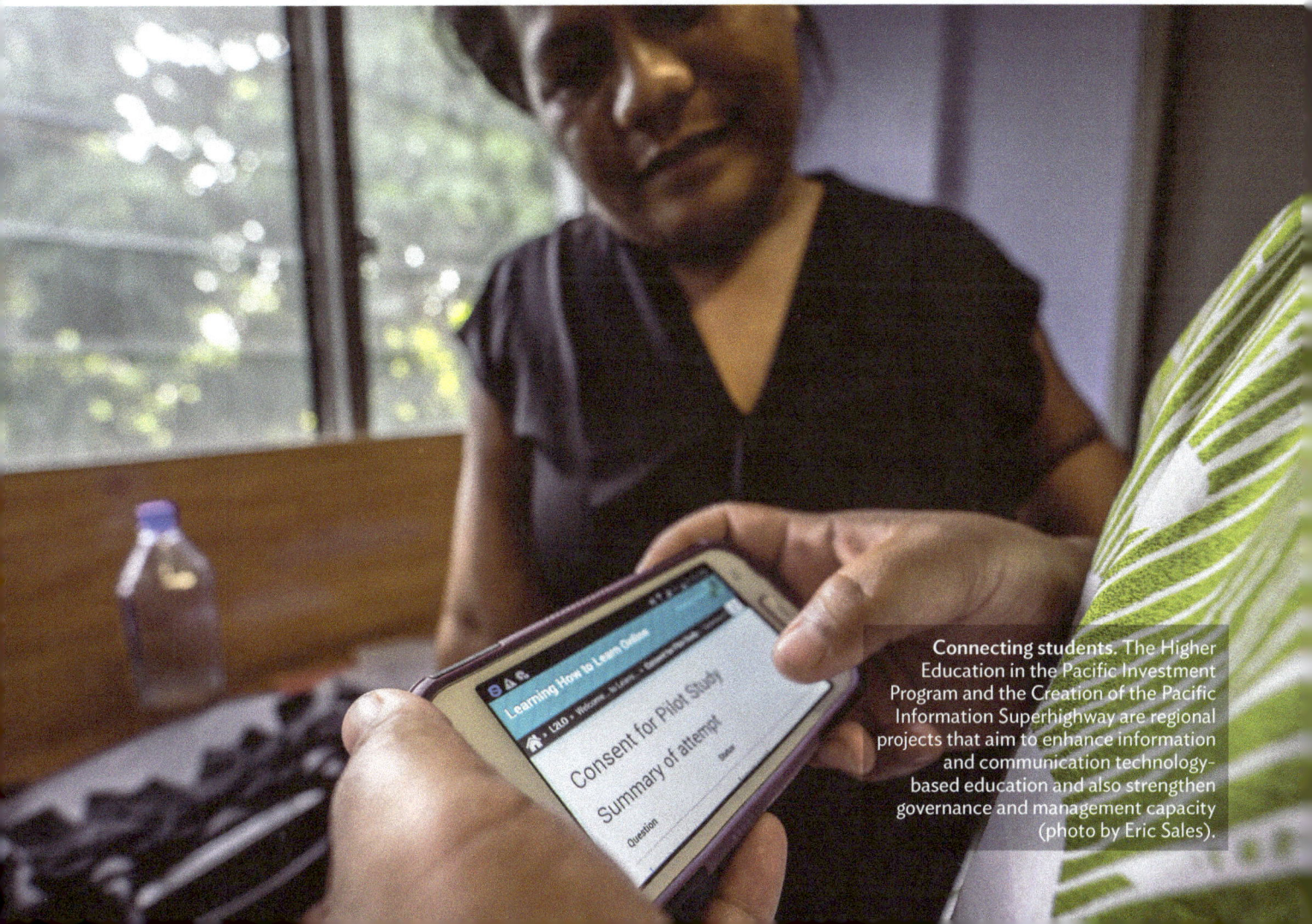

Connecting students. The Higher Education in the Pacific Investment Program and the Creation of the Pacific Information Superhighway are regional projects that aim to enhance information and communication technology-based education and also strengthen governance and management capacity (photo by Eric Sales).

Economic corridor development. ADB supported the training of officials to manage the Savan-Seno Special Economic Zone in Savannakhet, Lao People's Democratic Republic, and promote its features to investors (photo by Ariel Javellana).

CHAPTER 7

ADB'S SYSTEMS, PROCESSES, AND CAPACITY

Strategy 2030 calls on ADB to be stronger, better, and faster in its work to enhance development results in Asia and the Pacific. A stronger ADB requires a robust resource base, enhanced human resources, and the country presence necessary to be more attentive to the needs of its developing members. A better ADB demands more modern business processes, more efficient operations, and more use of country systems. A faster ADB will be achieved by ensuring that procurement is timely and provides value for money. To achieve greater operational effectiveness and efficiency, ADB must also have the right skill sets in place. This chapter assesses ADB's effectiveness in key performance areas, including operational systems and processes and organizational capacity. It also examines factors that affected performance in these areas during 2020 and highlights ADB's main advances in better managing its internal resources and processes.

ENSURING A ROBUST RESOURCE BASE

CAPITAL UTILIZATION RATIO (SOV AND NSO)	WEIGHTED AVERAGE RISK RATING (NSO)	IMPAIRED LOANS RATIO (NSO)
69.1% IN 2020	9.7 or B IN 2020	4.2% IN 2020

ENHANCING HUMAN RESOURCES

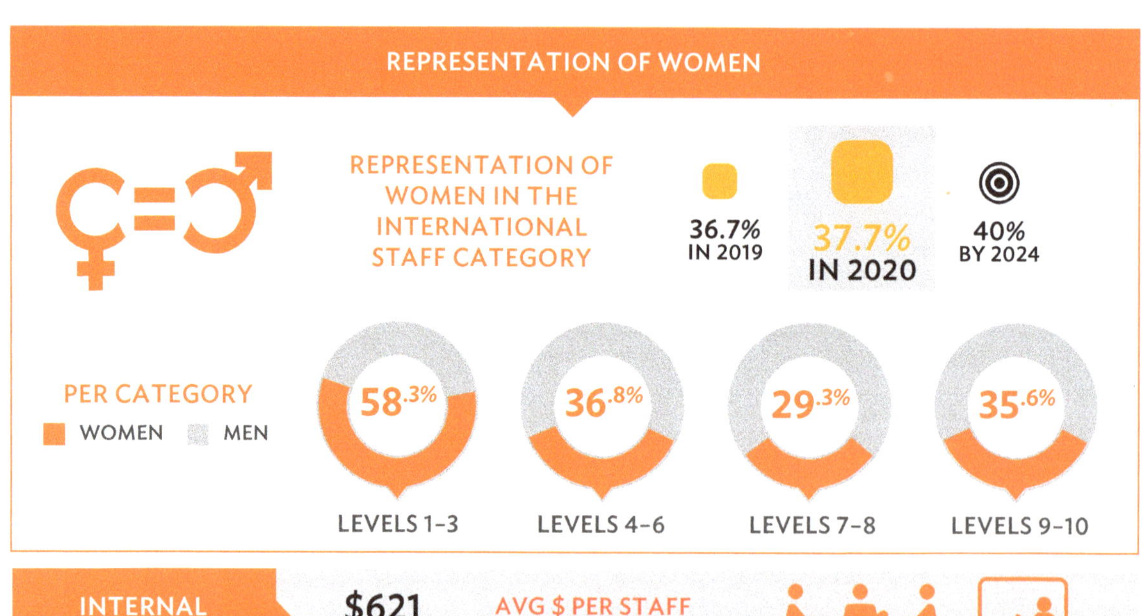

INTERNAL TRAINING BUDGET

$621 IN 2020

AVG $ PER STAFF PARTICIPANT

MAINTAINING A STRONG COUNTRY PRESENCE

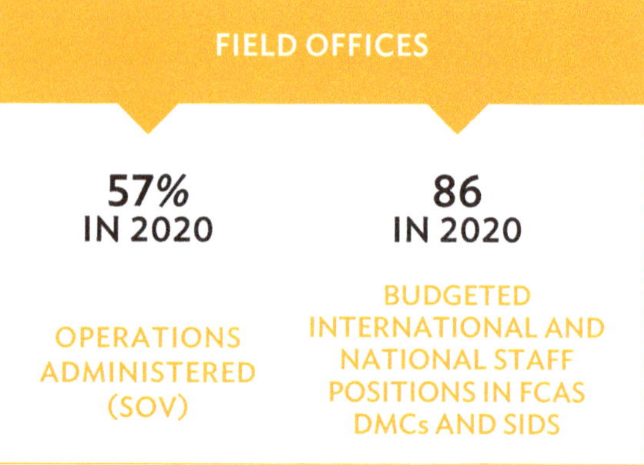

AVG = average, DMC = developing member country, FCAS = fragile and conflict-affected situations, NSO = nonsovereign operation, SIDS = small island developing state, SOV = sovereign operation.

A. ORGANIZATIONAL CAPACITY

147. **Robust capitalization.** ADB's capitalization remains robust and supports the planned expansion of operations in line with Strategy 2030. The capital utilization ratio increased to 69.1% in 2020 from 62.1% in 2019 mainly because of the increase in loan exposure caused by the strong growth of ADB's operations to respond to the coronavirus disease (COVID-19) crisis.[50]

148. **Nonsovereign credit quality weakened slightly.** Challenging credit and macroeconomic conditions triggered by the COVID-19 pandemic did not significantly change the weighted average risk rating of nonsovereign operations. The rating declined only slightly to 9.7 (B) from 9.6 (B) in 2019.[51] The impaired loans ratio improved to 4.2% in 2020 from 4.8% in the previous year because of growth in the credit portfolio, which was driven in part by COVID-19 support and some successful recoveries of impaired transactions.

149. **Representation of women *on track but watch*.** Women's share of ADB's international staff positions grew to 37.7% from 36.7% in 2019. Their representation in leadership roles (levels 7–8) rose sharply to 29.3% from 24.1% in the same period.

150. **Shift to virtual training programs reduced spending.** An average of $621 was spent on training per staff member trained in 2020 compared with $887 in 2019, with 5,295 individual staff attending one or more training program provided by ADB's Budget, People and Management Systems Department.[52] There was no training travel expenditure for in-house or external training programs after late February because of the pandemic, and many programs were deferred or canceled in the second quarter as staff relocated and adjusted to remote work arrangements. After March, all programs were held virtually, so the normal cost of trainer travel was not spent. Throughout the year, there were 214 sessions covering 59 different training programs, 3 blended learning programs, and 186 coaching sessions addressing various staff needs. There was a 43% year-on-year increase in learning and coaching sessions to support staff learning needs and well-being in response to increasing workloads and the challenges of working from home during the extended lockdown (Figure 7.1).

151. **Field office staffing ratio increased slightly.** The share of all ADB international and national staff positions in regional departments assigned to field offices rose by 1 percentage point to 46% in 2020.[53] Continued efforts to increase field office presence despite the difficulties of relocating staff during the pandemic, together with the extension of existing outposting arrangements to compensate for travel restrictions on headquarters staff, resulted in the addition of 25 positions. This was the net result of 9 fewer resident mission positions and 34 more outposted positions. By the end of 2020, 564 of ADB's staff positions were in its field offices.

152. **More field staff assigned in fragile, conflict-affected, and small island states.** Two budgeted international and national staff positions were added in the field offices in countries with fragile and conflict-affected situations (FCAS) and small island developing states (SIDS). The new total of 86, of which 59 are resident mission positions and 27 are outposted, was about 15% of the 564 such positions in all field offices in 2020. ADB's efforts to expand its field presence in response to Strategy 2030 calls for strengthening resident mission capacity and improving business processes in the field.

153. **More than half of operations administered by field offices.** About 57% (371) of the 655 active sovereign operations in 2020 were administered by ADB's field offices—52% (341) by field-office-based staff, and 4.6% (30) by staff posted from ADB headquarters. The share was slightly lower for the 143 active sovereign concessional assistance operations. About 47% (67) of them were administered by the field offices, 41% (59) by staff based in the field offices and 6% (8) by outposted headquarters staff.

Figure 7.1: Training Programs Conducted in 2019 and 2020

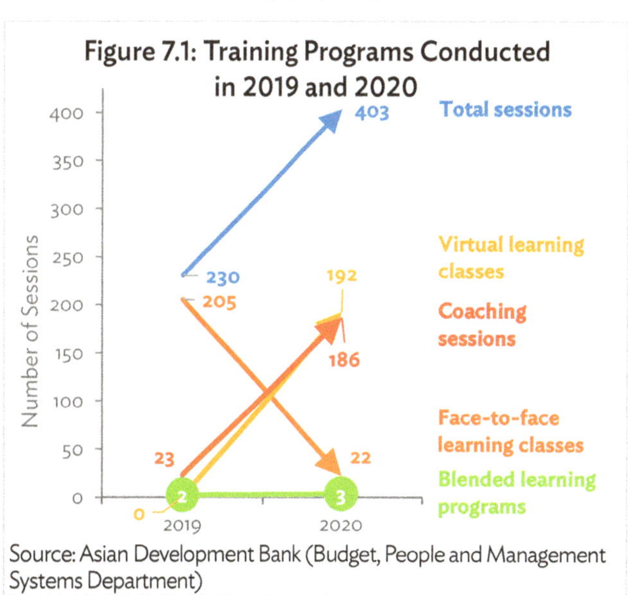

Source: Asian Development Bank (Budget, People and Management Systems Department)

MODERNIZING BUSINESS PROCESS AND IMPROVING OPERATIONAL EFFICIENCY

TIME FROM CONCEPT APPROVAL OR CLEARANCE TO FIRST DISBURSEMENT (MONTHS)

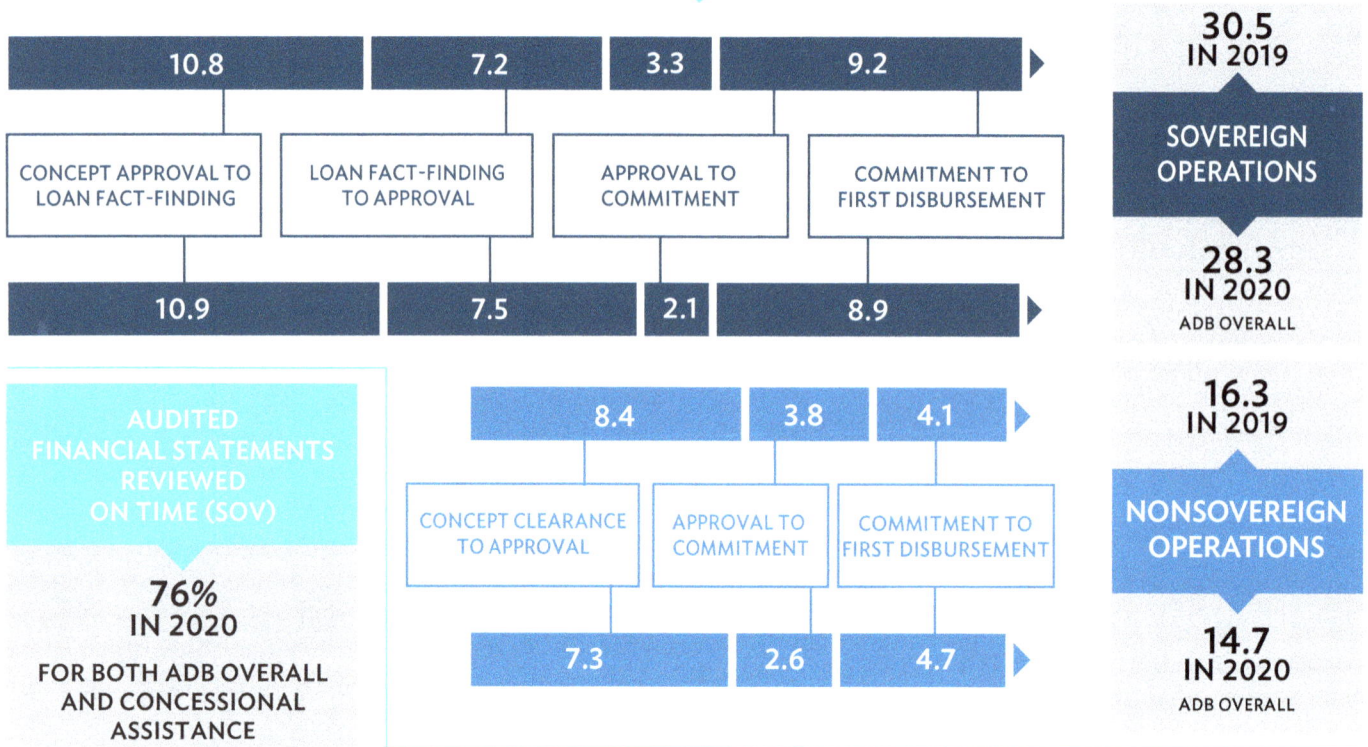

SOVEREIGN OPERATIONS

	CONCEPT APPROVAL TO LOAN FACT-FINDING	LOAN FACT-FINDING TO APPROVAL	APPROVAL TO COMMITMENT	COMMITMENT TO FIRST DISBURSEMENT	ADB OVERALL
2019	10.8	7.2	3.3	9.2	30.5 IN 2019
2020	10.9	7.5	2.1	8.9	28.3 IN 2020

NONSOVEREIGN OPERATIONS

	CONCEPT CLEARANCE TO APPROVAL	APPROVAL TO COMMITMENT	COMMITMENT TO FIRST DISBURSEMENT	ADB OVERALL
2019	8.4	3.8	4.1	16.3 IN 2019
2020	7.3	2.6	4.7	14.7 IN 2020

AUDITED FINANCIAL STATEMENTS REVIEWED ON TIME (SOV)

76%
IN 2020
FOR BOTH ADB OVERALL AND CONCESSIONAL ASSISTANCE

QUALITY OF BUDGET MANAGEMENT (%, UNUTILIZED IAE)

0%
IN 2019

5%
IN 2020
(including 2% carryover)

5% OR LESS
ANNUAL

SHARE OF OPERATIONAL EXPENSES FOR OPERATIONS DEPARTMENTS AND DIRECT OPERATIONS SUPPORT DEPARTMENTS (%)

82.9%
IN 2020

INTERNAL ADMINISTRATIVE EXPENSES ($'000)

37.8
IN 2020
PER $1 MILLION DISBURSEMENT

771
IN 2020
PER PROJECT UNDER ADMINISTRATION

4,242
IN 2020
PER PROJECT APPROVED

DEPARTMENTS WITH DOCUMENTED AND TESTED BUSINESS CONTINUITY PLANS IN PLACE

4
IN 2020

PROVIDED AN ENABLING CULTURE FOR S2030

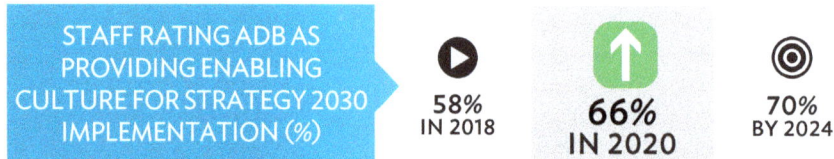

STAFF RATING ADB AS PROVIDING ENABLING CULTURE FOR STRATEGY 2030 IMPLEMENTATION (%)

58%
IN 2018

66%
IN 2020

70%
BY 2024

ADB = Asian Development Bank, IAE = internal administrative expenses, SOV = sovereign operation.

B. ORGANIZATIONAL SYSTEMS AND PROCESSES

154. **Sovereign processing time reduced substantially.** Sovereign operations were processed over an average of 28 months in 2020, 2.3 months faster than in 2019.[54] The disbursement time for the concessional assistance subset also shortened from 30 months to 28 months. Concept approval to fact-finding was the longest stage in both cases—almost 11 months for sovereign operations overall, and 12 months for those receiving concessional assistance. Two transport projects in Myanmar and Pakistan took between 31 and 53 months to complete this stage, lengthening the average time for ADB. In the Pakistan project, this was partly because the project design advance phase frontloaded the detailed design work, potentially saving time after loan approval. The difficult FCAS context and pandemic-related travel restrictions were also contributing factors.

155. **Nonsovereign operations start-up time faster.** The average time from concept clearance to first disbursement was 14.7 months for nonsovereign operations in 2020, 1.6 months shorter than in 2019.[55] The period from concept clearance to project approval, the longest processing stage, averaged 7 months.

156. **FAST deals speed COVID-19 response.** Use of the Faster Approach to Small Nonsovereign Transactions (FAST) in 2020 was instrumental in facilitating approvals and commitments of critical liquidity and working capital for clients across health care, agribusiness, energy, and finance in record time. The 11 FAST deals took an average of 8 months from concept clearance to first disbursement, 9.7 months less than regular nonsovereign deals (17.8 months). The five FAST deals that were COVID-19 related were processed in an average of 3.4 months. By comparison, the six non-COVID-19 related FAST deals took about 12 months.

157. **Larger share of audit result reviews completed on time.** ADB reviewed 76% (565) of the 743 audited project financial statements for sovereign operations submitted in 2020 within the target time (i.e., within 8 weeks of receipt from the executing or implementing agency) compared with 55% (466 of 847) in 2019. Acknowledging the unprecedented disruption brought by the COVID-19 pandemic, ADB provided a temporary 6-month extension for the submission of audited project financial statements with due dates from 31 March to 31 December 2020. As a result, ADB received 12% fewer financial statements in 2020 than in 2019. However, the improvement of on-time review was mainly driven by two factors: the implementation of online review checklists and approval workflow in e-Operations; and strengthened departmental internal review procedures, financial management scrutiny, and advice during the process.

158. **Budget utilization on target.** ADB's budget utilization rate in 2020 was 95%, including 2% carry-over. Excluding travel-related expenses, which were impacted by international travel restrictions, the utilization rate was 100%.

159. **Administrative and operational expenses reduced.** Internal administrative expenses (IAE) per $1 million in disbursements stood at $37,800 in 2020, down from $49,000 in 2019. IAE per project under administration dropped from $794,000 in 2019 to $771,000, and IAE per project approved also decreased from $4,877,000 to $4,242,000. Despite the travel restrictions, the decrease in IAE was not substantial because of the significant increase in the total number of operations in 2020. The share of operational expenses for operations departments and direct operations support departments decreased by 1 percentage point to 82.9% in 2020 because the operations business travel savings were greater than the increase in information technology and facility management expenses that enabled ADB's operations to continue through the COVID-19 crisis.

160. **More departments have continuity plans in place.** Given the unprecedented disruption caused by the pandemic, 2020 was a year in which all personnel at ADB headquarters and many in resident missions put into practice business continuity drills as they began an extended period of work-from-home arrangements. In lieu of the drills that usually take place in the fourth quarter, information technology disaster recovery testing took place in November 2020, in which four departments tested access to critical applications in the offshore data center that supports their essential business processes.

Systems and processes improving with culture change

161. **Development of Strategy 2030 culture *on track*.** ADB's success in providing an enabling culture for Strategy 2030 implementation is measured using staff perceptions of the key elements of ADB's culture required to support Strategy 2030 implementation. In the 2020 survey, 66% of respondents agreed (32%) or tended to agree (34%) that ADB has a culture for innovation and collaboration, rating this indicator *on track* toward meeting the 70% target. About 79% of respondents agreed with the statement "my supervisor is open to staff's suggestions for change" (the highest constituent score) while only 50% agreed that "typically, people are comfortable speaking up in ADB" (the lowest). Detailed scores are shown in Figure 7.2.[56]

Figure 7.2: Staff Rating ADB as Providing an Enabling Culture for Strategy 2030
(%)

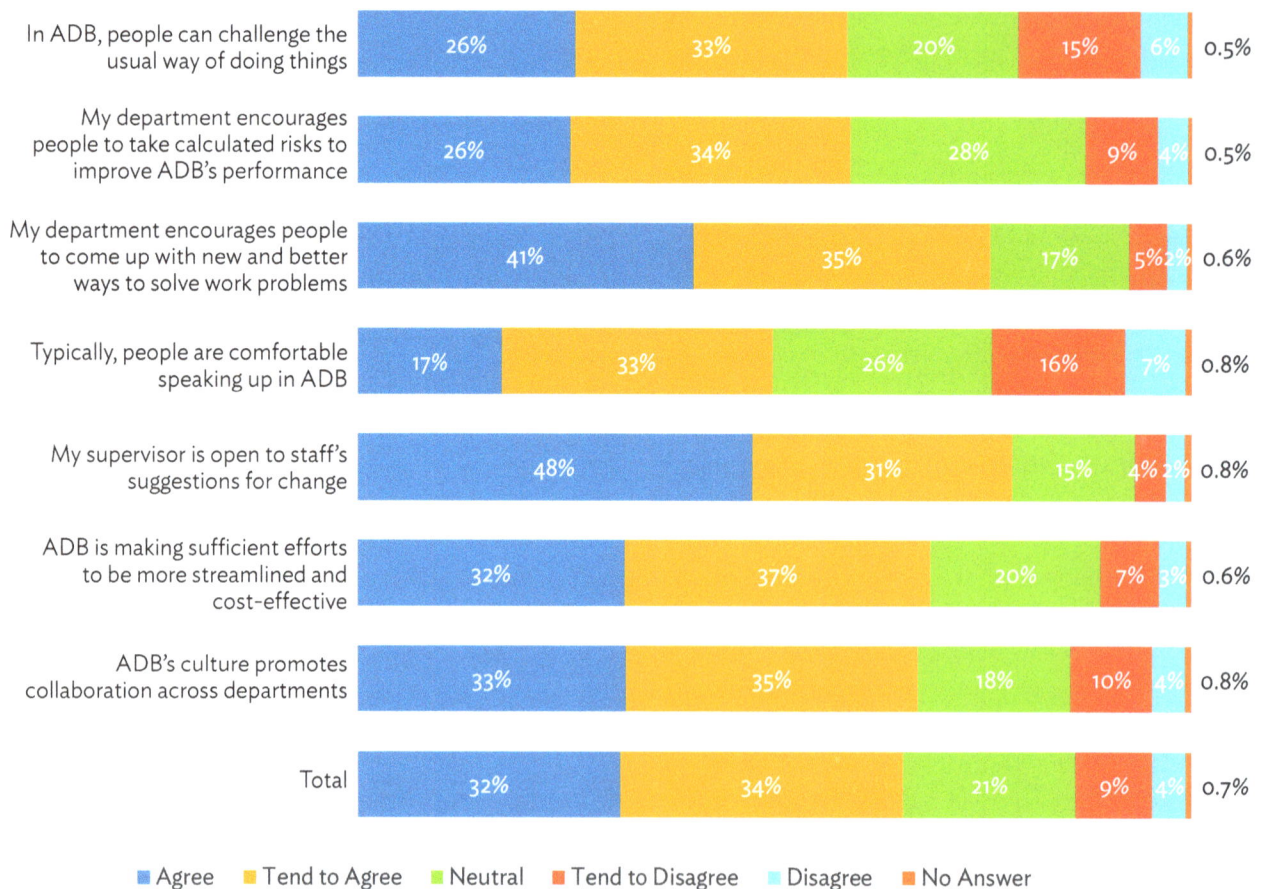

	Agree	Tend to Agree	Neutral	Tend to Disagree	Disagree	No Answer
In ADB, people can challenge the usual way of doing things	26%	33%	20%	15%	6%	0.5%
My department encourages people to take calculated risks to improve ADB's performance	26%	34%	28%	9%	4%	0.5%
My department encourages people to come up with new and better ways to solve work problems	41%	35%	17%	5%	2%	0.6%
Typically, people are comfortable speaking up in ADB	17%	33%	26%	16%	7%	0.8%
My supervisor is open to staff's suggestions for change	48%	31%	15%	4%	2%	0.8%
ADB is making sufficient efforts to be more streamlined and cost-effective	32%	37%	20%	7%	3%	0.6%
ADB's culture promotes collaboration across departments	33%	35%	18%	10%	4%	0.8%
Total	32%	34%	21%	9%	4%	0.7%

ADB = Asian Development Bank
Source: Asian Development Bank (Budget, People and Management Systems Department).

PROMOTING DIGITAL TRANSFORMATION

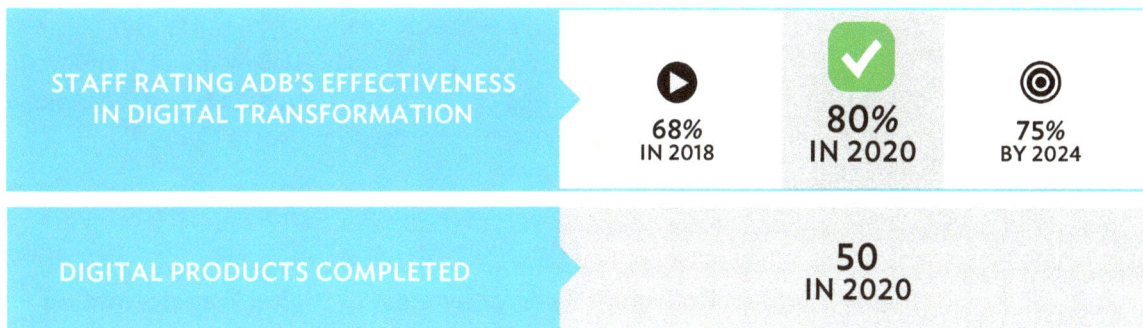

STAFF RATING ADB'S EFFECTIVENESS IN DIGITAL TRANSFORMATION

68%
IN 2018

80%
IN 2020

75%
BY 2024

DIGITAL PRODUCTS COMPLETED

50
IN 2020

ACHIEVING TIMELY AND VALUE-FOR-MONEY PROCUREMENT

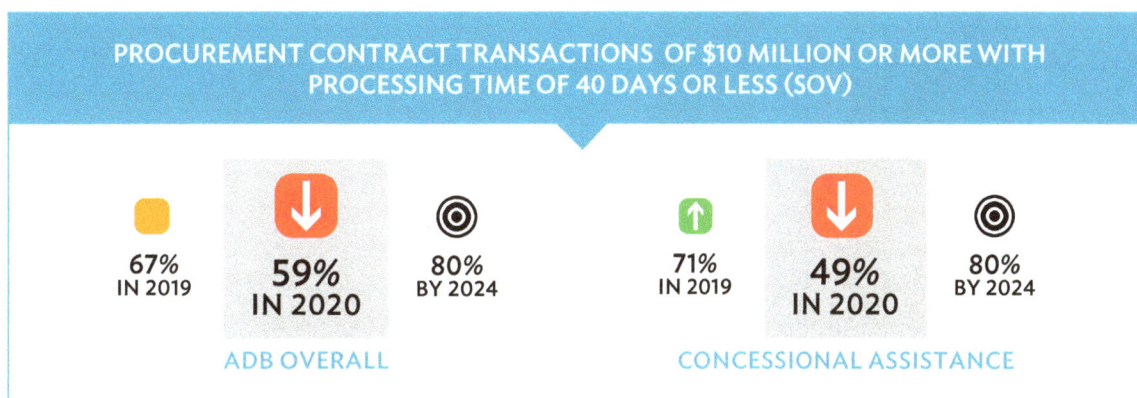

PROCUREMENT CONTRACT TRANSACTIONS OF $10 MILLION OR MORE WITH PROCESSING TIME OF 40 DAYS OR LESS (SOV)

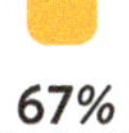
67%
IN 2019

59%
IN 2020

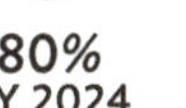
80%
BY 2024

ADB OVERALL

71%
IN 2019

49%
IN 2020

80%
BY 2024

CONCESSIONAL ASSISTANCE

PROCUREMENT TIME $10 MILLION OR MORE IN 2020 (SOV)

ADVERTISEMENT → CONCESSIONAL ASSISTANCE 332 DAYS → CONTRACT SIGNING

ADVERTISEMENT → ADB OVERALL 285 DAYS → CONTRACT SIGNING

CONSULTING SERVICES RECRUITMENT TIME FOR ADB-ADMINISTERED CONTRACTS IN 2020 (SOV)

RECRUITMENT NOTICE → ADB OVERALL 185 DAYS → CONTRACT SIGNING

INCREASING THE USE OF COUNTRY SYSTEMS

CONTRACTS USING GOVERNMENT E-PROCUREMENT SYSTEMS (SOV)

$4.6 BILLION
IN 2020

OPERATIONS USING COUNTRY PROCUREMENT SYSTEMS (SOV)

76%
IN 2020

ADB = Asian Development Bank, SOV = sovereign operation.

162. **First staff rating of ADB's effectiveness in digital transformation.** The corporate results framework (CRF) introduced a new results framework indicator to measure staff perspectives on the foundational elements for ADB's digital transformation. In the 2020 biennial staff engagement survey, the first to measure this progress, 80% of respondents agreed (42%) or tended to agree (38%) that ADB was successfully supporting digital transformation, surpassing the target of 75%. Detailed scores are shown in Figure 7.3.

Figure 7.3: Staff Rating ADB's Effectiveness in Digital Transformation (%)

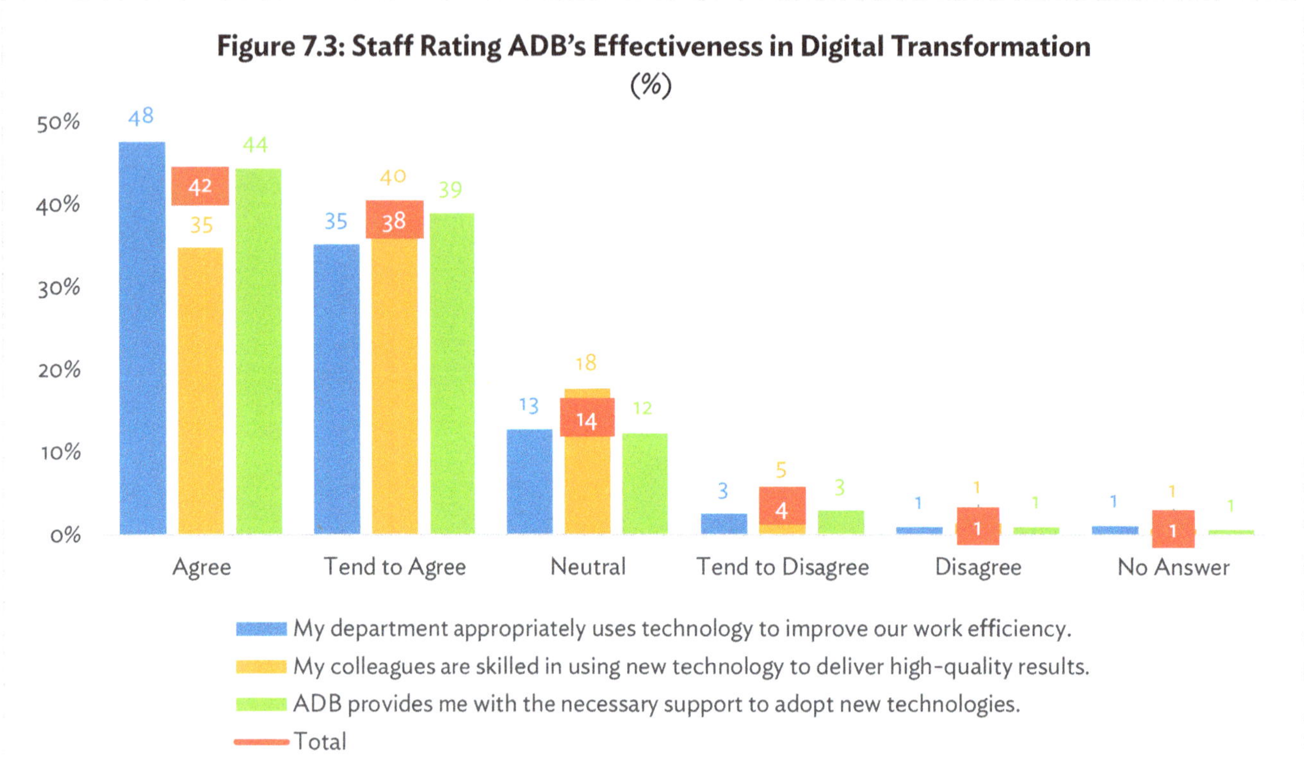

ADB = Asian Development Bank.
Source: Asian Development Bank (Budget, People and Management Systems Department).

163. **Digital transformation accelerated.** A total of 50 digital products were delivered in 2020, compared with 27 in 2019. The faster development and implementation of new digital tools and services was prompted by the need to support the sudden shift of ADB staff to remote work arrangements and to enable ADB's continued operation amid the pandemic. New digital tools and services related to supporting work-from-home arrangements included the Work from Home and COVID-19 Response dashboards; Pocket Wi-Fi; MS Teams and Zoom; the Management Approval System; Universal Access, which enables headquarters and field office users to securely connect to corporate applications even when not connected to the office internet; and the eSignature pilot.

164. **Procurement time *off track.*** The share of sovereign operation procurement transactions of $10 million or more that were processed within the target time of 40 days decreased by 8 percentage points to 59% overall and by 22 percentage points to 49% for concessional assistance operations, in both cases resulting in an *off track* rating for this indicator.[57]

165. **End-to-end procurement time longer.** The average end-to-end procurement time from the date an invitation to bid was advertised on ADB's website to the date a contract of $10 million or more was signed lengthened by 20 days to 285 in 2020. COVID-19 contributed to the delay in 17 (59%) of the 29 contracts with procurement times of longer than 300 days by causing the bid preparation period

to be extended. The slightly longer procurement time was because of the constrained capacities of the executing and implementing agencies and the need to allocate resources to addressing the pandemic and maintaining the health and safety of contractors in the field. The 20-day increase is therefore a manifestation of the working context amid the pandemic rather than a sign of underperformance.

166. **Slower onboarding of consulting firms.** Recruitment of consultants required an average of 185 days. It took 22 days longer than in 2019 to engage consulting firms for technical assistance (TA) projects through quality- and cost-based selection. Reasons for the delay included amendments to the terms of reference after launch of requests for proposals and prolonged contract negotiations to agree on contractual provisions to address COVID-19 related restrictions.

167. **Promoting use of country procurement systems.** ADB continues to help developing member countries (DMCs) establish and strengthen their procurement systems.[58] The share of disbursements made through open competitive bidding processes with national advertisement, results- and policy-based lending, and on-lending by financial intermediaries was 76% both for overall and concessional assistance operations. This was a substantial increase from the 2019 figures of 60% overall and 58% for concessional assistance operations.

168. **Shift to e-procurement.** ADB encourages the use of e-procurement at different stages of the procurement process because it promotes good governance, transparency, value for money, audit trails, and the broadest possible access to suppliers. Before the pandemic, more than two-thirds of ADB DMCs had some capacity and systems for conducting procurement electronically. After the onset of pandemic, ADB provided seven distinct e-government procurement installations in Georgia, India, and Viet Nam, and it contracted Ilion TenderLink to provide a Software-as-a-Service e-procurement portal to ADB borrowers with weak or no e-bidding platforms.

169. **Transition to e-procurement steady despite transborder trade limitations.** Very few national e-government procurement systems are approved for use in open competitive bidding with international advertisement. Many are limited to open competitive bidding with national advertisement only. Despite these restrictions, the volume of sovereign contracts using government e-procurement systems was $4.6 billion in 2020 compared with $4.5 billion in 2019.

170. **One ADB collaboration increased.** In the CRF, collaboration between ADB's sovereign and nonsovereign operations departments is monitored through a performance indicator measuring the number of projects or transactions with sovereign–nonsovereign collaboration. Operations departments have responded strongly to Strategy 2030's call for a One ADB approach to deliver solutions to the DMCs. In 2020, 14 projects brought together private sector and sovereign operations expertise and knowledge, giving a cumulative total of 22 and exceeding the cumulative target of 18 such projects by 2024. Boxes 7.1 and 7.2 provide examples of One ADB collaboration.

STRENGTHENING COLLABORATION

SOVEREIGN–NONSOVEREIGN COLLABORATION

PARD–OPPP

1. **PAL:** Solar Photovoltaic Independent Power Producer Project

SARD–PSOD

1. **IND:** Bengaluru Smart Energy Efficient Power Distribution Project

SARD–OPPP

1. **BAN:** Strengthening Bangladesh Infrastructure Finance Fund Limited Project
2. **IND:** Delhi–Meerut Regional Rapid Transit System Investment Project

CWRD–OPPP

1. **GEO:** Sustainable Water Supply and Sanitation Sector Development Program
2. **PAK:** Karachi Wastewater Treatment Project (Treatment Plant 4)
3. **TAJ:** Power Sector Development Program

CWRD–OPPP–PSOD

1. **UZB:** Solar Public-Private Partnership Program

CWRD–PSOD

1. **KGZ:** Rural Financial Inclusion for Women Project

SERD–PSOD

1. **CAM:** Agricultural Value Chain Competitiveness and Safety Enhancement Project
2. **VIE:** Binh Duong Water Treatment Expansion Project

SERD–OPPP

1. **PHI:** National ID System Project

EARD–PSOD

1. **MON:** Tavan Bogd COVID-19 Wheat Supply Chain Liquidity Support Project
2. **PRC:** Climate-Resilient and Smart Urban Water Infrastructure Project

PROJECTS OR TRANSACTIONS WITH SOVEREIGN–NONSOVEREIGN COLLABORATION (CUMULATIVE)

8 IN 2019

22 IN 2020

18 BY 2024

MEANINGFUL ENGAGEMENT WITH CIVIL SOCIETY ORGANIZATIONS

76% IN 2020
% OF COMPLETED OPERATIONS (SOV)

COLLABORATION WITH DEVELOPMENT PARTNERS

63% IN 2020
% OF STAKEHOLDERS SATISFIED

ADB = Asian Development Bank, BAN = Bangladesh, CAM = Cambodia, CWRD = Central and West Asia Department, EARD = East Asia Department, GEO = Georgia, IND = India, KGZ = Kyrgyz Republic, MON = Mongolia, OPPP = Office of Public–Private Partnership, PAK = Pakistan, PAL = Palau, PARD = Pacific Department, PHI = Philippines, PRC = People's Republic of China, PSOD = Private Sector Operations Department, SARD = South Asia Department, SERD = Southeast Asia Department, SOV = sovereign operation, TAJ = Tajikistan, UZB = Uzbekistan, VIE = Viet Nam.

Box 7.1: Tavan Bogd COVID-19 Wheat Supply Chain Liquidity Support Project in Mongolia

The Asian Development Bank (ADB) is providing collaborative "One ADB" assistance for a project in Mongolia that provides liquidity support to two subsidiaries of Tavan Bogd Group (TBG) to enable them to sustain their operations during the coronavirus disease (COVID-19) crisis. The project will help ensure a stable supply of wheat flour, the main staple in Mongolia, and flour products, and protect livelihoods. ADB's East Asia Department (EARD) held discussions with TBG and brokered the first meeting between TBG and ADB's Private Sector Operations Department (PSOD). PSOD provided a nonsovereign loan using FAST (Faster Approach to Small Nonsovereign Transactions), and EARD continues to play a key role in the investment process.

Source: ADB. 2020. *Fast Report: Loans to Ulaanbaatar Flour Limited Liability Company and Tavan Bogd Foods Limited Liability Company for the Tavan Bogd COVID-19 Wheat Supply Chain Liquidity Support Project in Mongolia*. Manila.

Box 7.2: Solar Public–Private Partnership Program in Uzbekistan

"One ADB" collaboration on the Solar Public–Private Partnership Program in Uzbekistan brings together a suite of transaction support services and financial instruments from the Central and West Asia Department (CWRD), the Office of Public–Private Partnership (OPPP), and the Private Sector Operations Department (PSOD) of the Asian Development Bank (ADB) for the deployment of up to 1 gigawatt of solar projects.

In coordination with CWRD and PSOD, OPPP provided transaction advisory support, including developing bankable and sustainable power project structures and replicable document templates, to prepare and structure the first project, a solar photovoltaic facility in the district of Sherabad—a site initially proposed by a CWRD solar energy study. A comprehensive sovereign-backed guarantee, prepared by CWRD and PSOD to mitigate off-taker credit risks, attracted international investors and lenders to the project.

Source: ADB. 2020. *Concept Paper: Proposed Partial Credit Guarantee Facility for Uzbekistan Solar Public-Private Partnership Program*. Manila.

171. **Engagement with civil society organizations.** ADB continues to track its important collaboration with civil society organizations (CSOs) and recognizes their unique strengths and extensive local presence. In 2020, ADB's NGO and Civil Society Center began reporting the achievements rather than the intent of CSO participation, as well as differentiating between the different types of CSO engagement. The redefined tracking indicator shows that 76% of the sovereign operations completed in 2020 achieved the planned meaningful CSO engagement. ADB defines meaningful CSO engagement as significant information sharing or consultation activities, or any type of collaboration or partnership with CSOs.

172. **First results show scope for more collaboration efforts.** Responses to the client survey question, "How effective is ADB in its collaboration with other development partners?" revealed that 63% primary clients were either *extremely* (10%) or *very* (53%) *satisfied* with ADB's performance.

Reliable electricity. Most of the 4 million residents of Afghanistan's capital, Kabul, now enjoy the benefits of power transmitted via 220-kilovolt electricity towers and lines on the outskirts of the city of Mazar-e-Sharif (photo by Jawad Jalali).

CHAPTER 8

DIFFERENTIATED APPROACHES IN FCAS AND SIDS

Strategy 2030 specifies the differentiated approaches ADB must take to meet the distinct needs and conditions of the diverse groups within its developing country membership. These include the low-income and lower middle-income developing member countries, as well as upper middle-income countries. Strategy 2030 calls for ADB to prioritize and tailor special support for the poorest and most vulnerable developing member countries, including those dealing with fragile and conflict-affected situations and the difficult challenges of small island developing states. This special support is markedly crucial during a global health pandemic.

FOCUSING OPERATIONS ON FCAS AND SIDS

SHARE OF COMMITMENTS IN FCAS DMCS AND SIDS

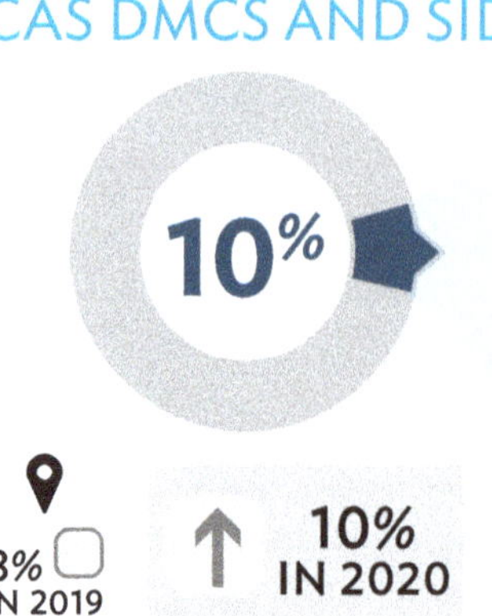

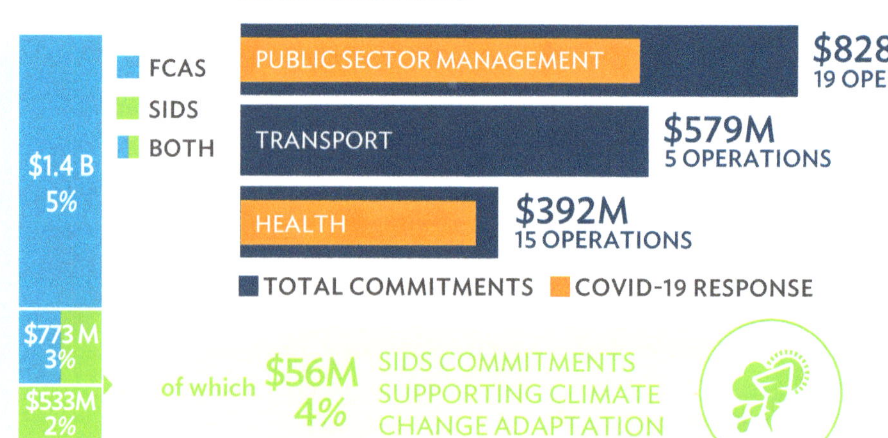

8% IN 2019 ↑ 10% IN 2020

of which $56M 4% SIDS COMMITMENTS SUPPORTING CLIMATE CHANGE ADAPTATION

PERFORMANCE OF COMPLETED OPERATIONS

COMPLETED FCAS OPERATIONS RATED *SUCCESSFUL*

57% IN 2017–2019 ↓ 50% IN 2018–2020

OVERALL SUCCESS RATE

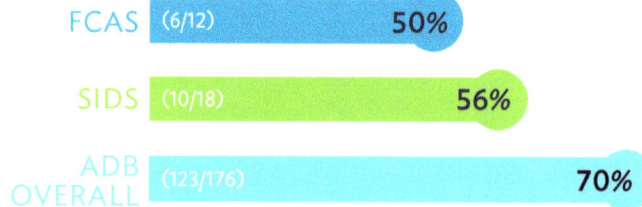

FCAS	(6/12)	50%
SIDS	(10/18)	56%
ADB OVERALL	(123/176)	70%

COMPLETED SIDS OPERATIONS RATED *SUCCESSFUL*

42% IN 2017–2019 ↑ 56% IN 2018–2020

ENHANCING ADB'S CAPACITY TO SUPPORT FCAS AND SIDS

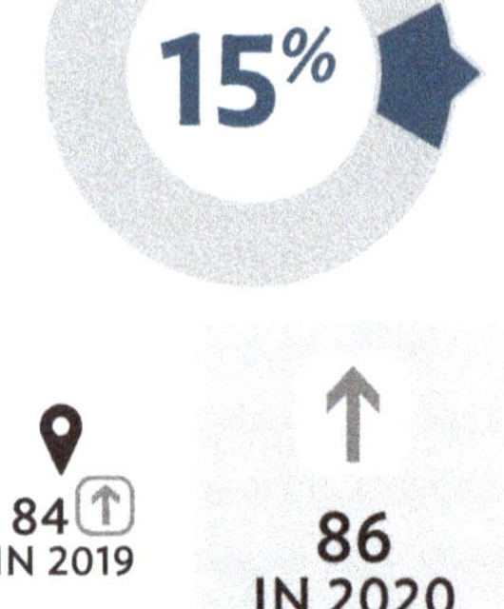

84 IN 2019 ↑ 86 IN 2020

In 2020, ADB had 86 budgeted staff positions in FCAS and SIDS field offices, of the total 564 budgeted international and national staff positions in operations departments' field offices

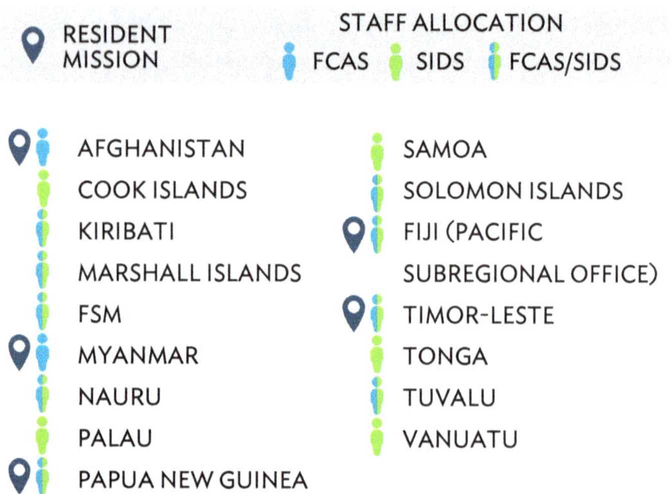

ADB = Asian Development Bank, B = billion, DMC = developing member country, FCAS = fragile and conflict-affected situations, FSM = Federated States of Micronesia, M = million, SIDS = small island developing state.

A. OPERATIONAL FOCUS

173. **Fragile and conflict-affected situations.** Context sensitivity is key to implementing Strategy 2030 successfully.[59] This demands knowledge and understanding of the local conditions and the flexibility needed to adjust with good effect when these change. These two elements are central to ADB's approach to fragile and conflict-affected situations (FCAS), and ADB put both to work to deliver tailored, context-sensitive support to FCAS countries during the 2020 COVID-19 crisis.

174. Of the ADB financing committed for FCAS-category developing member countries (DMCs) in 2020, $894 million (about 40%) was in direct response to the pandemic. The bulk (67%) of this went to Afghanistan, Myanmar, and Papua New Guinea for countercyclical expenditure programs. Another 22% of the total financing for FCAS DMCs supported non-urban road transport projects, and electricity transmission and distribution accounted for 14%. A $484 million sovereign commitment to Myanmar was the largest transport operation. It will build a safe, climate-resilient four-lane expressway for more efficient connectivity on the Greater Mekong Subregion East–West Economic Corridor.[60]

175. **Small island developing states.** Small island developing states (SIDS) generally share very similar structural constraints whether they are experiencing fragility and formally categorized as FCAS or not.[61] Elevated vulnerability to and an inability to resist or rebound from shocks are common features. So are weak institutions, governance, and basic service delivery, as well as deep indebtedness risks, limited private sectors, and narrowly based economies struggling to lift people out of poverty. Small size and remote isolation often compound their extreme exposure and sensitivity to the impacts of climate change, natural hazards, and global economic downturns.

176. ADB continued its focus on these long-standing SIDS challenges in 2020 while also swiftly providing these DMCs with help they urgently needed to cope with the COVID-19 pandemic and its economic shocks. These included the collapse of international tourism on which many depend and other threats to lives and well-being. About $769 million (59%) of ADB financing committed to the SIDS during the year was budgetary support for their governments' countercyclical pandemic response measures and health and livelihood protection programs. Of the total, 15% supported the reforms of state-owned enterprises in the SIDS.

B. PERFORMANCE OF COMPLETED OPERATIONS

177. The small number of sovereign operations completed in FCAS and SIDS countries each year makes annual success rates highly volatile. The average rate for ADB's FCAS operations has been declining since 2016. It reached a new low of 50% (6 of 12 operations were rated *successful*) in 2018–2020. Of 18 SIDS operations 10 were rated *successful*. Results from two *successful* completed operations are highlighted in Boxes 8.1 and 8.2.

178. Three FCAS and SIDS public sector management (PSM) and energy sector operations were rated *less than successful* after procurement delays, difficulties in implementing safeguard measures, and weakness in the government plans and policies to support them.[62] An energy project in Solomon Islands that did not proceed with construction because of land acquisition issues was eventually canceled. Recently completed technical assistance (TA) projects addressed some of these challenges. In 2020, all 10 TA projects in FCAS and SIDS were rated *successful* by self-evaluations. They helped governments adopt longer-term planning horizons, promoted cross-sector synergies, and supported more programmatic approaches.

C. ENHANCING ADB'S CAPACITY TO RESPOND

179. ADB added budgeted staff outpost positions in Afghanistan and Myanmar in 2020, raising the total in FCAS DMCs and SIDS from 84 to 86. Staff operating in ADB field offices were essential to scaling up ADB's support and monitoring project implementation during 2020 global travel restrictions. ADB also committed TA to design enhanced remote project management tools including drone technology.[63] These are expected to enable higher quality and frequency of monitoring at a lower cost. In addition, ADB developed an implementation approach for the Healthy Oceans Action Plan that will focus on SIDS (endnote 35).

Box 8.1: Response to Tropical Cyclones Ian and Winston

The readiness of the Asian Development Bank (ADB) to support recovery, reconstruction, and preparedness in the Pacific's disaster-prone small island developing states is illustrated by its response when category 5 Tropical Cyclone Ian directly hit Tonga's Ha'apai island group in 2014, affecting two-thirds of the population. After providing emergency solar lanterns and community solar chargers for outlying islands, ADB helped develop a new disaster- and climate-resilient main power grid. Residences, businesses, government offices, and a hospital were reconnected to electricity through new underground cables. Reconstruction, upgrading, and the asbestos remediation of all the islands' 12 primary and 4 secondary schools was completed within 2 years.

The ADB response to Tropical Cyclone Winston's destruction across large parts of rural Fiji in 2016 included support for social protection payments to 43,524 people, assistance to sustain and generate economic activity, and the reconstruction of homes and 134 schools. The government approved an ADB-supported disaster recovery framework in the same year to apply disaster resilience policies to budget preparation, reconstruction financing, social protection, and recovery activities.

Sources: ADB. 2020. *Completion Report: Cyclone Ian Recovery Project in Tonga*. Manila.; and ADB. 2020. *Completion Report: Emergency Assistance for Recovery from Tropical Cyclone Winston in Fiji*. Manila.

Box 8.2: Electricity Supply Security in Nauru

Asian Development Bank (ADB) support has often addressed one of the most damaging barriers to fuller socioeconomic development in small island developing states: poor basic services. A 2015 project helped greatly improve previously unreliable electricity service by upgrading the generators used by Nauru's lone power utility. The powerhouse was rehabilitated and personnel were trained in effective operation and maintenance. Residents responding to a 2019 survey reported that they can now reliably use refrigerators, washing machines, fans, and cooking stoves after years of enduring regular power interruptions. Revenues have risen for businesses and service sector operations, and operating costs have declined. Emergency generators and fuel to power them are no longer needed. A guaranteed supply on the tiny nation's power grid has made medical treatment more efficient and safer at Nauru's only hospital.

Source: ADB. 2019. *Completion Report: Electricity Supply Security and Sustainability Project in Nauru*. Manila.

D. IN FOCUS

1. Protecting the Most Vulnerable through a Pandemic in Fragile Situations

180. The pandemic created a perfect storm of health and economic shocks, and helping the most vulnerable withstand it was a special challenge in ADB's FCAS DMCs and SIDS. Basic service delivery, often poor at the best of times, was strained to unprecedented degrees, leaving populations affected by conflict, fragility, and undeveloped or unreformed public services even more exposed than normal. Medical systems, already inadequate, faced the threat of being overrun. Shutdowns, travel restrictions, and border closures drove unemployment up and crippled businesses large and small. A surge in poverty is now expected. So is a spike in the instability that is a frequent adverse feature of situations of fragility and/or conflict. Children, women, older persons, people with disabilities, and minorities have become more vulnerable.

181. ADB's COVID-19 emergency context-sensitive programs provided immediate support in FCAS DMCs and SIDS. These will also be vital in paving the way to recovery once the crisis ends. Examples from Afghanistan, Myanmar, and Timor-Leste illustrate

how ADB tailored these emergency-response programs to emphasize and address the unique needs of the most vulnerable.

182. **Mainstreaming gender in the pandemic response in Afghanistan.** Gender equality objectives formed an integral part of two COVID-19 response support packages for Afghanistan, where the pandemic was not only overtaxing an inadequate health care system but also exacerbating the country's gender-based inequalities.

183. Under a government social safety net program supported by a $100 million ADB countercyclical financing grant, households headed by women were given priority for assistance that covered the water and electricity bills of 350,000 users.[64] More than 36,000 women were among the 130,311 pensioners and their heirs who continued to receive their payments during the crisis with program support. The program also financed remuneration packages for at least an additional 32,000 disabled military personnel and civilians and the families of people killed during Afghanistan's conflicts, including their female heirs.

184. Female medical staff will be outfitted with properly sized PPE through a $40 million ADB emergency assistance grant, and 900 women will be among 3,000 health workers trained for public health emergencies.[65] This is critical in a country where social norms deny the half of the population that is female treatment by the males who make up 98% of the doctors and 85% of the nurses. A resilience strategy and capacity development plan will be prepared and implemented to help give women more access to sexual and reproductive health services and support for victims of gender-based violence. All the 15 hospitals and medical facilities to be constructed and equipped under the program and the 5 to be rehabilitated will feature women-friendly facilities.

185. **Making Myanmar's services more geographically inclusive.** ADB adjusted two ongoing operations and approved a third in 2020 to address vulnerabilities in Myanmar on both the immediate pandemic-related front and in minority areas.

186. Financing of $30 million was added to an existing subregional health security operation and $1.7 million committed to regional TA to support the government's COVID-19 contingency plan in the health sector.[66] Given that conflict can be sparked or fueled by inequities in access to government services and a relative lack of social and economic capital, this funding will provide essential medical supplies and equipment and expand clinical care, infection prevention and control, and human resource capacity for pandemic response mainly in district and township hospitals (23 of 31) in geographical areas accessible by Myanmar's many diverse ethnic minority groups.

187. Guided by updates from a panel of informed conflict advisors, ADB was able to better ensure that the $250 million countercyclical pandemic response loan it provided Myanmar in 2020, will finance inclusive development, provide equitable benefits, and neither exacerbate nor be disrupted by local conflicts. The emphasis is on reaching the poorest and most vulnerable populations, including minorities and people in the areas affected by past and current conflicts. The internally displaced now living in camps will receive cash and food transfers under the program.

188. **Ensuring food security amid the pandemic in Timor-Leste.** Young children are especially vulnerable in FCAS countries. International shipping and food supply chain disruptions during the 2020 pandemic threatened to seriously aggravate malnutrition and a 50% rate of stunting of boys and girls under 5 in Timor-Leste. A $1 million ADB grant through the Asia Pacific Disaster Response Fund helped address the problem in an innovative way.[67] The project, developed in coordination with United Nations agencies and local civil society organizations, purchased food for distribution to the vulnerable from local shops and farmers unable to sell their products because of pandemic restrictions. It thus benefited micro and small enterprises struggling to survive during the COVID-19 outbreaks and poor households in an FCAS DMC where food insecurity affects three-quarters of the population.

2. Meeting the Unique COVID-19 Needs of Small Island Developing States

189. ADB's member SIDS closed their borders early in the pandemic and had shown little sign of reopening them when 2020 ended. Like larger countries throughout the world, they took emergency steps to strengthen health systems, continue providing essential public services, and bolster economies rocked by the global crisis. Investments to protect themselves and build resilience against their exceptional exposure to the destructive impacts of climate change and other natural hazards continued.

190. **Building resilience against health emergencies.** Rapid ADB pandemic support included disbursement of contingent disaster financing to eight Pacific SIDS and 18 COVID-19 grants providing support to 14 Pacific SIDS through its Asia Pacific Disaster Response Fund. Phase 3 of the separate Pacific Disaster Resilience Program, approved in 2020, is providing contingent disaster financing to 10 SIDS—the Cook Islands, the Federated States of Micronesia, Kiribati, the Marshall Islands, Palau, Samoa, Solomon Islands, Tonga, Tuvalu, and Vanuatu.[68] The policy actions to be supported through Phase 3 were expanded to help enable these Pacific DMCs tackle public health threats and better prepare for health emergencies as well as such hazards as cyclones and earthquakes. The program disburses financing quickly when these events occur.

191. **Reducing disaster risk and improving climate change resilience in Maldives.** ADB continued during 2020 to support crucial efforts by Pacific SIDS to reduce the high risks they face from climate change and strengthen their resilience to frequent disasters. The design of an ADB-financed project to establish a sustainable solid waste management system for the Greater Male region and neighboring outer islands in Maldives takes into account the threats posed to the country's infrastructure by climate change-induced sea level rise and coastal erosion. The system is designed specifically for a small island country and features added resilience to disasters triggered by natural and climate-related hazards.[69] Effective solid waste management treatment services will minimize pollution; reduce the use of natural resources; and improve the environment, including ocean health. The spillover benefits for tourism and fisheries are expected to help Maldives' economy recover from the COVID-19 pandemic.

192. **Expanding reliable climate-resilient solar energy in the Pacific.** Another ADB project, committed in 2020, addresses a further fundamental, common, and ongoing challenge confronting the Pacific SIDS. Their heavy reliance on imported fossil fuels drags on their economies and adds to their vulnerability to adverse external events. Fuel imports, expensive to transport, liable to supply disruptions by increasingly frequent extreme weather events, and subject to price volatility on the international markets, drive up costs and diminish the reliability of electricity services for businesses and households. The new project, cofinanced by the Strategic Climate Fund and the Government of New Zealand, will aim to strengthen energy security, reduce electricity production costs, and make the power grid more reliable in Kiribati.[70]

193. New technologies—including a solar photovoltaic system and battery energy storage and rainwater collection in the solar arrays and water supply equipment—aim to help boost the share of renewable energy on the South Tarawa grid in Kiribati from 9% to 44%. Fossil fuel consumption is expected to reduce, alongside the associated greenhouse gas emissions that contribute to global warming, which is in turn contributing to the rising sea levels that pose a threat to SIDS such as Kiribati. The project supports the development of draft legislation for essential reforms in the energy sector to increase the deployment of renewable energy solutions, including through inviting private sector investment. Environmental and technological innovations include an enhanced tree-planting program to preserve the Bonriki freshwater lens; climate-resilient and aviation-safe design; and the use of drones for remote site visits to monitor application of safeguards, implementation, and operation and maintenance. ADB plans to replicate design elements of this energy project, its first in Kiribati, in the 11 smaller Pacific SIDS.[71]

Marketing produce. A street vendor takes shelter with his produce near a market on a rainy day in Dili , Timor-Leste (photo by Luis Enrique Ascui).

Water supply and sanitation. The Ebeye Water Supply and Sanitation Project is linking all households in Ebeye, Marshall Islands, to upgraded freshwater and sewerage facilities that reduce water leaks and sewage overflows (photo by Eric Sales).

ACTIONS TO ADDRESS CHALLENGES

This section describes the systems and processes ADB has in place to identify and monitor actions to improve its performance, including the Management Action Record System. It summarizes the actions ADB took in 2020 in response to the challenges highlighted in the 2019 Development Effectiveness Review (DEfR) that pose barriers to implementing Strategy 2030, as well as the challenges identified in the 2020 DEfR process that ADB needs to address in 2021 and beyond.

A. MANAGEMENT ACTION RECORD SYSTEM

194. ADB's results-based management systems and processes are designed to formulate, communicate, mobilize, and monitor the actions ADB undertakes to tackle its operational and development effectiveness challenges. Challenges identified in the annual development effectiveness review (DEfR) are highlighted in the President's planning directions for the year, along with the corresponding strategic guidance and targets. These are then reflected in the annual work program and budget framework and cascaded down into the work plans of the individual departments and staff members to make performance expectations clear.

195. ADB's electronic Management Action Record System (MARS) was introduced in 2009 to capture and monitor the implementation by Management of actions responding to the recommendations stemming from evaluations and reviews of ADB's Independent Evaluation Department (IED). Action plans needed to carry out these recommendations are uploaded by Management to MARS along with due dates for completing each action. At the end of 2020, MARS held the records of 518 actions. Figure 9.1 summarizes their implementation status.

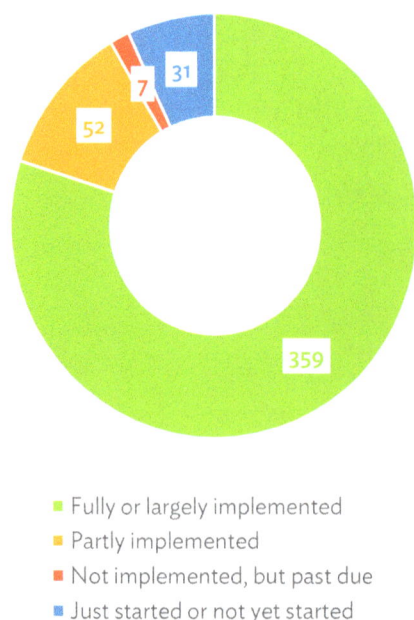

Figure 9.1: Status of Management Action Record System Actions at the End of 2020
(number)

196. **Assessment of actions completed in 2020.** ADB completed 32 actions in 2020. IED assessed the implementation of seven of them and downgraded two actions Management had self-assessed as *fully or largely implemented* to *partly implemented*.

197. **Action plans added in 2020.** The six evaluation reports discussed by the Development Effectiveness Committee of the ADB Board of Directors in 2020 made an average of five recommendations each. Of the 29 recommendations made overall, Management fully accepted 27 and partially agreed to 2 recommendations. The two were from the evaluation of ADB Support for Public–Private Partnerships, 2009–2019 and related to organizational changes proposed to promote a One ADB approach to such partnerships. By March 2021, action plans responding to four of the six evaluations had been uploaded, one was under discussion with IED, and one was not yet due to be uploaded.

198. **Action status in 2020.** In response to the 29 recommendations in 2020, 19 actions have been developed and uploaded to MARS. Only 1 action was due in 2020, and it has been self-assessed as *fully implemented*, while 18 actions are due in the next 3 years: 8 by 2021, 5 by 2022, and 5 by 2023. Once discussions are completed, 10 other actions contained in 2 action plans will be uploaded in 2021.

199. **Challenges delaying action implementation.** The delay for actions that were not fully implemented by their due date was attributed to project design weaknesses, prioritization of other ongoing work, and changes in context. Some actions were poorly specified and lacked a target completion date, and others had insufficient data to verify their completion. The experience highlights the importance of the quality of action formulation, monitoring, follow-up, and making midcourse adjustments in implementation.

200. **Action planning process improvements.** In 2020, ADB Management revived the practice of seeking IED's feedback on action plans during their formulation. Upon IED's suggestion, the time to upload the MARS action plans was also extended from 60 days to 90 days, and flexibility is now provided to adjust action plans during their implementation. Management will continue working closely with IED to improve the MARS process in 2021.

B. ACTIONS TO ADDRESS 2019 CHALLENGES

201. Two main performance areas were rated *off track* to achieve their 2024 targets in the 2019 DEfR scorecard: nonsovereign and sovereign success rates, including the share of sovereign projects completed on time. Two other areas were flagged as meriting close attention: financing for education and achievement of gender results. As explained in Chapter 3, supporting DMCs' urgent pandemic response needs shifted ADB's focus away from education financing in 2020. However, in addition to responding to urgent new challenges caused by the global health pandemic, ADB started, continued, and completed initiatives to address the ongoing challenges. This section summarizes the main actions taken during 2020.

1. Actions to Improve Success Rates of Completed Sovereign Projects

202. **Challenge.** The success rate of completed sovereign operations continued to decline in 2017–2019 and was 8 percentage points below the 2024 target of 80%. Of the four evaluation criteria, performance remained weakest on sustainability, followed by effectiveness.

203. **Steps taken to increase sustainability of development results.** ADB intensified efforts to address sustainability issues of sovereign operations in 2020. A One ADB approach was adopted by establishing a working group with the participation of 10 relevant departments to deliberate and exchange views on short- and long-term solutions for improving sovereign project sustainability. Building on its 2017 study on this topic, ADB's Strategy, Policy and Partnerships Department undertook a comparative study examining various practices for promoting and determining prospective sustainability across development partners and selected countries.[72] The working group is further reviewing and supplementing this study's findings and recommendations to explore approaches for sustaining the development outcomes of ADB-financed projects after their completion.

204. **Performance monitoring processes strengthened.** ADB completed the first full year of monitoring projects under implementation using the enhanced project performance rating methodology. The methodology was revised in 2019 to more accurately detect and flag issues with output delivery and compliance with safeguards and financial management covenants. The lower share of projects rated *on track* in 2019 using the new methodology (52% versus 74% using the old methodology) demonstrated the reform had met its objective of increased rigor. During 2020, project teams took swift action on many of the new issues flagged. They updated project design and monitoring frameworks to reflect changes in project scope and ensured performance indicators and targets were correctly entered into ADB's web-based monitoring system. They also addressed flagged safeguard compliance issues and better ensured timely submission of complete financial monitoring reports. These monitoring and supervision efforts bore fruit in 2020. The share of operations under implementation rated *successful* in 2020 increased by 12 percentage points to 64% despite the delays in project disbursement caused by the COVID-19 pandemic. Efforts to monitor active projects more rigorously are expected to aid project effectiveness and efficiency.

2. Actions to Improve Success Rates of Completed Nonsovereign Operations

205. **Challenge.** The success rate of completed nonsovereign operations remained *off track* in 2017–2019 and at 51% was considerably below the 2024 target of 70%. The poorest performers were the private equity fund operations. ADB work quality was the lowest-rated evaluation criterion, followed by achievement of development results.

206. **Development effectiveness improvement program underway.** ADB's Private Sector Operations Department (PSOD) continued to implement its development effectiveness change program. In 2020, PSOD fully rolled out a new monitoring system to measure the risk that ongoing nonsovereign operations will not achieve their targeted development results. The information is reported in a dashboard that gives Management insight into how the portfolio, and individual deals within it, are progressing toward their development objectives and identifies timely lessons. To foster timely use of this information, PSOD instituted the Development Effectiveness Forum as a platform to help ensure quality at entry and monitor (and remedy where required) development effectiveness during a project's life. The monitoring system also encourages more timely and complete progress monitoring and reporting.

207. In 2018–2020, the share of completed nonsovereign operations with a *satisfactory* rating for ADB work quality increased significantly (Chapter 5). While it is too soon to tell whether this is a sign of sustainable improvement, more timely and complete monitoring and reporting contributed to the improvement and are notable given that projects are sometimes rated *unsuccessful* because they lack data and evidence to show whether their intended development results were achieved. In 2020, PSOD also designed and tested an ex ante assessment tool that will more objectively evaluate the additionality and anticipated development results of each project under consideration. It is intended to be piloted in 2021.

208. **Continued focus on quality of equity investments.** In 2020, PSOD allocated staff resources to the Equity Investments Unit it had established the year prior to strengthen its ability to actively manage equity investments. The unit assumed management of the equity portfolio, providing a sounder governance structure and supporting the implementation of best market practices in the management of equity investments.

3. Actions to Better Deliver Gender Results

209. The share of completed ADB sovereign and nonsovereign operations delivering intended gender equality results continued a slow decline to 74% in 2017–2019 and remained *on track but watch* to reach the 80% target by 2024. These results emphasize the need for ADB to focus on quality and implementation of gender action plans as it continues to increase the gender mainstreaming of its operations. To this end, ADB's Sustainable Development and Climate Change Department, in partnership with operations departments, continued in 2020 to deliver gender equality training virtually for DMC officials and ADB staff. PSOD also hired an additional gender specialist.

C. ONGOING AND NEW CHALLENGES TO ADDRESS IN 2021 AND ONWARD

210. ***Off track* areas in 2020.** Sovereign and nonsovereign success rates remain *off track* in the 2020 DEfR. The success rate of completed sovereign operations in 2018–2020 was 10 percentage points below the 2024 target of 80%. A historic low of 33% of sovereign projects were completed on time. The success rate for ADB's operations in countries experiencing fragile and conflict-affected situations (FCAS) has been declining since 2016 and dipped to a low of 50% in 2018–2020. For nonsovereign operations, the success rate was 53%—still well below the 2024 target of 70%. The other indicators rated *off track* in 2020 are financing for health and education, sovereign disbursement rate, and nonsovereign operations committed as a share of the ADB total. They are measured on an annual basis rather than a 3-year average and are expected to readjust during 2021 and 2022 as ADB moves from providing urgent pandemic response support to its DMCs to supporting pandemic recovery and redoubling focus on achieving the Sustainable Development Goals (SDGs).

211. **New challenges for attaining the Sustainable Development Goals.** As highlighted in Chapter 1, ADB estimates that poverty has risen in Asia and the Pacific after many decades of almost uninterrupted decline. Existing fragilities and inequalities caused the effects of the COVID-19 pandemic to hurt the poorest the most.

212. ADB's rapid reorientation of its operations to help DMCs weather and manage the pandemic represents a remarkable effort to respond to a multidimensional shock that affected all countries in the region. ADB exceeded its health sector financing targets for the first time, while the emphasis on targeting the poorest and most vulnerable through emergency COVID-19 response operations expanded government programming that directly addressed these groups' needs. Toward this end, ADB's support for social protection systems also increased substantially and will need to continue to expand as the pandemic has reinforced the importance of strengthening these systems across the region. The need to empower women if the region's sustainable development aspirations are to be realized was also reinforced by the global health pandemic, which has put gender equality progress at risk. Although remote learning options have filled some gaps, education has been disrupted, reinforcing the need to build and deliver a robust pipeline of projects that provide digital skills and support more equitable access to distance learning.

213. Progress on environmental dimensions of the SDG agenda has been especially uneven in the region, as highlighted in Chapter 1, and although carbon intensity of the region's economies has improved, absolute emissions have continued to rise. In this context, Strategy 2030 sets out ambitious climate finance and climate mainstreaming targets for operations, and ADB has retained its focus on achieving these targets even though most emergency COVID-19 response operations had relatively few entry points to address climate change mitigation or resilience. The *on track but watch* status of progress toward climate finance targets in 2020 reinforces the imperative for ADB to continue to scale up these efforts. Support for low-carbon and climate-resilient COVID-19 recovery programming can play an important role in this context. ADB also recognizes the need to take integrated approaches to address issues related to air, water, and ocean pollution, including through the continued implementation of its Action Plan for Healthy Oceans (endnote 35).

214. Governance remains an enduring development challenge for the region. Strengthening governance is a key operational priority under Strategy 2030, and deepened engagement on these issues, including support for subnational implementation of the SDGs and strengthened domestic resource mobilization, will be critical to recovery efforts.

215. It will be vital for ADB to continue supporting SDG attainment through the implementation of its seven operational priorities and to deepen its engagement with countries on prospects for achieving the SDGs through green, inclusive, resilient, and sustainable COVID-19 recovery efforts.

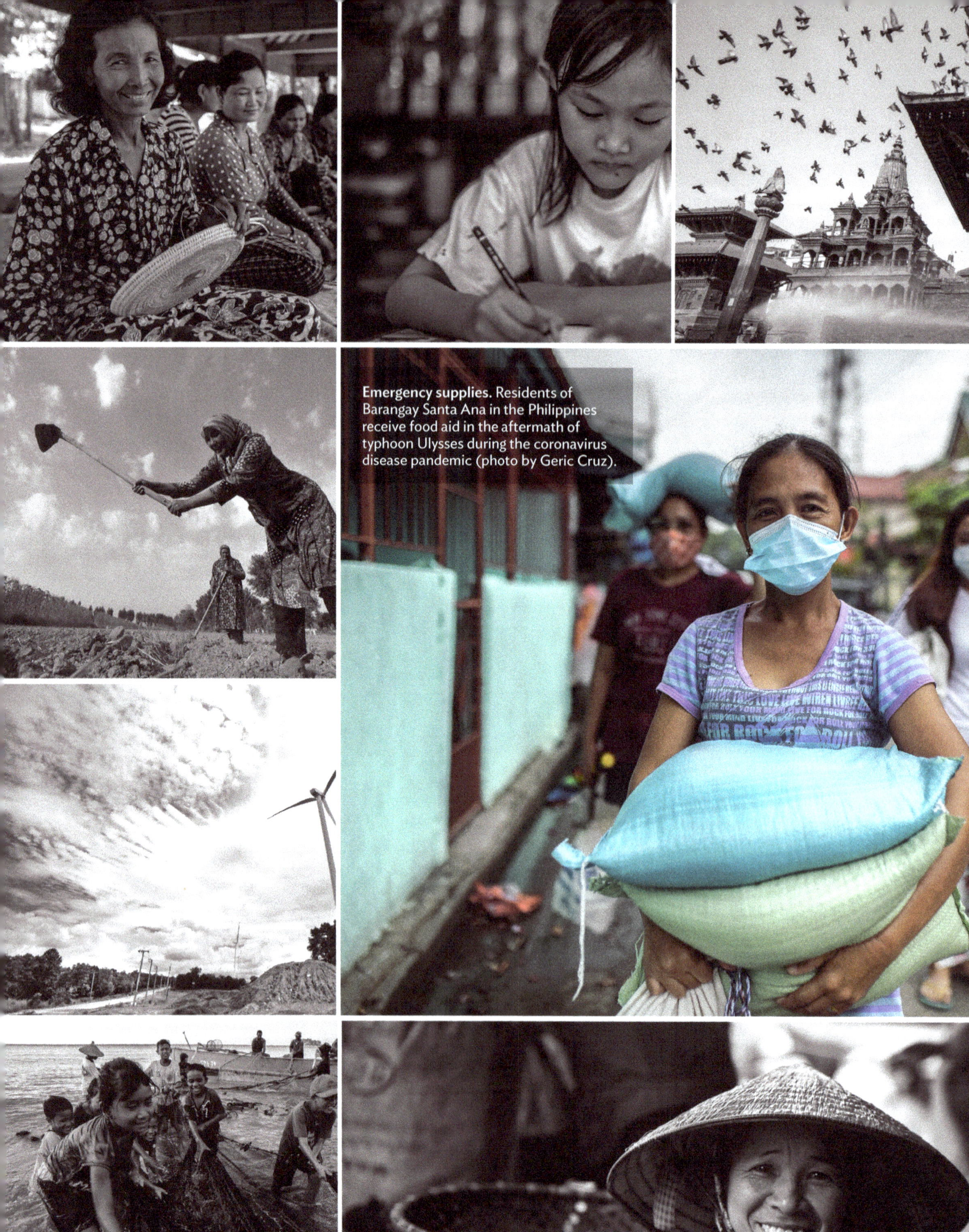

Emergency supplies. Residents of Barangay Santa Ana in the Philippines receive food aid in the aftermath of typhoon Ulysses during the coronavirus disease pandemic (photo by Geric Cruz).

PERFORMANCE HIGHLIGHTS

This section summarizes the main findings for the 60 indicators in the corporate results framework, 2019–2024, organized by indicator level. The 10 indicators at level 1 track regional development progress and challenges in Asia and the Pacific. Level 2 measures the results from completed operations, including 22 indicators monitoring delivery of results for the seven operational priorities in Strategy 2030 and 5 assessing the quality of completed operations. The 15 indicators at level 3 gauge how ADB manages its operations, focusing on design and implementation quality, development finance, and strategic alignment. Level 4 includes 8 indicators that measure ADB's organizational effectiveness in terms of systems, processes, and capacity.

SUMMARY PERFORMANCE SCORECARD 2020

REGIONAL DEVELOPMENT PROGRESS (SECTION I)

Development Progress in Asia and the Pacific (Level 1)

	ADB DMCs Overall			ADB Concessional Assistance DMCs		
	↑	↔	↓	↑	↔	↓
Strategy 2030: Achieving a Prosperous, Inclusive, Resilient, and Sustainable Asia and the Pacific	6	2	2	4	2	4

ADB'S DEVELOPMENT EFFECTIVENESS (SECTION II)

Results from ADB's Completed Operations (Level 2)	ADB	CA
Strategy 2030 Operational Priority Results	[good]	[good]
Quality of Completed Operations	[poor]	[poor]
ADB's Operational Management (Level 3)		
Design and Implementation Quality	--	--
Development Finance	[poor]	--
Strategic Alignment	[good]	--
ADB's Organizational Management (Level 4)		
Organizational Systems and Processes	[good]	--
Organizational Capacity	[good]	--

[good] = good, [mixed] = mixed, [poor] = poor, = not available until end of 2020, -- = not scored, ↑ = number of results progress indicators (RPIs) that have improved since the prior year, ↔ = number of RPIs that have remained constant since the prior year, ↓ = number of RPIs that have deteriorated since the prior year.
ADB = Asian Development Bank, CA = concessional assistance, DMC = developing member country.

A. PROGRESS ON REGIONAL DEVELOPMENT INDICATORS

1. Level 1: Development Progress in Asia and the Pacific

216. Social and economic shocks, crises, and chain reactions triggered in Asia and the Pacific by the COVID-19 pandemic highlighted the consequences of uneven progress on the Sustainable Development Goals (SDGs) across developing member countries (DMCs). For level 1 regional progress indicators, ADB tracks whether results have improved, stayed constant, or regressed relative to the baseline year.

217. **Economic contraction and people pushed back into poverty.** ADB estimates that economic growth in the region, already slowing in part because of pre-pandemic global trade tensions, turned negative in 2020 for the first time in more than 60 years. An estimated 78 million people were pushed back into extreme poverty and 162 million into near poverty, reversing a steadily declining trend.

218. **Learning, jobs, and health systems disrupted.** Existing fragilities and inequalities mean the poorest have been hurt the most. Unemployment and underemployment through substantial loss of working hours rose in 2020. Educational enrollment indicators had been improving, although attainment remained an issue. Education systems were upended by COVID-19, with remote learning options bridging the gap for some. The consequences of uneven access to social protection systems and health care were exposed by the crisis. These issues have severe implications for women, and United Nations projections suggest that more women than men may be pushed back into poverty or near poverty.

219. **Women's empowerment in the region has been put at further risk.** Early data suggest that the gap in labor force participation may have widened in 2020. Women's participation stood at only 48% compared with 81% for men. Women's burden of unpaid care, already triple that of men, has also grown, and there is emerging evidence of a global increase in gender-based violence in 2020.

220. **Pressing environmental challenges persist.** The region has made limited progress toward environmentally focused SDGs to promote sustainable consumption and production, protect life on land and below water, and take climate action. Despite substantial economic contraction in 2020, global emissions are estimated to have decreased by less than 7%. More than 5,000 deaths from disasters triggered by natural and climate-related hazards in a highly vulnerable region added to the toll from the pandemic.

221. **Cities on the front lines.** Access to basic services has improved, but the clean water and sanitation considered available in large informal and slum settlements proved difficult for many to access in practice, and overcrowding in close living quarters compounded transmission of COVID-19. Respites in air pollution that resulted from initial pandemic containment measures proved fleeting. Disruptions to rural–urban food supply chains and income opportunities in cities reversed the flow of migrants, forcing many to return to rural areas.

222. **Food insecurity worsening.** Asia and the Pacific was home to more than half of the world's undernourished people in 2019, with more than 22% of the region's people experiencing moderate or severe food insecurity and 28% of children under 5 stunted. The pandemic exacerbated this predicament. Avoidable food losses in weak agricultural supply chains add to these challenges. The problem of food scarcity for some is coupled with problems of plenty for others, as obesity remains a growing health issue in the DMCs.

223. **Governance remains to be strengthened.** The region's scores on the World Governance Index, already negative, improved slightly in 2019. Political stability has been a relative strength for the region, while the regulatory environment and controlling corruption present major challenges. Tax revenue to DMC gross domestic product is among the lowest in the world and showed volatility.

224. **Despite improving foundations for cooperation, countries looked inward.** Data for 2018 showed improvements in the Asia-Pacific Regional Cooperation and Integration Index. Financial and monetary cooperation scores returned to 2010–2015 levels. Although global tensions had weakened international trade, intraregional trade remained relatively strong. The onset of the pandemic disrupted cross-border trade and economic activity and exposed vulnerabilities in crucial global supply chains.

225. **Green, resilient, inclusive, and sustainable recovery delivering on the Sustainable Development Goals.** Renewed cooperation will be necessary to reconnect economies, strengthen inclusion and environmental sustainability, and make the best use possible of digitalization and innovation.

B. ADB'S ACHIEVEMENTS IN 2020

2. Level 2: Results from ADB's Completed Operations

226. Completed operations displayed uneven performance in 2020. While most achieved their expected outcomes across the seven operational priorities of Strategy 2030, success rates for sovereign and nonsovereign operations remained below target. The percentage of projects closed on time was a historic low, and the share delivering gender equality results continued a slow decline.

Strategy 2030 Operational Priority Results

227. **Strong delivery of results.** The corporate results framework, 2019–2024 (CRF) includes outcome indicators for measuring the results of ADB's sovereign and nonsovereign operations and TA in support of the seven operational priorities. In 2020, completed ADB operations overall delivered 80% or more of their expected results for 18 of 21 indicators for which results were expected. It was too early to assess achievement for the remaining 3 indicators. The concessional assistance subset of operations fell short on 1 of the 19 indicators for which results were expected, and achievement for 2 others was too early to assess. Appendix 3 highlights selected results from operations completed in 2020 by SDG.

Sovereign Operations Performance

228. **Slow but continued decline in success rate.** The share of the completed sovereign operations rated *successful* remained relatively constant in reporting years (RY) 2018–2020 and was 10 percentage points short of the 2024 target of 80%. The success rate of operations financed by concessional assistance was also *off track*, dropping to 65% from 70% in RY2017–2019. These declines were mainly caused by a widespread reduction in effectiveness ratings among infrastructure and public sector management (PSM) operations.

229. **Effectiveness and efficiency ratings mirrored success rate decline.** The share of operations rated *effective* in RY2018–2020 dropped by 4 percentage points to 64%. Efficiency ratings also declined by 3 percentage points to 72%. Completed sovereign operations continued to perform weakest on sustainability (62%) and best on relevance (82%).

230. **Success rates for fragile and conflict-affected situations lower but improved for small island developing states.** Only 50% of the 12 sovereign operations completed in countries with FCAS were rated *successful*, a 4-year low. The success rate of sovereign operations in small island developing states (SIDS) (18 operations) improved to 56% from 42%. This indicator is volatile because of the small number of operations.

231. **Fewer projects completed on time.** Only 33% of projects in 2018–2020 closed on time, a drop of 4 percentage points compared with 2017–2019, putting ADB's performance further *off track* from the 2024 target. Issues related to safeguards, procurement, and performance of contractors and consultants contributed to the delays. Concessional assistance projects were also *off track*, with only 31% closing on time in 2018–2020, a decline of 2 percentage points.

Nonsovereign Operations Performance

232. **Small improvement in success rate but still *off track*.** The share of completed nonsovereign operations rated *successful* was up by 2 percentage points to 53% but remained below the baseline performance of 54% and *off track* on the 2024 target of 70%. A bigger share of infrastructure operations, historically the best performing sector among completed nonsovereign operations, lifted overall performance. This shift offset a decline in the success rates of infrastructure operations to 76% and of private equity fund operations to 10%.

233. **ADB work quality most improved.** The rating for the ADB work quality criterion improved by 13 percentage points driven primarily by stronger project team efforts to prepare, monitor, and supervise infrastructure operations. Performance on this criterion remains weakest, however, alongside that for development results. Private sector operations performed best on investment profitability during this reporting period.

Gender Equality Results

234. **Delivery of gender equality results *on track but watch*.** For ADB as a whole, the share of completed operations that were assessed as having achieved their envisaged gender equality results declined by 1 percentage point to 73% for the third successive period, keeping the indicator *on track but watch* to meet the 80% target by 2024. On the other hand, operations financed by concessional assistance recorded an increase of 1 percentage point to 78% for the third consecutive period and were also rated *on track but watch*.

Client Feedback on ADB Knowledge Solutions

235. **Client satisfaction rate above baseline at 79% but shy of target.** ADB conducted a survey in 2020 to gauge the reach, quality, use, and benefits to its developing member country (DMC) clients of the knowledge products and services (KPS) it delivers. Of the 1,153 clients who responded to the survey, 79% rated ADB's KPS "very useful," a result just short of the 80% satisfaction rate targeted.

3. Level 3: ADB's Operational Management

236. Performance was good overall on indicators measuring implementation readiness and performance of ADB operations under implementation. ADB continued to perform well on aligning its new operations with Strategy 2030 priorities. However, indicators measuring the financing mobilized and transferred to DMCs displayed uneven performance in 2020.

Design and Implementation Quality

237. **Design and procurement readiness remained strong.** The share of sovereign infrastructure projects that were design-ready before approval was 81%, 1 percentage point higher than the annual target. At 51%, the share of sovereign infrastructure projects that are procurement-ready remained roughly constant, and was *on track but watch* toward the 2024 target of 60%.

238. **Performance of active portfolio improved.** In 2020, ADB fully rolled out enhanced methodologies for rating the performance of operations under implementation. About 64% of sovereign projects under implementation were rated *satisfactory* for both ADB overall and the concessional assistance subset, an improvement from 52% for ADB overall and 53% for concessional assistance in 2019 when the methodology was piloted. Of the nonsovereign operations under implementation, 32% were assessed as being *at risk* of not achieving their targeted development results.

Mobilization and Transfer of Development Finance

239. **Faster project start-up time.** The average time from concept approval to first disbursement of all sovereign operations with first disbursement in 2020 was 28.3 months. For nonsovereign operations, it was 14.7 months. In both cases this is about 2 months quicker than in 2019.

240. **Sovereign disbursement rate *off track*.** ADB disbursed 88% ($9.2 billion) of its targeted $10.5 billion of financing for sovereign projects and results-based lending to its DMCs, below the 90% annual target.

241. **Nonsovereign cofinancing ratio higher.** The volume of long-term cofinancing for nonsovereign operations signed in 2018–2020 totaled $9.1 billion, lower than the $10.1 billion in 2017–2019. Every $1.00 in financing ADB committed for its nonsovereign operations was matched by $1.45 in long-term cofinancing, achieving a 145% cofinancing ratio. With this slight improvement on the 143% ratio achieved in 2017–2019, ADB remained *on track but watch* to reach a ratio of 200% by 2024 and inched closer to the Strategy 2030 target of 250% by 2030.

242. **Record high volume of sovereign cofinancing.** In 2020, ADB mobilized $11.1 billion in sovereign cofinancing to contribute to the intended development outcomes of 180 projects, more than double the volume mobilized in 2019. About $8.2 billion supports COVID-19 response operations while the remaining $2.9 billion supports regular development operations.

243. **Health finance overshoots target.** Financing for health rose to a record of 12.03% of total ADB commitments in 2020. The fivefold increase in financing for health operations, 90% of which went to combat COVID-19, overshot the 3%–5% range targeted for more normal times. Performance on this indicator is therefore considered to have declined and fallen off track. Health financing supported more than three times as many loans and grants than in the previous year (44 versus 13 in 2019).

244. **Education financing down.** Financing for education fell to 3.76% in 2020 from 5.23% in 2019, keeping performance *off track* to meet the 2024 target of 6%–10%. With $1.05 billion committed for 9 loans and grants, the volume of financing for education was slightly lower than the $1.13 billion committed in 2019 for 16 loans and grants.

Alignment with Strategy 2030 Priorities

245. **Exceptional gender mainstreaming performance in 2020.** The share of committed operations classified *gender equity as a theme* (GEN) or *effective gender mainstreaming* (EGM) increased by 9 percentage points to 64% in 2018–2020, as did the share classified GEN, EGM, or *some gender elements* (SGE) to 89%. ADB's COVID-19 response operations were strong contributors. Performance on both indicators exceeded the 2024 targets of 50% (for GEN or EGM) and 71% (for GEN, EGM, or SGE) for the second year running, maintaining early progress toward the Strategy 2030 targets of 55% (GEN or EGM) and 75% (GEN, EGM, or SGE).

246. **Climate change mitigation and adaptation steady.** At 58% in 2018–2020, the share of committed ADB operations supporting climate change mitigation and/or adaptation was roughly steady and remained *on track but watch* to achieve the 2024 target of 65% and the 2030 target of 75%. The share of operations supporting both mitigation and adaptation increased to 22% in 2018–2020 from 17% in 2017–2019, while support for mitigation alone declined to 14% from 16% and support for adaptation alone declined to 22% from 26%. The share was steady at 63% for the concessional assistance subset.

247. **Climate finance *on track but watch.*** During 2019–2020, ADB committed $10.8 billion for climate change mitigation and/or adaptation, *on track but watch* to reach the 2024 target of a cumulative total of $35 billion. Strategy 2030 targets committing a cumulative total of $80 billion toward this priority from 2019 to 2030. Commitments for operations supporting both mitigation and adaptation reached a cumulative total of $6.5 billion, operations supporting only mitigation reached $3.2 billion, and operations supporting only adaptation $1.1 billion.

248. **Share of nonsovereign operations lower.** The proportion of committed nonsovereign operations to total ADB commitments dropped to 21% in 2020 from 24% in 2019. Although the number of nonsovereign operations remained unchanged at 38, ADB increased its sovereign commitments to respond to the COVID-19 pandemic. The volume of financing for nonsovereign operations also declined as ADB focused more on supplying shorter-term, smaller-scale liquidity and working capital support than traditional large-scale financing for infrastructure. Financing for nonsovereign operations was 6.2% of total ADB financing in 2020 compared with 17.5% in 2019.

249. **Continuing strong nonsovereign diversification.** In 2020, 58% of committed nonsovereign operations were in frontier economies and/or in nontraditional sectors, slightly lower than 61% the year before but still higher than the 2024 target of 55%. Of these operations, 32% were in underserved markets (group A and B DMCs [Appendix 4]) and 39% were in new sectors. Operations in health care and agribusiness contributed to the COVID-19 response.

250. **Poverty reduction and inclusiveness strengthened.** The share of committed operations supporting poverty reduction and inclusiveness rose to 79% in 2018–2020, 5 percentage points higher than in 2017–2019. Social protection was an important pillar of ADB's COVID-19 response, and as a result the number of social protection operations increased markedly in 2020 driving up the share of total commitments to 10% in 2018–2020 from 5% in 2017–2019.

251. **More projects supporting disability inclusion.** The share of committed operations supporting disability inclusion was 32% (55 of 173), compared with 22% in 2019. Three operations (2% of 2020 commitments) were rated *principally or significantly disability inclusive.* Eleven operations (6% of 2020 commitments) have some disability inclusion elements and involve the differently abled in project planning, monitoring, or providing feedback. Most operations (41 of 55, or 24% of 2020 commitments overall) have enabling conditions for disability inclusion without setting specific disability inclusiveness indicators or explicitly including people with disabilities in their design, monitoring, or implementation.

4. Level 4: ADB's Organizational Effectiveness

252. Performance was good overall on indicators measuring organizational systems and processes, as well as organizational capacity.

Organizational Systems and Processes

253. **Budget utilization on target.** ADB's budget utilization rate in 2020 was 95%, including 2% carry-over. Excluding travel-related expenses, which were impacted by international travel restrictions, the 2020 utilization rate was 100%.

254. **Robust capitalization.** ADB's capitalization remains robust and supports the planned expansion of operations in line with Strategy 2030. The capital utilization ratio increased to 69.1% in 2020 from 62.1% in 2019 on the strong growth of ADB's operations.

255. **Nonsovereign credit quality in good standing.** Challenging credit and macroeconomic conditions triggered by the COVID-19 pandemic did not significantly change the weighted average risk rating of nonsovereign operations, which was 9.7 or B in 2020. The impaired loans ratio improved to 4.2% from 4.8% in 2019 because of growth in the credit portfolio, which was driven in part by COVID-19 support and some successful recoveries of impaired transactions.

256. **Representation of women remains *on track but watch.*** Women's share of ADB's international staff positions grew to 37.7% in 2020 from 36.7% in 2019. Their representation in leadership roles (levels 7–8) rose to 29.3% from 24.1% in the same period.

257. **Procurement time *off track.*** The share of sovereign operation procurement transactions of $10 million or more that were processed within the target time of 40 days decreased by 8 percentage points to 59% overall and by 22 percentage points to 49% for concessional assistance operations, in both cases resulting in an *off track* rating for this indicator.

258. **One ADB collaboration target met.** Operations departments responded strongly to Strategy 2030's One ADB imperative in 2020, with 14 projects bringing together private sector and sovereign operations expertise and knowledge, giving a cumulative total of 22 and exceeding the cumulative target of 18 such projects by 2024.

Enhancing Organizational Capacity

259. **Staff rate ADB effective in digital transformation.** In the 2020 biennial staff engagement survey, the first to measure this progress, 80% of respondents agreed or tended to agree that ADB was successfully supporting digital transformation, surpassing the 2024 target of 75%.

260. **Development of Strategy 2030 culture *on track.*** ADB's success in providing an enabling culture for Strategy 2030 implementation is measured using staff perceptions of the key elements of ADB's culture required to support Strategy 2030 implementation. In the 2020 survey, 66% of respondents agreed or tended to agree that ADB has a culture for innovation and collaboration, rating this indicator *on track* toward the 70% target.

261. **Staff share in field offices steady with slight increase in fragile, conflict-affected, and small island states.** The share of all ADB staff assigned to field offices was roughly steady at 46% in 2020, while ADB staff in FCAS and SIDS increased from 84 positions in 2019 to 86 in 2020. Strategy 2030 calls for strengthening resident mission capacity, and staff operating in these offices were essential for scaling up ADB's support and monitoring project implementation during 2020 global travel restrictions.

262. **Further transformation into a knowledge and learning institution taking place.** ADB's transformation into a knowledge and learning institution requires the right culture, processes, and capacity. ADB's performance on the eight drivers of a knowledge-driven enterprise, based on its latest globally benchmarked Most Admired Knowledge Enterprise (MAKE) survey of all staff, rose by 4 percentage points from 2019 to 69% (55.42 out of 80 points). This puts ADB *on track but watch* on the CRF indicator.

Responding to the health emergency. Health workers prepare to carry out tests for coronavirus disease in Colombo, Sri Lanka (photo by M.A. Puspha Kumara).

APPENDIXES
ENDNOTES

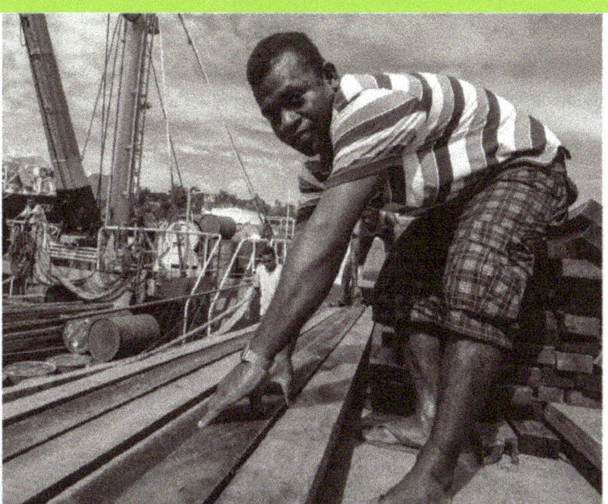

APPENDIX 1: INDICATOR INDEX

This index identifies the page reference(s) for each results framework indicator (RFI) and tracking indicator (TI) discussed in this report. Some indicators are featured across several chapters. Data for the remaining indicators are in the scorecard that accompanies this report.

DEVELOPMENT PROGRESS IN ASIA AND THE PACIFIC (LEVEL 1 RESULTS PROGRESS INDICATORS)

RESULTS FROM COMPLETED OPERATIONS—STRATEGY 2030 OPERATIONAL PRIORITY RESULTS (LEVEL 2A)

OP 1: Addressing Remaining Poverty and Reducing Inequalities

OP 2: Accelerating Progress in Gender Equality

RESULTS FROM COMPLETED OPERATIONS—QUALITY OF COMPLETED OPERATIONS (LEVEL 2B)

1		Completed operations rated *successful* (%) (sovereign), 62–65, 67, 107, 109, 114
	1	Completed operations rated *successful* (%) (sovereign)—a. Investment projects; b. Policy-based operations; c. FCAS DMCs; d. Small island developing states, 62–64, 66, 98-99, 114
	2	Completed operations rated *successful* (%) (sovereign)—a. Relevance; b. Efficiency; c. Effectiveness; d. Sustainability, 62–67, 114
2		Projects closed on time (%) (sovereign), 62, 66, 114
3		Completed operations rated *successful* (%) (nonsovereign), 70–71, 74–75, 108–109, 114
	3	Completed operations rated *successful* (%) (nonsovereign)—a. Development results; b. ADB's additionality; c. ADB's investment profitability; d. ADB's work quality, 70–71, 74–75, 114
4		Completed operations delivering intended gender equality results (%) (sovereign and nonsovereign), 108, 114
5		Clients satisfied with the use of ADB knowledge products (%), 78
	4	Web-distributed knowledge solutions (number of downloads), 32, 80
	5	Engagement on social media (number)—a. Subscribers and followers; b. Active engagement, 80
	6	Event participants reporting increased knowledge and/or skills (number), 78
	8	Completed technical assistance projects rated *successful* (%) (sovereign and nonsovereign), 78–79, 99
	10	Impact evaluations completed (number), 81
	11	Operations with meaningful civil society organization engagement (%) (number), 25, 27, 34, 94–95

ADB'S OPERATIONAL MANAGEMENT (LEVEL 3)

Level 3A. Design and Implementation Quality

1		Infrastructure projects that are design-ready (%) (sovereign), 62–63, 115
2		Infrastructure projects that are procurement-ready (%) (sovereign), 62–63, 115
3		Performance of operations at implementation rated *satisfactory* (%) (sovereign), 62–63, 115
	1	Performance of operations at implementation rated *satisfactory* (%) (sovereign)-a. Output; b. Contract award; c. Disbursement; d. Financial management; e. Safeguards, 62–63
4		Operations at risk of not achieving development results (%) (nonsovereign), 70–71, 108, 115

Level 3B. Development Finance

	2	Time from concept approval to first disbursement (months) (sovereign)—a. From concept approval to loan fact-finding; b. From loan fact-finding to approval; c. From approval to commitment; d. From commitment to first disbursement, 88–89, 115
	3	Time from concept approval to first disbursement (months) (nonsovereign)—a. From mandate approval to project approval; b. From approval to signing; c. From signing to first disbursement, 88–89, 115
5		Disbursement rate (%) (sovereign), 48–49, 109, 115
	4	Overall disbursement ($ billion) (sovereign), 48–49, 115
	6	Approvals ($ billion) (sovereign and nonsovereign), 48-49
	7	Commitments ($ billion) (sovereign and nonsovereign), 48-49
	8	Commitments in concessional assistance countries (group A + group B) (%) (sovereign and nonsovereign), 48-49
	9	Commitments in FCAS DMCs and SIDS (%) (sovereign and nonsovereign), 98-99
6		Cofinancing ratio (%) (nonsovereign), 48-49, 54, 115
	11	Sovereign cofinancing ($ billion) (sovereign), 115
7		Financing for education (%) (sovereign and nonsovereign), 48–49, 56, 109, 116
8		Financing for health (%) (sovereign and nonsovereign), 48–49, 54–55, 109, 115–116

Level 3C. Strategic Alignment

9		Committed operations classified gender equity theme or effective gender mainstreaming (%) (sovereign and nonsovereign), 48–50, 116
	12	Committed operations that promote gender equality (%) (sovereign and nonsovereign)—a1. GEN—sovereign operations; a2. GEN—nonsovereign operations; b1.EGM—sovereign operations; b2. EGM—nonsovereign operations; c1.SGE—sovereign operations; c2. SGE—nonsovereign operations; d1.NGE—sovereign operations; d2. NGE—nonsovereign operations, 50
10		Committed operations classified gender equity theme, effective gender mainstreaming, or some gender elements (%) (sovereign and nonsovereign), 48–50, 70–71, 116
	13	Financing for gender equality (%) (sovereign and nonsovereign), 50

11		Committed operations that support climate change mitigation and adaptation (%) (sovereign and nonsovereign), 48–49, 51–52, 109, 116
	14	Committed operations supporting climate change (%) (sovereign and nonsovereign)–a. Mitigation; b. Adaptation; c. Both, 51–52, 116
12		Financing for climate change mitigation and adaptation ($ billion, cumulative) (sovereign and nonsovereign), 48–49, 52–53, 70–71, 109, 116
	15	Financing for climate change ($ billion, cumulative) (sovereign and nonsovereign)–a. Mitigation; b. Adaptation; c. Both, 52–53, 116
13		Nonsovereign operations as a share of total ADB operations (%, number) (nonsovereign), 48–49, 70–72, 116
	16	Nonsovereign operations as a share of total ADB operations (%, $) (nonsovereign), 72, 116
14		Operations in frontier economies and/or in new sectors (%) (nonsovereign), 70–71, 73, 116
15		Operations supporting poverty reduction and inclusiveness (%) (sovereign and nonsovereign), 56, 116
	17	Operations or transactions supporting inclusive business (number) (nonsovereign), 70–71, 74
	18	Knowledge products and services delivered (%), 30–31, 81
	19	Operations that are green, sustainable, inclusive, and resilient (%) (sovereign and nonsovereign), 58
	20	Operations contributing to each of seven operational priorities (%) (sovereign and nonsovereign), 56–57
	21	Operations contributing to social protection (%) (sovereign and nonsovereign), 48–49, 55, 109, 116
	22	Disability-inclusive operations (%) (sovereign and nonsovereign), 57, 116
	23	Operations aligned with Sustainable Development Goals (%, number)(sovereign and nonsovereign), 58
	24	Operations using country procurement systems (%) (sovereign), 91, 93
	25	Contracts using government e-procurement systems ($ billion) (sovereign), 91, 93
	26	Innovative operations and technical assistance projects (%) (sovereign and nonsovereign), 81

ADB'S ORGANIZATIONAL EFFECTIVENESS (LEVEL 4)

Level 4A. Organizational Systems and Processes

1		Quality of budget management (%), 88–89
	1	Capital utilization ratio (%) (sovereign and nonsovereign), 86–87
	2	Impaired loans ratio % (nonsovereign), 86–87
	3	Weighted average risk rating of the nonsovereign portfolio (nonsovereign), 86–87
	4	Internal administrative expenses per $1 million disbursement ($'000), 88–89
	5	Internal administrative expenses per project under administration ($'000), 88–89
	6	Internal administrative expenses per project approved ($'000), 88–89
2		Procurement contract transactions of $10 million or more with processing time of 40 days or less (%) (sovereign), 91–92
	7	Procurement time from advertisement to contract signing, $10 million or more (days) (sovereign), 91–93
	8	Consulting services recruitment time for ADB-administered contracts, from consulting services recruitment notice to consultant contract signing (days) (sovereign), 91, 93
	9	Audited financial statements reviewed on time (%) (sovereign), 88–89
3		Representation of women in the international staff category (%), 86–87
	10	Representation of women in the international staff category (%)—a. Levels 4–6; b. Levels 7–8; c. Levels 9–10, 86–87
4		Projects or transactions with sovereign–nonsovereign collaboration (number, cumulative) (sovereign and nonsovereign), 93–94

Level 4B. Organizational Capacity

5		Staff rating ADB's effectiveness in digital transformation (%), 91-92
	13	Digital products completed (number), 91–92
6		Staff rating ADB as providing enabling culture for Strategy 2030 implementation (%), 88, 90
	14	Internal training budget (average $ per staff), 86–87
	15	Departments with documented and tested business continuity plans in place (number), 88–89
7		Budgeted international and national staff positions in field offices (% of total operations departments), 86–87
	16	Budgeted international and national staff positions in FCAS DMCs and SIDS field offices (number), 86–87
	17	Operations administered in field offices (%) (sovereign), 86–87
	18	Share of operational expenses for direct operations support (%), 88-89
8		Staff rating ADB as an effective knowledge and learning organization (%), 82
	19	Knowledge products and services drawn from k-Nexus (number), 81

APPENDIX 2: ADB'S RESPONSE TO THE COVID-19 PANDEMIC

A. EARLY RESPONSES TO THE COVID-19 PANDEMIC

Box A2.1: Repurposing of Ongoing Projects: Examples from East Asia

The East Asia Department of the Asian Development Bank quickly repurposed additional three projects in Mongolia, one in the People's Republic of China (PRC), and two regional technical assistance projects to provide personal protective equipment and medical supplies and support small businesses in the early stages of the pandemic.

A health project in Mongolia added the procurement of $1.2 million of essential medical equipment for early detection of coronavirus disease (COVID-19) and management complications, and a border services improvement project was updated to allow procurement of $75,000 worth of equipment for border crossing points. An economic diversification project was given added flexibility and funds to provide small and medium-sized enterprises with credit to mitigate uncertainties posed by pandemic.

Ambulances and medical and personal protective equipment were procured using part of the loan proceeds from a flood and environmental risk management project in the PRC that were redirected to assist the COVID-19 response. An ongoing regional technical assistance project had a change in scope to survey the impacts of COVID-19 on businesses and households under lockdown and prepare guidelines for conducting virtual gender assessments to support project processing during the pandemic.

Source: Asian Development Bank (East Asia Department).

Box A2.2: Use of the COVID-19 Pandemic Response Option in Palau and the Philippines

Isolated locations and prompt preparedness and response measures have spared many Pacific developing member countries of the Asian Development Bank (ADB) from the potentially catastrophic direct health impacts of coronavirus disease (COVID-19). However, they have not been unscathed by the pandemic. Palau has had no confirmed cases, but its tourist-dependent economy is likely to contract by 10% in fiscal year 2020 and 13% in 2021 because of global travel restrictions. Annual arrivals are expected to halve, with a loss of more than 3,100 jobs—more than a quarter of the total workforce.

This pause in economic activity is creating large shortfalls in government revenue. Reserve funds are being drawn down to keep government services running; cover emergency supplies and additional screening, testing, and monitoring of COVID-19; and support affected businesses and workers.

ADB's concessional loan of $20 million for the *Health Expenditure and Livelihoods Support Program* under the Countercyclical Support Facility COVID-19 Pandemic Response Option supports the government's COVID-19 response. Funds are being deployed to strengthen the health system's COVID-19 response measures including by training frontline health workers on the proper use of personal protective equipment, installing additional ventilators, and testing all domestic high-risk groups; implement social assistance for the unemployed; and deliver economic relief to affected businesses.

Unlike Palau, the Philippines has suffered devastating health impacts because of active community transmission of COVID-19. By 15 April 2020, there were almost 5,500 confirmed cases in the country and 349 deaths. Strict but necessary quarantine measures imposed to limit spread of the disease put Filipinos' livelihoods at risk and threatened to reverse poverty reduction gains. The poor and vulnerable were disproportionately affected.

In April 2020, ADB provided $1.5 billion in budget support to the Government of the Philippines through the COVID-19 Pandemic Response Option for the *COVID-19 Active Response and Expenditure Support Program* (CARES program) to manage the spread of COVID-19 in the country and contain poverty. The critically needed support helped the government increase testing capacity, provide conditional cash transfers and emergency subsidy to millions of vulnerable households, deliver economic stimulus and assistance for agriculture and other severely affected sectors, and provide relief to small businesses.

Source: Asian Development Bank (Pacific Department and Southeast Asia Department).

B. PANDEMIC-RELATED KNOWLEDGE SOLUTIONS OF ADB'S REGIONAL DEPARTMENTS

Box A2.3: Knowledge Solutions in Mongolia and the People's Republic of China

In 2020, the Mongolia Resident Mission of the Asian Development Bank (ADB) issued *COVID-19 Impact Monitoring Report and Quarterly Economic Updates* to assess the economic consequences of the coronavirus disease (COVID-19) pandemic in the country and help formulate and support pandemic response measures. These reports, covering risk and impact assessments across a broad range of sectors, were used internally by ADB and shared with government clients to support economic and policy dialogue and shape policy actions under the COVID-19 Rapid Response Program and other assistance.

As lockdowns and mobility restrictions in Mongolia and the People's Republic of China increasingly prevented processing and implementation teams from undertaking due diligence and monitoring implementation progress, ADB's East Asia Department piloted the use of virtual surveys to conduct gender and social assessments. Guidelines on *Using Virtual Surveys to Gather Project Data in the New Normal* were published in *Development Asia* to share the lessons learned with a broader ADB and external audience.

Source: Asian Development Bank (East Asia Department).

Box A2.4: Knowledge Solutions in India and Sri Lanka

In India, technical assistance supported the development of 50 e-learning courses targeting doctors, nurses, police, technicians, and other frontline workers as part of the Department of Personnel and Training's coronavirus disease (COVID-19) response strategy. By December 2020, 2.5 million people had enrolled and 2.0 million had completed courses. Follow-on technical assistance is expanding this work to improve the technical content of other courses, including to teach physicians how to manage stress brought on by the COVID-19 workload.

As COVID-19 abruptly forced Sri Lanka's tertiary education system to shift to online learning, the government needed to understand how the transition was working. An online survey of university administrations, faculty members, and students by the Asian Development Bank found an impressive digital transformation taking place: nearly 90% were able to access online tertiary education, similar to developed countries such as Japan, and faculty needed only a brief period of training. Limited access to laptops and a stable internet connection and the need for a credible online examination were among the main challenges identified.

Source: Asian Development Bank (South Asia Department).

Box A2.5: Knowledge Solutions in Southeast Asia

Early in the pandemic, before other support commenced, the Asian Development Bank (ADB) One ADB team processed and approved a technical assistance grant of $5 million in just 4 days to deliver critical food supplies to the most vulnerable households in the Philippines' National Capital Region and neighboring provinces. In collaboration with the Department of Social Welfare and Development and Armed Forces of the Philippines, ADB selected the contents of the food parcels, identified the beneficiaries, and developed a procurement chain and distribution logistics. The Rapid Emergency Supplies Provision "Bayan Bayanihan" Project distributed food packs to 174,000 households, about 870,000 Filipinos.

Policy Actions for COVID-19 Economic Recovery (PACER) Dialogues, supported by ADB under the Brunei Darussalam–Indonesia–Malaysia–Philippines East ASEAN Growth Area, Indonesia–Malaysia–Thailand Growth Triangle, and Greater Mekong Subregion Capacity Building Program, provided a platform for these countries to collectively explore knowledge solutions on COVID-19 with leading experts in a structured and robust manner. The knowledge solutions developed are summarized in the 13 policy briefs produced after each PACER dialogue with detailed information on policy design, implementation experience, outcomes and concrete recommendations on COVID-19 response and recovery measures and policy actions.

Source: Asian Development Bank (Southeast Asia Department).

APPENDIX 3: SELECTED RESULTS OF 2020 COMPLETED OPERATIONS BY SUSTAINABLE DEVELOPMENT GOAL

- **4,872,000 people benefiting from improved health services, education services, or social protection**
- **30,521,000 poor and vulnerable people with improved standards of living**
- Seven social protection schemes established or improved
- Four dedicated crisis-responding social assistance schemes for women and girls implemented or established

- **18,943,000 people enrolled in improved education and/or training**
- **30,000 women enrolled in TVET and other job training**

- **1,748,000 jobs generated**
- **One enhanced labor policy or standards implemented**
- **One new financial product and services made available to the poor and vulnerable**
- **10,000 women opening new accounts**
- Four models for business development and financing established or improved

- **11 national and subnational disaster risk reduction and/or management plans supported in implementation**
- 14,150,000 people benefiting from improved services in urban areas

- **361,000 hectares of land with higher productivity**
- **1,200 rural infrastructure assets established or improved**
- 27,605,000 people benefiting from increased rural investment
- 2,800 farmers with improved market access
- 17,000 hectares of land improved through climate-resilient irrigation infrastructure and water delivery services

- **115,000 women represented in decision-making structures and processes**
- **997,000 women and girls with increased time savings**
- Three solutions to prevent or address gender-based violence implemented
- 32,000 time-saving or gender-responsive infrastructure assets and/or services established or improved

- Four measures for increased inclusiveness supported in implementation

- **561,000 people with strengthened climate and disaster resilience**
- **$1.53 billion climate finance mobilized**
- 19,325,000 tCO_2e/year total annual greenhouse gas emissions reduction
- 1,300 people with increased capacity in implementing mitigation and low-carbon development actions

- **11 health services established or improved**
- **One health service for women and girls established or improved**

- **5,000 MW renewable energy capacity installed**
- **82,000 infrastructure assets established or improved**
- **100 low-carbon infrastructure assets established or improved**
- **86 new and existing infrastructure assets made climate- and disaster-resilient**
- 24 measures to improve the efficiency and/or productivity of cross-border connectivity supported in implementation

- **54,000 hectares of terrestrial, coastal, and marine areas conserved, restored, and/or enhanced**
- **Eight solutions to conserve, restore, and/or enhance terrestrial, coastal, and marine areas implemented**
- 244,000 hectares of area with reduced flood risk

- 890 entities with improved management functions and financial stability

- $1.37 billion trade and investment facilitated

MW = megawatt, tCO_2e = tons of carbon dioxide equivalent, TVET = technical and vocational education and training.
Note: Indicators in bold are derived from or aligned with official Sustainable Development Goal indicators. Others are linked to the Goal and associated targets.

APPENDIX 4: ADB DEVELOPING MEMBER COUNTRIES

Table A3.1: ADB Developing Member Countries

Afghanistan	India	Mongolia	Solomon Islands
Armenia	Indonesia	Myanmar	Sri Lanka
Azerbaijan	Kazakhstan	Nauru	Tajikistan
Bangladesh	Kiribati	Nepal	Thailand
Bhutan	Kyrgyz Republic	Niue[a]	Timor-Leste
Cambodia	Lao People's Democratic Republic	Pakistan	Tonga
China, People's Republic of	Malaysia	Palau	Turkmenistan
Cook Islands	Maldives	Papua New Guinea	Tuvalu
Fiji	Marshall Islands	Philippines	Uzbekistan
Georgia	Micronesia, Federated States of	Samoa	Vanuatu
			Viet Nam

ADB = Asian Development Bank.
Note: Five developing members—Brunei Darussalam; Hong Kong, China; the Republic of Korea; Singapore; and Taipei,China—have graduated from regular ADB assistance and are not included in this table.
[a] Niue became an ADB member country on 11 March 2019.

Table A3.2: 2018 Classification of ADB Developing Member Countries

Regular OCR-Only Countries (group C)	CA Countries		FCAS	SIDS
	OCR Blend Countries (group B)	CA-Only Countries (group A)		
Armenia[a]	Bangladesh	**COL-only countries**	Afghanistan	Cook Islands
Azerbaijan[b]	Mongolia[e]	Cambodia	Kiribati	Fiji
China, People's Republic of	Pakistan	Myanmar	Marshall Islands	Kiribati
Cook Islands	Palau	Nepal	Micronesia, Federated States of	Maldives
Fiji	Papua New Guinea	**ADF blend countries**	Myanmar	Marshall Islands
Georgia[c]	Sri Lanka[f]	Bhutan	Nauru	Micronesia, Federated States of
India [d]	Timor-Leste[g]	Kyrgyz Republic	Papua New Guinea	Nauru
Indonesia	Uzbekistan	Solomon Islands	Solomon Islands	Niue[k]
Kazakhstan	Viet Nam[h]	Vanuatu	Timor-Leste	Palau
Malaysia		**Grants-only countries**	Tuvalu	Papua New Guinea
Philippines		Afghanistan		Samoa
Thailand		Kiribati		Solomon Islands
Turkmenistan		Lao People's Democratic Republic		Timor-Leste
		Maldives		Tonga
		Marshall Islands[i]		Tuvalu
		Micronesia, Federated States of[j]		Vanuatu
		Nauru		
		Samoa		
		Tajikistan		
		Tonga		
		Tuvalu		

ADB = Asian Development Bank, ADF = Asian Development Fund, CA = concessional assistance, COL = concessional ordinary capital resources lending, FCAS = fragile and conflict-affected situation, OCR = ordinary capital resources, SIDS = small island developing state.

Notes:

a ADB. 2014. *Armenia: Review of Classification under ADB's Graduation Policy*. Manila (R77-14).

b ADB. 2013. *Azerbaijan: Review of Classification under ADB's Graduation Policy.* Manila (R89-13).

c ADB. 2013. *Georgia: Review of Classification under ADB's Graduation Policy.* Manila (R78-14).

d India is classified under group B but has no access to concessional assistance based on OM Section A1 (23 April 2019).

e ADB. 2011. *Review of the Classification of Mongolia under the Asian Development Bank's Graduation Policy.* Manila (115-11).

f ADB. 2017. *Sri Lanka: Review of Classification under ADB's Graduation Policy.* Manila (R67-17). Sri Lanka's reclassification to group C (regular OCR-only) was effective from 1 January 2019.

g ADB. 2011. *Review of the Classification of Timor-Leste under the Asian Development Bank's Graduation Policy*. Corrigendum 1. Manila (172-11).

h ADB. 2017. *Viet Nam: Review of Classification under ADB's Graduation Policy.* Manila (R66-17). Viet Nam's reclassification to group C (regular OCR-only) was effective from 1 January 2019.

i ADB. 2013. *Marshall Islands: Review of Classification under ADB's Graduation Policy.* Manila (R61-13).

j ADB. 2017. *Federated States of Micronesia: Review of Classification under ADB's Graduation Policy.* Manila (R1-17).

k Niue became an ADB member country on 11 March 2019. Assessment of its lending eligibility is ongoing.

Sources: ADB. 2013. *Operational Plan for Enhancing ADB's Effectiveness in Fragile and Conflict-Affected Situations.* Manila; ADB. 2018. Classification and Graduation of Developing Member Countries. Operations Manual. OM A1/BP. Manila; and ADB Strategy, Policy and Partnerships Department.

ENDNOTES

1 ADB. 2020. *Asian Development Outlook Update 2020: Wellness in Worrying Times.* Manila.

2 World Bank. *World Bank Education COVID-19 School Closures Map* (accessed 19 February 2021).

3 ADB. 2021. *COVID-19 and Education in Asia and the Pacific: Guidance Note.* Manila.

4 World Bank. 2021. *Urgent, Effective Action Required to Quell the Impact of COVID-19 on Education Worldwide.* Washington, DC.

5 UN Women. 2020. *From Insight to Action: Gender Equality in the Wake of COVID-19.* New York.

6 The most recent data for the official SDG indicator on social assistance coverage, as listed in the Development Effectiveness Review 2020 scorecard tracking indicators, is from 2014 and suggests a coverage rate of 47.5%. Data from 2015 compiled for the ADB social protection indicator suggested that social protection covered only 55.1% of intended beneficiaries (ADB. 2019. *The Social Protection Indicator for Asia: Assessing Progress.* Manila).

7 International Labour Organization. 2020. *ILO Monitor: COVID-19 and the World of Work. Fifth Edition.* Geneva.

8 C. Park and A. Inocencio. 2020. *COVID-19 Is No Excuse to Regress on Gender Equality. ADB Briefs.* No. 157. Manila: ADB.

9 N. Affoum and I. Santagostino Recavarren. 2020. *Child Marriage: The Unspoken Consequence of COVID-19.* World Bank. Washington DC.

10 ADB. 2020. *Managing Infectious Medical Waste During the COVID-19 Pandemic.* Manila.

11 S. Praveena and A. Aris. 2021. *The Impacts of COVID-19 on the Environmental Sustainability: A Perspective from the Southeast Asian Region. Environmental Science and Pollution Research.* 6 January.

12 J. Tollefson. 2021. *COVID Curbed Carbon Emissions in 2020—but Not by Much. Nature.* 589, 343; P. Friedlingstein et al. 2020.*Global Carbon Budget 2021. Earth Syst. Sci. Data.* 12. pp. 3269–3340.

13 IQAir. *World's Most Polluted Cities 2019 (PM2.5)* (accessed 19 February 2021).

14 ADB. 2020. *COVID-19 and Livable Cities in Asia and the Pacific: Guidance Note.* Manila.

15 The Third Pole. 2020. *Air Pollution Could Worsen Covid-19 Outbreak in South Asia.*

16 N. Nixon, M. Surie, and K. McQuay. 2020. *Covid Lays Bare the Flaws in Asia's Booming Megacities.* The Asia Foundation.

17 Food and Agriculture Organization (FAO), International Fund for Agricultural Development, United Nations Children's Fund (UNICEF), World Food Programme, and World Health Organization. 2020. *The State of Food Security and Nutrition in the World 2020. Transforming Food Systems for Affordable Healthy Diets.* Rome: FAO.

18 K. Kim, S. Kim, and C. Park. 2020. *Food Security in Asia and the Pacific amid the COVID-19 Pandemic. ADB Briefs.* No. 139. Manila: ADB.

19 ADB. 2021. *Asian Economic Integration Report 2021: Making Digital Platforms Work for Asia and the Pacific.* Manila.

20 The $16.3 billion committed includes $16.1 billion in new sovereign and nonsovereign commitments and $0.2 billion in repurposed sovereign financing. Data on the number and amount of COVID-19 related 2020 commitments are as of 17 March 2021.

21 The 88 sovereign operations include 20 special assistance grants funded through the Asia Pacific Disaster Response Fund. Twenty-eight operations worth $0.2 billion were repurposed and 157 were new, dedicated COVID-19 response projects.

22 The calculation of processing time is based on Level 3 tracking indicator in the corporate results framework "Time from concept approval to first disbursement (months)" using the operations that have verified milestones recorded in the e-Operations system. Three Countercyclical Support Facility operations launched in 2009, 2015, and 2016 took an average of 3.9 months from concept clearance to fact-finding, 1.4 months to approval, and 1.2 months to first disbursement.

23 Client ratings for 2020 presented throughout this report are based on responses to a client perceptions survey GlobeScan conducted on behalf of ADB from December 2020 to January 2021. In total, 1,216 ADB clients working in governments, civil society organisations, the private sector, media, university, think tanks or academia, and other organisations responded to the main survey. The findings presented in para. 42 are based on responses from the 318 primary clients who responded to that survey question. The ADB will publish the detailed report of survey findings during 2021.

24 Total cofinancing of $10.8 billion includes $8.2 billion in cofinancing for new and repurposed COVID-19 related sovereign projects and $2.6 billion for nonsovereign COVID-19 projects.

25 The remaining 30% is dedicated to other sectors—agriculture, natural resources, and rural development; education; energy; finance; industry and trade; information and communication technology; public sector management; transport; and water and other urban infrastructure and services.

26 Using 11 types of indicators in the 6 main categories, the expected results were mapped for 149 COVID-19 related projects by reviewing reports and recommendations of the President, TA reports, supply list requirements, and other project documents.

27 ADB's total commitments from its own resources for lending, grants, guarantees, equity investments, and technical assistance reached $31.6 billion in 2020. Commitment volumes used by corporate results framework indicators exclude financing for nonsovereign revolving fund programs, technical assistance, cofinancing, special funds, investment facilities, and loans and grants supporting project preparation and design activities.

28 ADB. 2020. *FAST Report: Loan to PT Cisarua Mountain Dairy for the Dairy Farmer Support and Food Security Project in Indonesia.* Manila.

29 ADB. 2015. *ADB to Double Annual Climate Financing to $6 Billion for Asia-Pacific by 2020.* News release. 25 September.

30 ADB. 2020. *Report and Recommendation of the President to the Board of Directors: Proposed Multitranche Financing Facility to India for the Delhi–Meerut Regional Rapid Transit System Investment Project.* Manila.

31 ADB. 2020. *Report and Recommendation of the President to the Board of Directors: Proposed Loans to the Republic of the Philippines for the Epifanio de los Santos Avenue Greenways Project.* Manila.

32 ADB. 2020. *Report and Recommendation of the President to the Board of Directors: Proposed Grant to the Islamic Republic of Afghanistan for the Emergency Assistance for COVID-19 Pandemic Response.* Manila; and ADB. 2020. *Report and Recommendation of the President to the Board of Directors: Proposed Loan and Administration of Grant to the Islamic Republic of Pakistan for the Emergency Assistance for Fighting the COVID-19 Pandemic.* Manila.

33 ADB. 2020. *Report and Recommendation of the President to the Board of Directors: Proposed Loan and Administration of Loan to "Nur Navoi Solar" Foreign Enterprise Limited Liability Company for the Navoi Solar Power Project in Uzbekistan.* Manila.

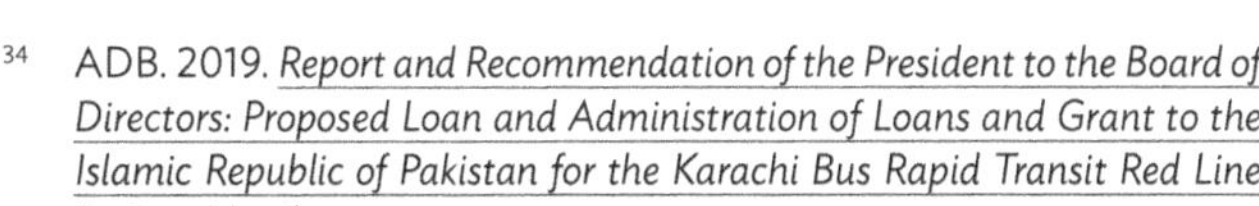

34 ADB. 2019. *Report and Recommendation of the President to the Board of Directors: Proposed Loan and Administration of Loans and Grant to the Islamic Republic of Pakistan for the Karachi Bus Rapid Transit Red Line Project.* Manila.

35 ADB. 2019. *Action Plan for Healthy Oceans: Investing in Sustainable Blue Economies for Poverty Alleviation in Asia and the Pacific.* Manila.

36 ADB. 2020. *Report and Recommendation of the President to the Board of Directors: Proposed Loan to the Republic of the Philippines: Expanded Social Assistance Project.* Manila.

37 ADB. 2020. *Report and Recommendation of the President to the Board of Directors: Proposed Equality Investment in Mekong Enterprise Fund IV L.P. in Viet Nam. Manila; and ADB. 2020. Regional: Follow-on Investment in OrbiMed Asia Partners IV.* Project Overview. Manila.

38 ADB. 2020. *Report and Recommendation of the President to the Board of Directors: Proposed Loan to the People's Republic of China for the Chongqing Innovation and Human Capital Development Project.* Manila.

39 ADB (Sustainable Development and Climate Change Department). 2020. ADB's Social Protection Operational Plan: An Assessment Paper. 25 January (internal).

40 The new poor are a combination of those who would have exited poverty in the absence of COVID-19 but are now projected to remain poor and those projected to fall into poverty because of COVID-19.

41 ADB. 2020. *Report and Recommendation of the President to the Board of Directors: Proposed Programmatic Approach, Policy-Based Loan for Subprogram 1, and Project Loan to Georgia for the Modern Skills for Better Jobs Sector Development Program.* Manila.

42 ADB. 2020. *Report and Recommendation of the President to the Board of Directors: Proposed Grant and Administration of Grant to the Republic of Tajikistan for the Skills and Employability Enhancement Project.* Manila.

43 ADB's methodology for classifying operations as disability-inclusive is based on the Organisation for Economic Co-operation and Development's disability marker. It aligns with the United Nations Economic and Social Commission for Asia and the Pacific's 2012 Incheon Strategy and the 2017 Beijing Declaration and Action Plan to Accelerate the Implementation of the Incheon Strategy, which introduced goals, indicators, and targets for implementing the Convention on the Rights of Persons with Disabilities in the Asia and Pacific region. All committed operations are reviewed for disability-inclusiveness, excluding project readiness financing facilities.

44 ADB. 2019. *Operational Plan for Private Sector Operations, 2019–2024.* Manila.

45 ADB. 2020. *FAST Report: Loan to Imexpharm Corporation for the Imexpharm COVID-19 Generic Pharmaceutical Project in Viet Nam.* Manila.

46 ADB. 2020. *FAST Report: Loans to Ulaanbaatar Flour Limited Liability Company and Tavan Bogd Foods Limited Liability Company for the Tavan Bogd COVID-19 Wheat Supply Chain Liquidity Support Project in Mongolia.* Manila; and ADB. 2020. *Report and Recommendation of the President to the Board of Directors: Proposed Loan to Olam International Limited and Olam Treasury Private Limited for the Olam COVID-19 Smallholder Farmer Livelihood Support Project in Indonesia, Papua New Guinea, and Viet Nam.* Manila.

47 ADB's client survey results are based on GlobeScan's report dated 18 March 2021. The respondents are grouped into two categories: "primary clients," which includes government officials and private companies directly involved in ADB-funded projects; and "others," which refers to participants in ADB-organized events. All survey questions are mandatory unless otherwise stated.

48 Knowledge-related events include forums, conferences, seminars, meetings, workshops, and training programs in which DMC officials and others participated.

49 This includes followers on Facebook, Instagram, LinkedIn, and Twitter.

50 Starting in 2020, ADB's Office of Risk Management reports the capital utilization ratio, defined as the ratio of the total economic capital used to total available capital. Economic capital covers the capital requirement for credit, market, operational, and other risk types. This indicator replaces reporting on the equity–loan ratio.

51 Starting in 2020, the Office of Risk Management reports the weighted average risk rating based on outstanding exposure rather than exposure at default in the previous methodology.

52 The count is based on staff participants and includes training expenses directly managed by the Budget, People and Management Systems Department.

53 The figure refers to budgeted international and national staff positions on 31 December each year. Field offices include resident missions, regional offices (i.e., the Pacific Liaison and Coordination Office in Sydney and the Pacific Subregional Office in Suva), and country offices in the Pacific.

54 The 2020 sample for sovereign operations comprises 47 projects. These include 5 COVID-19 related projects of which 4 are emergency assistance loans and 1 is a results-based loan. Of the total of 65 loans and grants, 18 were removed from the computations—8 were project readiness financing and 10 had missing data on concept approval and fact-finding dates.

55 The 2020 sample for nonsovereign operations comprises 35 projects, including 8 COVID-19 related transactions.

56 A total of 2,567 staff participated in the survey—995 administrative staff, 682 national staff, and 890 international staff.

57 Procurement processing time is the period from receipt of the bid evaluation report to ADB's approval of the executing or implementing agency's recommendation.

58 ADB approved a new TA project amounting to $2 million in October 2020 to improve the approach for financial management and procurement assessments and thus strengthen DMC fiduciary systems for use in ADB operations.

59 ADB. 2018. *Strategy 2030: Building a Prosperous, Inclusive, Resilient, and Sustainable Asia and the Pacific.* Manila. ADB uses the multilateral development bank harmonized methodology to classify fragile and conflict-affected situations (FCAS) countries. A country is considered FCAS if it has an average rating of 3.2 or less based on the ADB country performance assessment and the World Bank Group country policy and institutional assessment. A country is also considered FCAS if a United Nations and/or regional peacekeeping or peace-building mission has been present during the past 3 years. Based on 2020 harmonized methodology, ADB classified 11 developing member countries (DMCs) FCAS: Afghanistan, the Federated States of Micronesia, Kiribati, the Lao People's Democratic Republic, the Marshall Islands, Myanmar, Nauru, Papua New Guinea, Solomon Islands, Timor-Leste, and Tuvalu. However, to reduce data volatility because of changing DMC assessments, the FCAS listing for this review is based on the country classification in 2018. This may be updated during the midterm review of the corporate results framework, 2019–2024.

60 ADB. 2020. *Report and Recommendation of the President to the Board of Directors: Proposed Loan to the Republic of the Union of Myanmar for the Second Greater Mekong Subregion Highway Modernization Project.* Manila.

[61] There are 16 SIDS. Of these, eight are also classified as FCAS: the Federated States of Micronesia, Kiribati, the Marshall Islands, Nauru, Papua New Guinea, Solomon Islands, Timor-Leste, and Tuvalu. ADB follows the United Nations classification of SIDS.

[62] Independent Evaluation Department (IED). 2020. *Validation Report: Fiscal Resilience Improvement Program (Subprograms 1 and 2) in Samoa.* Manila: ADB; IED. 2020. *Validation Report: Provincial Renewable Energy Project in Solomon Islands*. Manila: ADB; and IED. 2020. *Validation Report: Yap Renewable Energy Development Project in the Federated States of Micronesia*. Manila: ADB.

[63] ADB. 2020. *Digital Twin Capabilities in Project Management*. Manila.

[64] ADB. 2020. *Report and Recommendation of the President to the Board of Directors: Proposed Countercyclical Support Facility Grant to the Islamic Republic of Afghanistan for the COVID-19 Active Response and Expenditure Support Program*. Manila.

[65] ADB. 2020. *Report and Recommendation of the President to the Board of Directors: Proposed Grant to the Islamic Republic of Afghanistan for the Emergency Assistance for COVID-19 Pandemic Response*. Manila.

[66] ADB. 2020. *Technical Assistance Report: Regional Support to Address the Outbreak of Coronavirus Disease 2019 and Potential Outbreaks of Other Communicable Diseases*. Manila; and ADB. 2020. *Report and Recommendation of the President to the Board of Directors: Proposed Loan for Additional Financing to the Republic of the Union of Myanmar for the Greater Mekong Subregion Health Security Project*. Manila.

[67] ADB. 2020. *Timor-Leste: COVID-19 Food Security Emergency Response*. Manila.

[68] ADB. 2020. *Report and Recommendation of the President to the Board of Directors for the Proposed Contingent Disaster Financing Facility, Policy-Based Loan, and Policy-Based Grants for the Pacific Disaster Resilience Program (Phase 3)*. Manila.

[69] ADB. 2020. *Report and Recommendation of the President to the Board of Directors: Proposed Loan, Grant, Technical Assistance Grant, and Administration of Loan and Grant to the Republic of Maldives for the Greater Malé Waste-to-Energy Project*. Manila.

[70] ADB. 2020. *Periodic Financing Request Report: Pacific Renewable Energy Investment Facility for the Republic of Kiribati for the South Tarawa Renewable Energy Project*. Manila.

[71] ADB. 2017. *Report and Recommendation of the President to the Board of Directors: Proposed Facility for Pacific Renewable Energy Investment.* Manila. The smaller Pacific SIDS consist of the Cook Islands, the Federated States of Micronesia, Kiribati, the Marshall Islands, Nauru, Palau, Samoa, Solomon Islands, Tonga, Tuvalu, and Vanuatu.

[72] ADB Strategy, Policy and Partnerships Department. Improving the Sustainability of Results in ADB Financed Operations: Operations Research Study. Unpublished.

Regional road links. The 244-kilometer Noi Bai–Lao Cai Highway is an integral section of the eastern link of the Greater Mekong Subregion Northern Economic Corridor, connecting Kunming in Yunnan Province of the People's Republic of China with Ha Noi, and Hai Phong and Cai Lan ports in Viet Nam (photo by Ariel Javellana).

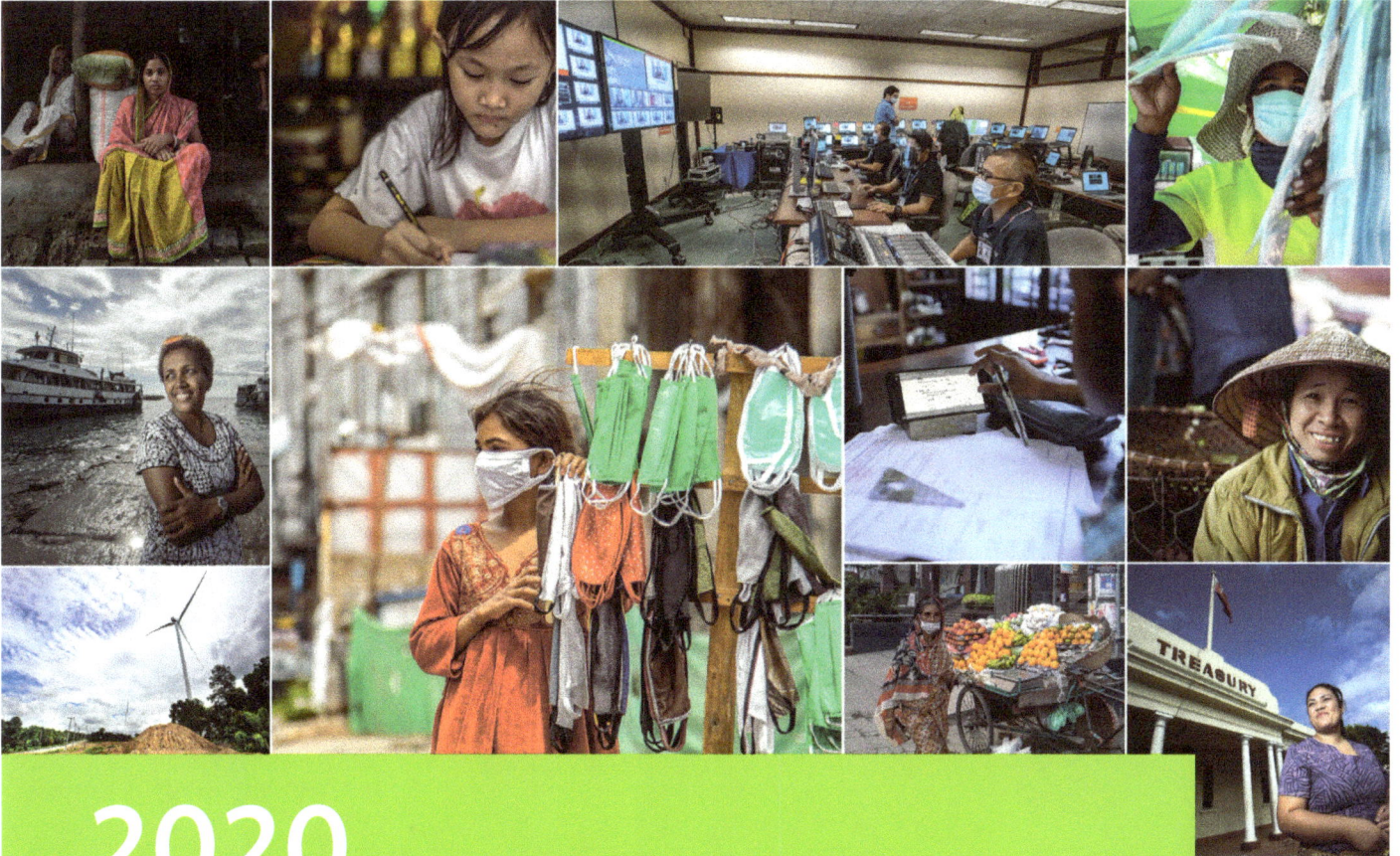

2020 DEVELOPMENT EFFECTIVENESS REVIEW

SCORECARD AND RELATED INFORMATION

APRIL 2021

ASIAN DEVELOPMENT BANK

CONTENTS

SIGNALS AND SCORING METHODS

RESULTS FRAMEWORK INDICATORS

TRACKING INDICATORS

Notes:
1. In this report, "$" refers to United States dollars.
2. The Asian Development Bank's Strategy, Policy and Partnerships Department is the source of all information in tables, figures, boxes, and infographics in this report, unless otherwise stated.
3. Totals may not sum precisely because of rounding.

TREASURY

SIGNALS AND SCORING METHODS

Alignment with the Sustainable Development Goals

	SDG Indicator	Official Sustainable Development Goal (SDG) Indicator
	SDG Derived	***Directly*** related to an official SDG indicator
	SDG Aligned	***Closely*** linked to SDG indicator or captures certain elements of the official indicator
	SDG Proxy Indicator	***Relates*** to overall SDG and associated targets but not to an official SDG indicator

Results Framework Indicators Level 1: Signals

Scoring Method	Signal[a]	Change
Improved—region's performance improved relative to prior year of available data	↑	Improved
Unchanged—region's performance unchanged relative to prior year of available data	↔	Stayed constant
Regressed—region's performance deteriorated relative to prior year of available data	↓	Deteriorated

[a] A change of more than 2.5% constitutes an improvement or deterioration.

Results Framework Indicators Levels 2–4: Signals

Scoring Method	Signal	Annual Change[a]
At or above target—performance at or above target		
On track—performance exceeded desired progress to attain target		Improved
		Remained constant
		Deteriorated
On track but watch—performance met desired progress to attain 2024 target but requires close monitoring		Improved
		Remained constant
		Deteriorated
Off track—performance fell short of desired progress to attain target		Improved
		Remained constant
		Deteriorated
Monitor—no performance assessment		Increased
		Remained constant
		Decreased

[a] An arrow indicates a significant (≥ 3%) change from previous performance.

Results Framework Indicators Levels 2–4: Composite Signals

Signal		Explanation
(green circle)	*Good*	Two-thirds or more of RFIs in the group achieved a green or amber signal and half or more achieved a green signal.
(amber circle)	*Mixed*	More than half but less than two-thirds of RFIs in the group achieved a green or amber signal, or two-thirds or more of RFIs in the group achieved a green or amber signal but less than half achieved a green signal.
(red circle)	*Poor*	Half or less of RFIs in the group achieved a green or amber signal.
(empty circle)		No signal generated because data is not yet available for three or more indicators in the group.
--		Group not scored because data are reported for less than three indicators that have a specific target.

RFI = results framework indicator.

Results Framework Indicators Levels 2–4: Scoring Methods for 2019–2023

Scoring Method	Target	Note	Signal	Applied to[a]
Achievement rate[b]	Annual	• At or above 80% of expected results • Below 80% of expected results	(green check) (red)	Level 2A: RFIs 1–22
Point target	2024	• At or above target • Above band from baseline to target • Within band from baseline to target • Below band from baseline to target	(green check) (green) (amber) (red)	Level 2B: RFIs 1–4 Level 3: RFIs 2 (ADB overall only), 6, 9–11 (ADB overall only), 13–14 Level 4: RFIs 2–3, 5–6, and 8
Range	2024	• Within the target range • Above band from baseline to target • Within band from baseline to target • Below band from baseline to target	(green check) (green) (amber) (red)	Level 3: RFIs 7, 8
Performance standard	Annual	• Performance standard or better • Worse than the performance standard	(green check) (red)	Level 2B: RFI 5 Level 3: RFI 5 Level 4: RFI 1

continued on next page

Results Framework Indicators Levels 2–4: Scoring Methods for 2019–2023 (continued)

Scoring Method	Target	Note	Signal	Applied to[a]
Maintain	Annual	• Baseline or better • Worse than the baseline	✓ (green) (red)	Level 3: RFI 1 (ADB overall only)
Cumulative	2024	• Above cumulative target • Performance is expected to increase each year and add up to the cumulative target • Performance is on track to reach the target but requires close monitoring • Below cumulative target	✓ (green) (green) (yellow) (red)	Level 3: RFI 12 Level 4: RFI 4
Monitor[c]	2024	• Increased • Remained stable • Decreased	↑ (gray) ↓	Level 3: RFIs 1–2 (CA only), 3–4, 9–11 (CA only), and 15 Level 4: RFI 7

ADB = Asian Development Bank, CA = concessional assistance, RFI = results framework indicator.

[a] Refers to the RFI numbers used in the ADB Corporate Results Framework, 2019–2024.

[b] Achievement rate for Level 2A indicators is only calculated once the count of cumulative planned results has reached a threshold of at least 20.

[c] Only arrows are shown, no impact on summary scorecard.

Results Framework Indicators Levels 2–4: Scoring Methods for 2024

Scoring Method	Target	Note	Signal	Applied to[a]
Achievement rate	Annual	• Better than target • Worse than target	✓ (green) (red)	Level 2A: RFIs 1–22
Point target	2024	• At or above target • Below target, but within 1% buffer zone • Below target	✓ (green) (yellow) (red)	Level 2B: RFIs 1–4 Level 3: RFIs 2 (ADB overall only), 6, 9–11 (ADB overall only), 13–14 Level 4: RFIs 2–3, 5–6, and 8

continued on next page

Results Framework Indicators Levels 2–4: Scoring Methods for 2024 (continued)

Scoring Method	Target	Note	Signal	Applied to[a]
Range	2024	• Within the target range • Outside the target range		Level 3: RFIs 7, 8
Performance standard	Annual	• Performance standard or better • Worse than the performance standard		Level 2B: RFI 5 Level 3: RFI 5 Level 4: RFI 1
Maintain	Annual	• Baseline or better • Worse than the baseline		Level 3: RFI 1 (ADB overall only)
Cumulative indicator	2024	• Above cumulative target • Performance is expected to increase each year and add up to the cumulative target • Performance is on track to reach the target but requires close monitoring • Below cumulative target		Level 3: RFI 12 Level 4: RFI 4
Monitor[b]	2024	• Increased • Remained stable • Decreased	↑ ↓	Level 3: RFIs 1–2 (CA only), 3–4, 9–11 (CA only), and 15 Level 4: RFI 7

ADB = Asian Development Bank, CA = concessional assistance, RFI = results framework indicator.

[a] Refers to the RFI numbers used in the ADB Corporate Results Framework, 2019–2024.
[b] Only arrows are shown, no impact on summary scorecard.

RESULTS FRAMEWORK INDICATORS

LEVEL 1: Development Progress in Asia and the Pacific

ADB Developing Member Countries Overall

Indicator	SDG	Baseline Year(s)	Latest Year	Baseline Value(s)	Latest Value	2020 Signal
1. **Population living on less than $1.90 a day** (%, number)[a]	1	2015	2017	7.20 273,000,000	5.10 198,000,000	↑
2. **Growth rates of household expenditure or income per capita among the bottom 40% and the total population** (percentage point difference)	10	2000–2017	2000–2018	(0.12)	0.14	↑
3. **Annual growth rate of real GDP per capita in 2010 constant United States dollars** (%)	8	2017	2019	5.54	4.11	↓
4. **Unemployment rate** (%)	8	2018	2020	3.49	4.57	↓
a. **Female**				3.79	4.46	↓
b. **Male**				3.51	4.70	↓
5. **CO_2 emissions per unit of GDP** (kg per $ constant 2010 PPP GDP)	9	2014	2017	1.04	0.90	↑
6. **Deaths attributed to climate-related and geophysical hazards** (number)[b]	13	2018	2020	8,761	5,050	↑
7. **PM2.5 air pollution, mean annual exposure** (micrograms per cubic meter)	11	2016	2017	60.07	60.65	↔
8. **Prevalence of stunting among children under 5 years** (%)	2	2006–2016	2008–2018	28.93	28.19	↔

LEVEL 1: Development Progress in Asia and the Pacific

ADB Concessional Assistance Countries

Indicator	SDG	Baseline Year(s)	Latest Year	Baseline Value(s)	Latest Value	2020 Signal
1. **Population living on less than $1.90 a day** (%, number)[a]	1	2015	2017	8.06 49,680,000	5.58 35,398,456	↑
2. **Growth rates of household expenditure or income per capita among the bottom 40% and the total population** (percentage point difference)	10	2000–2017	2000–2018	0.13	0.15	↑
3. **Annual growth rate of real GDP per capita in 2010 constant United States dollars** (%)	8	2017	2019	4.48	3.14	↓
4. **Unemployment rate** (%)	8			3.13	4.00	↓
a. **Female**		2018	2020	4.38	4.90	↓
b. **Male**				2.68	3.67	↓
5. **CO_2 emissions per unit of GDP** (kg per $ constant 2010 PPP GDP)	9	2014	2017	0.64	0.68	↓
6. **Deaths attributed to climate-related and geophysical hazards** (number)[b]	13	2018	2020	397	2,078	↓
7. **PM2.5 air pollution, mean annual exposure** (micrograms per cubic meter)	11	2016	2017	49.39	49.43	↔
8. **Prevalence of stunting among children under 5 years** (%)	2	2006–2016	2008–2018	37	35.39	↔

LEVEL 1: Development Progress in Asia and the Pacific

ADB Developing Member Countries Overall (continued)

Indicator	SDG	Baseline Year(s)	Latest Year	Baseline Value(s)	Latest Value	2020 Signal
9. **Worldwide Governance Indicators** (average score)[c]	9	2017	2019	(0.32)	(0.28)	↑
10. **Regional cooperation and integration index** (average score)[d]	17	2010–2015	2018	0.43	0.45	↑

ADB Concessional Assistance Countries (continued)

Indicator	SDG	Baseline Year(s)	Latest Year	Baseline Value(s)	Latest Value	2020 Signal
9. **Worldwide Governance Indicators** (average score)[c]	9	2017	2019	(0.34)	(0.31)	↑
10. **Regional cooperation and integration index** (average score)[d]	17	2010–2015	2018	0.42	0.44	↑

() = negative, ADB = Asian Development Bank, CO_2 = carbon dioxide, GDP = gross domestic product, kg = kilogram, PM2.5 = atmospheric particulate matter with a diameter of less than 2.5 micrometers, PPP = purchasing power parity, SDG = Sustainable Development Goal.

Notes:
1. "Concessional assistance countries" refers to a subset of ADB developing member countries that have access to Asian Development Fund grants and concessional ordinary capital resources loans (group A and B countries except India).
2. Estimates are averages of actual country values or imputed country values wherever data are missing for the year required, weighted by population size or by GDP.
3. Gray shading in cells indicates the column heading does not apply.

[a] The World Bank introduced the $1.90 income per day international poverty threshold in 2015 and revised its estimates in September 2020 reflecting 2011 Purchasing Power Parity (PPP). The new poverty estimates combine revised PPP exchange rates for household consumption from the 2011 International Comparison Program published in May 2020 with data from more than 1,500 household surveys across 166 economies in the world. World Bank. 2020. PovcalNet Update: What's New. *Global Poverty Monitoring Technical Note. No. 14.* Washington, D.C.
[b] Climate-related hazards include climatological, hydrological, and meteorological hazards.
[c] The Worldwide Governance Indicators report on six broad dimensions of governance: voice and accountability, government effectiveness, control of corruption, rule of law, regulatory quality, and political stability and absence of violence.
[d] ADB's Economic Research and Regional Cooperation Department adapted the Asia-Pacific Regional Cooperation and Integration Index to capture the following dimensions: trade and investment integration, regional value chains, infrastructure and connectivity, movement of people, and institutional and social integration.

Sources: Regional aggregates were prepared by ADB's Strategy, Policy and Partnerships Department using country data from the following sources: ADB Economic Research and Regional Cooperation Department; World Bank. PovcalNet. http://iresearch.worldbank.org/PovcalNet/povOnDemand.aspx (accessed 12 October 2020); Centre for Research on the Epidemiology of Disasters. Emergency Events Database. https://www.emdat.be/database (accessed 13 January 2021); World Bank. Worldwide Governance Indicators. https://datacatalog.worldbank.org/dataset/worldwide-governance-indicators (accessed 15 January 2021); and World Bank. World Development Indicators. https://databank.worldbank.org/source/world-development-indicators (accessed 15 February 2020). Population data used as weights are from the following sources: World Bank. World Development Indicators. https://databank.worldbank.org/source/world-development-indicators (accessed 12 January 2021); and International Labour Organization. ILOSTAT. https://ilostat.ilo.org/ (accessed 18 January 2021).

LEVEL 2: Results from Completed Operations

ADB Operations Overall

Indicator		SDG	Number of Completion Reports (PCR / XARR / TCR)	Results Achieved	Achievement Rate (%)	Signal
LEVEL 2A. STRATEGY 2030 OPERATIONAL PRIORITY RESULTS						✔ (green)
Operational Priority 1: Addressing Remaining Poverty and Reducing Inequalities						
1.1	People benefiting from improved health services, education services, or social protection (number)	1	PCR 6	4,872,000	85	✔
1.2	Jobs generated (number)	8	PCR 16, XARR 10	1,748,000	100+	✔
1.3	Poor and vulnerable people with improved standards of living (number)	1	PCR 11	30,521,000	100+	✔
Operational Priority 2: Accelerating Progress in Gender Equality						
2.1	Skilled jobs for women generated (number)	8	PCR 15	317,000	100+	✔
2.2	Women and girls completing secondary and tertiary education, and/or other training (number)	4	PCR 3	67,000	100+	✔
2.3	Women represented in decision-making structures and processes (number)	5	PCR 6	115,000	100+	✔
2.4	Women and girls with increased time savings (number)	5	PCR 3	997,000	100	✔
2.5	Women and girls with increased resilience to climate change, disasters, and other external shocks (number)	13	PCR 1	870	100	✔
Operational Priority 3: Tackling Climate Change, Building Climate and Disaster Resilience, and Enhancing Environmental Sustainability						
3.1	Total annual greenhouse gas emissions reduction (tCO_2e/year)	13	PCR 17, XARR 8	19,325,000	100+	✔
3.2	People with strengthened climate and disaster resilience (number)	13	PCR 3, TCR 2	561,000	100+	✔
3.3	People benefiting from strengthened environmental sustainability (number)	12	PCR 6	3,127,000	88	✔

LEVEL 2: Results from Completed Operations

Operations Financed by Concessional OCR Loans and ADF Grants

	Indicator	SDG	Number of Completion Reports (PCR / TCR)	Results Achieved	Achievement Rate (%)	Signal
LEVEL 2A. STRATEGY 2030 OPERATIONAL PRIORITY RESULTS						●
Operational Priority 1: Addressing Remaining Poverty and Reducing Inequalities						
1.1	**People benefiting from improved health services, education services, or social protection** (number)	1	5	4,379,000	83	✓
1.2	**Jobs generated** (number)	8	7	175,000	99	✓
1.3	**Poor and vulnerable people with improved standards of living** (number)	1	7	4,823,000	100+	✓
Operational Priority 2: Accelerating Progress in Gender Equality						
2.1	**Skilled jobs for women generated** (number)	8	9	115,000	98	✓
2.2	**Women and girls completing secondary and tertiary education, and/or other training** (number)	4	3	67,000	100+	✓
2.3	**Women represented in decision-making structures and processes** (number)	5	4	850	79	■
2.4	**Women and girls with increased time savings** (number)	5	1	90,000	100	✓
2.5	**Women and girls with increased resilience to climate change, disasters, and other external shocks** (number)	13				
Operational Priority 3: Tackling Climate Change, Building Climate and Disaster Resilience, and Enhancing Environmental Sustainability						
3.1	**Total annual greenhouse gas emissions reduction** (tCO_2e/year)	13	7	810,000	100+	✓
3.2	**People with strengthened climate and disaster resilience** (number)	13	2 / 1	81,000	100+	✓
3.3	**People benefiting from strengthened environmental sustainability** (number)	12	3	304,000	100+	✓

LEVEL 2: Results from Completed Operations

ADB Operations Overall (continued)

Indicator		SDG	Number of Completion Reports (PCR / XARR / TCR)	Results Achieved	Achievement Rate (%)	Signal
Operational Priority 4: Making Cities More Livable						
4.1	**People benefiting from improved services in urban areas** (number)	11	PCR 13	14,150,000	100+	✓
4.2	**Entities with improved urban planning and financial sustainability** (number)	11	PCR 3	7		
4.3	**Zones with improved urban environment, climate resilience, and disaster risk management** (number)	11	PCR 2	2		
Operational Priority 5: Promoting Rural Development and Food Security						
5.1	**People benefiting from increased rural investment** (number)	2	PCR 12, XARR 2	27,605,000	100+	✓
5.2	**Farmers with improved market access** (number)	2	TCR 1	2,800	100+	✓
5.3	**Land with higher productivity** (hectares)	2	PCR 3	361,000	100+	✓
Operational Priority 6: Strengthening Governance and Institutional Capacity						
6.1	**Entities with improved management functions and financial stability** (number)	16	PCR 13, XARR 4, TCR 10	890	100+	✓
6.2	**Entities with improved service delivery** (number)	16	PCR 19, XARR 1, TCR 5	320	100	✓
Operational Priority 7: Fostering Regional Cooperation and Integration						
7.1	**Cargo transported and energy transmitted across borders** ($)	17				
7.2	**Trade and investment facilitated** ($)	17	PCR 1	1,374,000,000	100	✓

LEVEL 2: Results from Completed Operations

Operations Financed by Concessional OCR Loans and ADF Grants (continued)

Indicator		SDG	Number of Completion Reports (PCR)	Number of Completion Reports (TCR)	Results Achieved	Achievement Rate (%)	Signal
Operational Priority 4: Making Cities More Livable							
4.1	**People benefiting from improved services in urban areas** (number)	11	7		1,595,000	89	✓
4.2	**Entities with improved urban planning and financial sustainability** (number)	11	2		2		
4.3	**Zones with improved urban environment, climate resilience, and disaster risk management** (number)	11					
Operational Priority 5: Promoting Rural Development and Food Security							
5.1	**People benefiting from increased rural investment** (number)	2	8		8,773,000	100+	✓
5.2	**Farmers with improved market access** (number)	2		1	2,800	100+	✓
5.3	**Land with higher productivity** (hectares)	2	3		361,000	100+	✓
Operational Priority 6: Strengthening Governance and Institutional Capacity							
6.1	**Entities with improved management functions and financial stability** (number)	16	6	9	880	100+	✓
6.2	**Entities with improved service delivery** (number)	16	12	4	290	100	✓
Operational Priority 7: Fostering Regional Cooperation and Integration							
7.1	**Cargo transported and energy transmitted across borders** ($)	17					
7.2	**Trade and investment facilitated** ($)	17	1		1,374,000,000	100	✓

LEVEL 2: Results from Completed Operations

ADB Operations Overall (continued)

Indicator	SDG	Number of Completion Reports (PCR / XARR / TCR)	Results Achieved	Achievement Rate (%)	Signal
7.3 Regional public goods initiatives successfully reducing cross-border environmental or health risks, or providing regional access to education services (number)	17	1 (PCR)	1		

LEVEL 2: Results from Completed Operations

Operations Financed by Concessional OCR Loans and ADF Grants (continued)

Indicator	SDG	Number of Completion Reports (PCR / TCR)	Results Achieved	Achievement Rate (%)	Signal
7.3 Regional public goods initiatives successfully reducing cross-border environmental or health risks, or providing regional access to education services (number)	17	1	1		

ADB = Asian Development Bank, ADF = Asian Development Fund, OCR = ordinary capital resources, PCR = project completion report, SDG = Sustainable Development Goal, tCO_2e/year = tons of carbon dioxide equivalent per year, TCR = technical assistance completion report, XARR = extended annual review report.

Notes:

1. "ADB Operations Overall" refers to ADB operations financed by regular and concessional OCR and/or ADF grants.
2. Results delivered as reported in PCRs, XARRs, and TCRs circulated from 16 November 2019 to 15 November 2020.
3. An annual achievement rate of 80% is used as a benchmark for satisfactory performance. "100+" achievement rate means that achieved results exceeded the planned results. In cases where annual results are too few in number to permit accurate achievement rate scoring (i.e., below 20), results will be cumulated over the years until the minimum value of 20 is reached and achievement rate and score will be reported starting from that year.
4. Achieved results over 10,000 are rounded to the nearest 1,000. Values smaller than 10,000 are rounded to the nearest 100. Values smaller than 1,000 are rounded to the nearest 10. Values smaller than 99 are not rounded.
5. Gray shading in cells indicates the column heading does not apply.

LEVEL 2: Results from Completed Operations

ADB Operations Overall

	Indicator	SDG	Baseline Year(s)	Baseline Value	RY2019	RY2020	2024 Target	2020 Signal
LEVEL 2B. QUALITY OF COMPLETED OPERATIONS								
1.	Completed operations rated ***successful*** (%) (sovereign)		RY2016–RY2018	77	72[a]	70	80	
2.	Projects closed on time (%) (sovereign)[b]		2016–2018	40	37[c]	33	45	
3.	Completed operations rated ***successful*** (%) (nonsovereign)		RY2016–RY2018	54	51[d]	53	70	
4.	Completed operations delivering intended gender equality results (%) (sovereign and nonsovereign)	5	RY2016–RY2018	75	74	73	80	
5.	Clients satisfied with the use of ADB knowledge products (%)[e]		2018	78		79	80	

LEVEL 2: Results from Completed Operations

Operations Financed by Concessional OCR Loans and ADF Grants

Indicator		SDG	Baseline Year(s)	Baseline Value	RY2019	RY2020	2024 Target	2020 Signal
LEVEL 2B. QUALITY OF COMPLETED OPERATIONS								
1.	**Completed operations rated** ***successful*** (%) (sovereign)		RY2016–RY2018	77	70	65	80	
2.	**Projects closed on time** (%) (sovereign)[a]		2016–2018	40	33[c]	31	45	
3.	**Completed operations rated** ***successful*** (%) (nonsovereign)							
4.	**Completed operations delivering intended gender equality results** (%) (sovereign and nonsovereign)	5	RY2016–RY2018	76	77	78	80	
5.	**Clients satisfied with the use of ADB knowledge products** (%)[b]							

⦿ = periodic performance target, ADB = Asian Development Bank, ADF = Asian Development Fund, OCR = ordinary capital resources, RY = reporting year, SDG = Sustainable Development Goal.

Notes:

1. "ADB Operations Overall" refers to ADB operations financed by regular and concessional OCR and/or ADF grants.
2. The reporting year is 1 July–30 June and is based on the circulation year of completion reports reviewed. For example, RY2020 refers to 1 July 2018–30 June 2020.
3. Success rates of completed operations are ratings evaluated by the Independent Evaluation Department based on validations of project and/or program completion reports and project and/or program performance evaluations.
4. Success rates in delivering intended gender equality results are ratings by the Gender Equity Thematic Group based on project and/or program completion reports.
5. Gray shading in cells indicates the column heading does not apply.

[a] The value changed from 71% in the 2019 report. Five project performance evaluation reports with *successful* ratings were done in 2020. Two were for projects completed in RY2019 that had no previous validation reports.

[b] Indicator is reported by calendar year.

[c] The value changed from 36% in the 2019 report. Inputs of actual financial closing dates were revised for two projects completed in calendar year 2019. The value for the concessional assistance subset was also adjusted from 30%.

[d] The value changed from 52% in the 2019 report. Two project performance evaluations reports, one with *successful* and another with *less than successful* ratings were done in 2020. The two projects were completed in RY2019 and had no previous validation reports.

[e] Periodic performance target, assessed biennially.

Sources: ADB (Strategy, Policy and Partnerships Department; and Sustainable Development and Climate Change Department).

LEVEL 3: ADB's Operational Management

ADB Operations Overall

Indicator	SDG	Baseline Year(s)	Baseline Value	2019	2020	2024 Target	2020 Signal
LEVEL 3A. DESIGN AND IMPLEMENTATION QUALITY							--
1. **Infrastructure projects that are design-ready** (%) (sovereign)	9	2018	80	83 ✓	81	Maintain ⊙	✓
2. **Infrastructure projects that are procurement-ready** (%) (sovereign)	9	2018	46	50 ↑	51	60	
3. **Performance of operations at implementation rated *satisfactory*** (%) (sovereign)[a]				52	64	Monitor	↑
4. **Operations at risk of not achieving development results** (%) (nonsovereign)[a]					32	Monitor	
LEVEL 3B. DEVELOPMENT FINANCE							
5. **Disbursement rate** (%) (sovereign)		2018		93 ✓	88	90 ⊙	
6. **Cofinancing ratio** (%) (nonsovereign)	17	2018	120	143 ↑	145	200	
7. **Financing for education** (%) (sovereign and nonsovereign)	4	2016–2018	5.43	5.23 ↓	3.76	6–10	↓
8. **Financing for health** (%) (sovereign and nonsovereign)	3	2016–2018	1.75	2.95 ↑	12.03	3–5	↓
LEVEL 3C. STRATEGIC ALIGNMENT							
9. **Committed operations classified *gender equity theme or effective gender mainstreaming*** (%) (sovereign and nonsovereign)	5	2016–2018	47	55 ✓	64	50	✓

LEVEL 3: ADB's Operational Management

Operations Financed by Concessional OCR Loans and ADF Grants

	Indicator	SDG	Baseline Year(s)	Baseline Value	2019	2020	2024 Target	2020 Signal
LEVEL 3A. DESIGN AND IMPLEMENTATION QUALITY								--
1.	**Infrastructure projects that are design-ready** (%) (sovereign)	9	2018	77	84 ↑	77	Monitor	↓
2.	**Infrastructure projects that are procurement-ready** (%) (sovereign)	9	2018	37	38	45	Monitor	↑
3.	**Performance of operations at implementation rated *satisfactory*** (%) (sovereign)[a]				53	64	Monitor	↑
4.	**Operations at risk of not achieving development results** (%) (nonsovereign)[a]							
LEVEL 3B. DEVELOPMENT FINANCE								
5.	**Disbursement rate** (%) (sovereign)							
6.	**Cofinancing ratio** (%) (nonsovereign)	17						
7.	**Financing for education** (%) (sovereign and nonsovereign)	4						
8.	**Financing for health** (%) (sovereign and nonsovereign)	3						
LEVEL 3C. STRATEGIC ALIGNMENT								--
9.	**Committed operations classified *gender equity theme* or *effective gender mainstreaming*** (%) (sovereign and nonsovereign)	5	2016–2018	62	73 ↑	76	Monitor	↑

ADB Operations Overall (continued)

Indicator	SDG	Baseline Year(s)	Baseline Value	2019	2020	2024 Target	2020 Signal
10. **Committed operations classified *gender equity theme, effective gender mainstreaming,* or *some gender elements*** (%) (sovereign and nonsovereign)	5	2016–2018	70	80	89	71	
11. **Committed operations that support climate change mitigation and adaptation** (%) (sovereign and nonsovereign)	13	2016–2018	56	59	58	65	
12. **Financing for climate change mitigation and adaptation** ($ billion, cumulative) (sovereign and nonsovereign)	13			6.5	10.8	35	
13. **Nonsovereign operations as a share of total ADB operations** (%, number) (nonsovereign)		2018	20	24	21	33	
14. **Operations in frontier economies and/or in new sectors** (%) (nonsovereign)	8	2016–2018	48	61	58	55	
15. **Operations supporting poverty reduction and inclusiveness** (%) (sovereign and nonsovereign)	1	2016–2018	[70]	[74]	[79]	Monitor	

Operations Financed by Concessional OCR Loans and ADF Grants (continued)

Indicator	SDG	Baseline Year(s)	Baseline Value	2019	2020	2024 Target	2020 Signal
10. Committed operations classified ***gender equity theme, effective gender mainstreaming***, or ***some gender elements*** (%) (sovereign and nonsovereign)	5	2016–2018	82	91 ↑	94	Monitor	↑
11. **Committed operations that support climate change mitigation and adaptation** (%) (sovereign and nonsovereign)	13	2016–2018	58	63 ↑	63	Monitor	
12. **Financing for climate change mitigation and adaptation** ($ billion, cumulative) (sovereign and nonsovereign)	13						
13. **Nonsovereign operations as a share of total ADB operations** (%, number) (nonsovereign)							
14. **Operations in frontier economies and/or in new sectors** (%) (nonsovereign)	8						
15. **Operations supporting poverty reduction and inclusiveness** (%) (sovereign and nonsovereign)	1						

⦿ = periodic performance target, assessed annually; ADB = Asian Development Bank; ADF = Asian Development Fund; OCR = ordinary capital resources; SDG = Sustainable Development Goal.

Notes:

1. "ADB Operations Overall" refers to ADB operations financed by regular and concessional OCR and/or ADF grants.
2. Gray shading in cells indicates the column heading does not apply.
3. Values presented in square brackets ([x]) were calculated using interim methodologies that will be revised in 2021.

[a] A new methodology for this indicator was introduced during the corporate results framework period. Data are reported starting from the first year that the new methodology was fully applied.

Sources: ADB (Central and West Asia Department; Controller's Department; East Asia Department; Pacific Department; Private Sector Operations Department; Procurement, Portfolio and Financial Management Department; South Asia Department; Southeast Asia Department; Strategy, Policy and Partnerships Department; and Sustainable Development and Climate Change Department).

LEVEL 4: ADB's Organizational Effectiveness

ADB Operations Overall

Indicator	Baseline Year(s)	Baseline Value	2019	2020	2024 Target	2020 Signal
LEVEL 4A. ORGANIZATIONAL SYSTEMS AND PROCESSES						
1. **Quality of budget management** (%)	2018	5.4	0.0	5.0	5.0 or less	
2. **Procurement contract transactions of $10 million or more with processing time of 40 days or less** (%) (sovereign)	2017–2018	67	67	59	80	
3. **Representation of women in the international staff category** (%)	2018	36.3	36.7	37.7	40.0	
4. **Projects or transactions with sovereign–nonsovereign collaboration** (number, cumulative) (sovereign and nonsovereign)	2016–2018	2	8	22	18	
LEVEL 4B. ORGANIZATIONAL CAPACITY						
5. **Staff rating ADB's effectiveness in digital transformation** (%)[a]	2018	68		80	75	
6. **Staff rating ADB as providing enabling culture for Strategy 2030 implementation** (%)[a]	2018	58		66	70	
7. **Budgeted international and national staff positions in field offices** (% of total operations departments)	2018	48	45	46	Monitor	
8. **Staff rating ADB as an effective knowledge and learning organization** (%)	2018	63	65	69	75	

LEVEL 4: ADB's Organizational Effectiveness

Operations Financed by Concessional OCR Loans and ADF Grants

Indicator	Baseline Year(s)	Baseline Value	2019	2020	2024 Target	2020 Signal
LEVEL 4A. ORGANIZATIONAL SYSTEMS AND PROCESSES						--
1. **Quality of budget management** (%)						
2. **Procurement contract transactions of $10 million or more with processing time of 40 days or less** (%) (sovereign)	2017–2018	60	71 ↑	49	80	↓
3. **Representation of women in the international staff category** (%)						
4. **Projects or transactions with sovereign–nonsovereign collaboration** (number, cumulative) (sovereign and nonsovereign)						
LEVEL 4B. ORGANIZATIONAL CAPACITY						
5. **Staff rating ADB's effectiveness in digital transformation** (%)[a]						
6. **Staff rating ADB as providing enabling culture for Strategy 2030 implementation** (%)[a]						
7. **Budgeted international and national staff positions in field offices** (% of total operations departments)						
8. **Staff rating ADB as an effective knowledge and learning organization** (%)						

⦿ = periodic performance target, assessed anually; ADB = Asian Development Bank; ADF = Asian Development Fund; OCR = ordinary capital resources.

Notes:

1. "ADB Operations Overall" refers to ADB operations financed by regular and concessional OCR and/or ADF grants.
2. Concessional assistance is the subset of ADB's overall operations financed by concessional OCR loans and ADF grants.
3. Gray shading in cells indicates the column heading does not apply.

[a] Data for this indicator is measured at least every 2 years.

Sources: ADB (Central and West Asia Department; Controller's Department; East Asia Department; Pacific Department; Private Sector Operations Department; Procurement, Portfolio and Financial Management Department; South Asia Department; Southeast Asia Department; Strategy, Policy and Partnerships Department; Sustainable Development and Climate Change Department).

TRACKING INDICATORS

LEVEL 1: Development Progress in Asia and the Pacific

ADB Developing Member Countries Overall

Indicator	SDG	Baseline Year	Latest Year	Baseline Value	Latest Value
1. Population living on less than $3.20 a day (%, number)[a]	1				
a. Population living on less than $3.20 a day (% of population)		2015	2017	29.3	24.30
b. Population living on less than $3.20 a day (number)		2015	2017	1,113,000,000	941,000,000
2. Youth not in education or training (%)	4	2017	2019	22.29	26.27
a. Female		2017	2019	31.28	40.12
b. Male		2017	2019	13.29	13.54
3. Lower secondary education graduation rate (%)	4	2017	2019	86.78	93.43
a. Female		2017	2019	88.46	95.63
b. Male		2017	2019	85.66	93.50
4. Universal healthcare coverage service index (%)	3	2015	2017	61.44	64.31
5. Proportion of adults (15 years and older) with an account at a bank, financial institution, and/or mobile money service provider (%)	8	2014	2017	58.35	69.54
a. Female		2014	2017	53.61	65.89
b. Male		2014	2017	62.92	73.08
6. Income inequality (average Gini coefficient)	10	2016	2018	33.84	34.44
7. Labor force participation rate (%)	8	2017	2020	66.46	65.04
a. Female		2017	2020	49.85	47.82
b. Male		2017	2020	82.41	81.46

LEVEL 1: Development Progress in Asia and the Pacific

ADB Concessional Assistance Countries

Indicator	SDG	Baseline Year	Latest Year	Baseline Value	Latest Value
1. **Population living on less than $3.20 a day** (%, number)[a]	1				
a. **Population living on less than $3.20 a day** (% of population)		2015	2017	35.85	29.30
b. **Population living on less than $3.20 a day** (number)		2015	2017	220,970,000	185,935,000
2. **Youth not in education or training** (%)	4	2017	2019	19.85	14.73
a. **Female**		2017	2019	36.88	18.47
b. **Male**		2017	2019	11.91	10.91
3. **Lower secondary education graduation rate** (%)	4	2017	2019	84.39	90.07
a. **Female**		2017	2019	85.18	91.30
b. **Male**		2017	2019	84.12	88.99
4. **Universal healthcare coverage service index** (%)	3	2015	2017	51.67	53.75
5. **Proportion of adults (15 years and older) with an account at a bank, financial institution, and/or mobile money service provider** (%)	8	2014	2017	26.47	34.40
a. **Female**		2014	2017	22.24	26.16
b. **Male**		2014	2017	30.63	42.49
6. **Income inequality** (average Gini coefficient)	10	2016	2018	33.32	32.03
7. **Labor force participation rate** (%)	8	2017	2020	66.36	64.32
a. **Female**		2017	2020	47.09	45.61
b. **Male**		2017	2020	83.25	83.12

LEVEL 1: Development Progress in Asia and the Pacific

ADB Developing Member Countries Overall (continued)

Indicator	SDG	Baseline Year	Latest Year	Baseline Value	Latest Value
8. Proportion of time spent on unpaid domestic and care work (%)					
a. Female	5	2013	2018	10.42	15.38
b. Male		2013	2018	2.50	5.90
9. Forest area as a proportion of total land area (%)	15	2015	2016	34.81	34.81
10. Coverage of protected areas in relation to marine areas (%)	14	2017	2018	4.38	4.38
11. Environmental performance index score (average number)	12	2008	2020	46.67	36.68
12. Deaths attributed to climate-related and geophysical hazards (number)[b]	13	2018	2020	8761	5,050
a. Climate-related hazards		2018	2020	3097	5,045
b. Geophysical hazards		2018	2020	5664	5
13. Access to social protection—social assistance (%)	1	2013	2014	39.70	47.47
14. Proportion of population with primary reliance on clean fuels and technology for cooking (%)	7	2015	2016	48.87	49.88
15. Debt sustainability	17				
a. Present value of debt (% of GNI)			2018		4.89
b. Total debt service (% of GNI)		2017	2019	2.36	2.65
16. Tax revenue (% of GDP)	17	2017	2019	11.64	12.21
17. Time to start a business (days)	8	2017	2019	23.56	21.46
18. Regional cooperation and integration index—Money and finance (average score)	17	2015	2018	0.41	0.39

ADB Concessional Assistance Countries (continued)

Indicator	SDG	Baseline Year	Latest Year	Baseline Value	Latest Value
8. Proportion of time spent on unpaid domestic and care work (%)					
a. Female	5	2013	2015	10.42	16.62
b. Male		2013	2015	2.50	9.10
9. Forest area as a proportion of total land area (%)	15	2015	2016	37.15	37.10
10. Coverage of protected areas in relation to marine areas (%)	14	2017	2018	5.98	5.98
11. Environmental performance index score (average number)	12	2008	2020	43.79	34.28
12. Deaths attributed to climate-related and geophysical hazards (number)[b]	13	2018	2020	397	2,078
a. Climate-related hazards		2018	2020	380	2,078
b. Geophysical hazards		2018	2020	17	0
13. Access to social protection—social assistance (%)	1	2013	2014	11.08	17.50
14. Proportion of population with primary reliance on clean fuels and technology for cooking (%)	7	2015	2016	37.15	38.61
15. Debt sustainability	17				
a. Present value of debt (% of GNI)			2018		19.50
b. Total debt service (% of GNI)		2017	2019	3.46	5.04
16. Tax revenue (% of GDP)	17	2017	2019	12.06	11.11
17. Time to start a business (days)	8	2017	2019	25.72	24.96
18. Regional cooperation and integration index—Money and finance (average score)	17	2015	2018	0.42	0.42
19. Proportion of population with access to electricity (%)	7	2016	2018	80.24	84.03

LEVEL 1: Development Progress in Asia and the Pacific

ADB Developing Member Countries Overall (continued)

Indicator	SDG	Baseline Year	Latest Year	Baseline Value	Latest Value
19. **Proportion of population with access to electricity** (%)	7	2016	2018	92.66	95.32
20. **Proportion of population using basic drinking water services** (%)	6	2016	2017	91.62	92.26
a. **Rural**		2016	2017	87.52	88.46
b. **Urban**		2016	2017	97.28	97.32
21. **Proportion of population using basic sanitation services** (%)	6	2016	2017	70.10	71.89
a. **Rural**		2016	2017	60.61	62.84
b. **Urban**		2016	2017	86.12	86.81
22. **Paved roads** (kilometers per 10,000 people)	9	2015	2018	22.45	24.44
23. **Proportion of population covered by a mobile network and/or information and communication technology** (%)	9	2017	2019	97.46	97.83

ADB Concessional Assistance Countries (continued)

Indicator	SDG	Baseline Year	Latest Year	Baseline Value	Latest Value
20. Proportion of population using basic drinking water services (%)		2016	2017	89.47	90.04
a. **Rural**		2016	2017	86.30	86.98
b. **Urban**		2016	2017	95.99	96.06
21. Proportion of population using basic sanitation services (%)		2016	2017	62.11	63.37
a. **Rural**		2016	2017	56.14	57.67
b. **Urban**		2016	2017	76.57	76.29
22. Paved roads (kilometers per 10,000 people)		2015	2018	9.68	8.36
23. Proportion of population covered by a mobile network and/or information and communication technology (%)		2017	2019	94.14	94.89

ADB = Asian Development Bank, GDP = gross domestic product, GNI = gross national income, SDG = Sustainable Development Goal.

Notes:
1. Estimates are averages of actual country values or imputed country values wherever data are missing for the year required, weighted by population size.
2. "Concessional assistance countries" refers to a subset of ADB developing member countries that have access to Asian Development Fund grants and concessional ordinary capital resources loans (group A and B countries except India).
3. Gray shading in cells indicates the column heading does not apply.

[a] Poverty estimates using the $3.20 poverty line introduced by the World Bank based on national poverty lines typically found in lower middle-income countries.
[b] Climate-related hazards include climatological, hydrological, and meteorological hazards.

Sources: Regional aggregates were prepared by ADB's Strategy, Policy and Partnerships Department using country data from the following sources: ADB Economic Research and Regional Cooperation Department; Yale Center for Environmental Law & Policy. Environmental Performance Index. https://epi.envirocenter.yale.edu (accessed 22 January 2021); Centre for Research on the Epidemiology of Disasters. Emergency Events Database. https://www.emdat.be/database (accessed 13 January 2021); United Nations Economic and Social Commission for Asia and the Pacific. SDG Gateway Data Explorer. http://data.unescap.org/sdg (accessed 18 December 2020); World Bank. PovcalNet. http://iresearch.worldbank.org/PovcalNet/povOnDemand.aspx (accessed 20 October 2020); International Road Federation. World Road Statistics. https://www.worldroadstatistics.org/ (accessed 7 February 2020); and World Bank. World Development Indicators. https://databank.worldbank.org/source/world-development-indicators (accessed 25 January 2021). Population and GNI data used as weights are from the following sources: World Bank. World Development Indicators. https://databank.worldbank.org/source/world-development-indicators (accessed 12 January 2021); and United Nations. Department of Economic and Social Affairs, Population Division. World Population Prospects: The 2017 Revision (DVD edition).

LEVEL 2: Results from Completed Operations

ADB Operations Overall

Indicator		SDG	Results Achieved 2020
LEVEL 2A. STRATEGY 2030 OPERATIONAL PRIORITY RESULTS			
Operational Priority 1: Addressing Remaining Poverty and Reducing Inequalities			
1.1.1	**People enrolled in improved education and/or training** (number)	4	18,943,000
1.1.2	**Health services established or improved** (number)	3	11
1.1.3	**Social protection schemes established or improved** (number)	1	7
1.2.1	**Business development and financial sector measures supported in implementation** (number)	8	120
1.2.2	**Models for business development and financing established or improved** (number)	8	4
1.2.3	**Enhanced labor policies or standards implemented** (number)	8	1
1.3.1	**Infrastructure assets established or improved** (number)	9	82,000
1.3.2	**New financial products and services made available to the poor and vulnerable** (number)	8	1
1.3.3	**Measures for increased inclusiveness supported in implementation** (number)	10	4
Operational Priority 2: Accelerating Progress in Gender Equality			
2.1.1	**Women enrolled in TVET and other job trainings** (number)	4	30,000
2.1.2	**Women opening new accounts** (number)	8	10,000
2.1.3	**Women-owned or -led SME loan accounts opened or women-owned or -led SME end borrowers reached** (number)	5	5,500
2.1.4	**Women and girls benefiting from new or improved infrastructure** (number)	5	24,187,000
2.2.1	**Women and girls enrolled in STEM or nontraditional TVET** (number)	4	–
2.2.2	**Health services for women and girls established or improved** (number)	3	1

LEVEL 2: Results from Completed Operations

Operations Financed by Concessional OCR Loans and ADF Grants

Indicator		SDG	Results Achieved 2020
LEVEL 2A. STRATEGY 2030 OPERATIONAL PRIORITY RESULTS			
Operational Priority 1: Addressing Remaining Poverty and Reducing Inequalities			
1.1.1	**People enrolled in improved education and/or training** (number)	4	18,390,000
1.1.2	**Health services established or improved** (number)	3	6
1.1.3	**Social protection schemes established or improved** (number)	1	2
1.2.1	**Business development and financial sector measures supported in implementation** (number)	8	2
1.2.2	**Models for business development and financing established or improved** (number)	8	4
1.2.3	**Enhanced labor policies or standards implemented** (number)	8	–
1.3.1	**Infrastructure assets established or improved** (number)	9	74,000
1.3.2	**New financial products and services made available to the poor and vulnerable** (number)	8	1
1.3.3	**Measures for increased inclusiveness supported in implementation** (number)	10	1
Operational Priority 2: Accelerating Progress in Gender Equality			
2.1.1	**Women enrolled in TVET and other job trainings** (number)	4	16,000
2.1.2	**Women opening new accounts** (number)	8	1,200
2.1.3	**Women-owned or -led SME loan accounts opened or women-owned or -led SME end borrowers reached** (number)	5	5,500
2.1.4	**Women and girls benefiting from new or improved infrastructure** (number)	5	392,000
2.2.1	**Women and girls enrolled in STEM or nontraditional TVET** (number)	4	–
2.2.2	**Health services for women and girls established or improved** (number)	3	–

LEVEL 2: Results from Completed Operations

ADB Operations Overall (continued)

Indicator		SDG	Results Achieved 2020
2.2.3	**Solutions to prevent or address gender-based violence implemented** (number)	5	3
2.3.1	**Women with strengthened leadership capacities** (number)	5	360
2.3.2	**Measures on gender equality supported in implementation** (number)	5	26
2.4.1	**Time-saving or gender-responsive infrastructure assets and/or services established or improved** (number)	5	32,000
2.4.2	**Child and elderly care services established or improved** (number)	5	–
2.5.1	**Community-based initiatives to build resilience of women and girls to external shocks implemented** (number)	1	–
2.5.2	**Climate- and disaster-resilient infrastructure assets and/or services for women and girls established or improved** (number)	9	–
2.5.3	**Savings and insurance schemes for women implemented or established** (number)	8	1
2.5.4	**Dedicated crisis-responding social assistance schemes for women and girls implemented or established** (number)	1	4
Operational Priority 3: Tackling Climate Change, Building Climate and Disaster Resilience, and Enhancing Environmental Sustainability			
3.1.1	**Additional climate finance mobilized** ($)	13	1,526,710,000
3.1.2	**People with increased capacity in implementing mitigation and low-carbon development actions** (number)	13	1,300
3.1.3	**Low-carbon infrastructure assets established or improved** (number)	9	100
3.1.4	**Installed renewable energy capacity** (megawatts)	7	5,000
3.1.5	**Low-carbon solutions promoted and implemented** (number)	13	13
3.2.1	**Area with reduced flood risk** (hectares)	14	244,000
3.2.2	**Gender-inclusive climate and disaster resilience capacity development initiatives implemented** (number)	5	–

LEVEL 2: Results from Completed Operations

Operations Financed by Concessional OCR Loans and ADF Grants (continued)

Indicator		SDG	Results Achieved 2020
2.2.3	**Solutions to prevent or address gender-based violence implemented** (number)	5	–
2.3.1	**Women with strengthened leadership capacities** (number)	5	360
2.3.2	**Measures on gender equality supported in implementation** (number)	5	18
2.4.1	**Time-saving or gender-responsive infrastructure assets and/or services established or improved** (number)	5	32,000
2.4.2	**Child and elderly care services established or improved** (number)	5	–
2.5.1	**Community-based initiatives to build resilience of women and girls to external shocks implemented** (number)	1	–
2.5.2	**Climate- and disaster-resilient infrastructure assets and/or services for women and girls established or improved** (number)	9	–
2.5.3	**Savings and insurance schemes for women implemented or established** (number)	8	1
2.5.4	**Dedicated crisis-responding social assistance schemes for women and girls implemented or established** (number)	1	–
Operational Priority 3: Tackling Climate Change, Building Climate and Disaster Resilience, and Enhancing Environmental Sustainability			
3.1.1	**Additional climate finance mobilized** ($)	13	600,000
3.1.2	**People with increased capacity in implementing mitigation and low-carbon development actions** (number)	13	1,300
3.1.3	**Low-carbon infrastructure assets established or improved** (number)	9	4
3.1.4	**Installed renewable energy capacity** (megawatts)	7	200
3.1.5	**Low-carbon solutions promoted and implemented** (number)	13	4
3.2.1	**Area with reduced flood risk** (hectares)	14	244,000
3.2.2	**Gender-inclusive climate and disaster resilience capacity development initiatives implemented** (number)	5	–

ADB Operations Overall (continued)

Indicator		SDG	Results Achieved 2020
3.2.3	**Financial preparedness instruments provided** (number)	1	1
3.2.4	**National and subnational disaster risk reduction and/or management plans supported in implementation** (number)	13	11
3.2.5	**New and existing infrastructure assets made climate and disaster resilient** (number)		86
3.3.1	**Pollution control-enhancing infrastructure assets established or improved** (number)	3	16
3.3.2	**Solutions to enhance pollution control and resource efficiency implemented** (number)	12	9
3.3.3	**Terrestrial, coastal, and marine areas conserved, restored, and/or enhanced** (hectares)	14	54,000
3.3.4	**Solutions to conserve, restore, and/or enhance terrestrial, coastal, and marine areas implemented** (number)	14	8
3.3.5	**Sustainable water–food–energy security nexus solutions implemented** (number)	6	–
Operational Priority 4: Making Cities More Livable			
4.1.1	**Service providers with improved performance** (number)	11	670
4.1.2	**Urban infrastructure assets established or improved** (number)	11	380
4.2.1	**Measures to improve regulatory, legal, and institutional environment for better planning supported in implementation** (number)	11	10
4.2.2	**Measures to improve financial sustainability supported in implementation** (number)	11	1
4.3.1	**Solutions to enhance urban environment implemented** (number)	11	9
4.3.2	**Urban climate and disaster resilience capacity development initiatives implemented** (number)		3
Operational Priority 5: Promoting Rural Development and Food Security			
5.1.1	**Rural infrastructure assets established or improved** (number)		1,200

Operations Financed by Concessional OCR Loans and ADF Grants (continued)

Indicator		SDG	Results Achieved 2020
3.2.3	**Financial preparedness instruments provided** (number)	1	1
3.2.4	**National and subnational disaster risk reduction and/or management plans supported in implementation** (number)	13	10
3.2.5	**New and existing infrastructure assets made climate and disaster resilient** (number)	9	81
3.3.1	**Pollution control-enhancing infrastructure assets established or improved** (number)	3	5
3.3.2	**Solutions to enhance pollution control and resource efficiency implemented** (number)	12	4
3.3.3	**Terrestrial, coastal, and marine areas conserved, restored, and/or enhanced** (hectares)	14	48,000
3.3.4	**Solutions to conserve, restore, and/or enhance terrestrial, coastal, and marine areas implemented** (number)	14	1
3.3.5	**Sustainable water–food–energy security nexus solutions implemented** (number)	6	–
Operational Priority 4: Making Cities More Livable			
4.1.1	**Service providers with improved performance** (number)	11	670
4.1.2	**Urban infrastructure assets established or improved** (number)	11	220
4.2.1	**Measures to improve regulatory, legal, and institutional environment for better planning supported in implementation** (number)	11	5
4.2.2	**Measures to improve financial sustainability supported in implementation** (number)	11	1
4.3.1	**Solutions to enhance urban environment implemented** (number)	11	1
4.3.2	**Urban climate and disaster resilience capacity development initiatives implemented** (number)	11	–
Operational Priority 5: Promoting Rural Development and Food Security			
5.1.1	**Rural infrastructure assets established or improved** (number)	2	870

LEVEL 2: Results from Completed Operations

ADB Operations Overall (continued)

Indicator		SDG	Results Achieved 2020
5.1.2	**Companies providing new or improved nonagricultural goods and services** (number)	2	–
5.1.3	**Health care, education, and financial services established or improved** (number)	8	1
5.1.4	**Rural economic hubs supported** (number)	2	3
5.2.1	**Wholesale markets established or improved** (number)	2	–
5.2.2	**Storages, agri-logistics, and modern retail assets established or improved** (number)	2	–
5.2.3	**Agribusinesses integrating farmers in efficient value chains** (number)	2	640
5.2.4	**Food safety and traceability standards improved** (number)	2	1
5.3.1	**Land improved through climate-resilient irrigation infrastructure and water delivery services** (hectares)	2	17,000
5.3.2	**Farmers using quality farm inputs and sustainable mechanization** (number)	2	–
5.3.3	**Commercial farming land supported** (hectares)	2	–
5.3.4	**Modern knowledge-intensive corporate farming models introduced** (number)	2	–
Operational Priority 6: Strengthening Governance and Institutional Capacity			
6.1.1	**Government officials with increased capacity to design, implement, monitor, and evaluate relevant measures** (number)	16	93,000
6.1.2	**Measures supported in implementation to improve capacity of public organizations to promote the private sector and finance sector** (number)	17	160
6.1.3	**Measures supported in implementation that promote resilience and responsiveness to economic shocks in a timely manner** (number)	1	9
6.1.4	**Transparency and accountability measures in procurement and financial management supported in implementation** (number)	16	31
6.2.1	**Service delivery standards adopted and/or supported in implementation by government and/or private entities** (number)	16	8

LEVEL 2: Results from Completed Operations

Operations Financed by Concessional OCR Loans and ADF Grants (continued)

Indicator		SDG	Results Achieved 2020
5.1.2	**Companies providing new or improved nonagricultural goods and services** (number)	2	–
5.1.3	**Health care, education, and financial services established or improved** (number)	8	1
5.1.4	**Rural economic hubs supported** (number)	2	3
5.2.1	**Wholesale markets established or improved** (number)	2	–
5.2.2	**Storages, agri-logistics, and modern retail assets established or improved** (number)	2	–
5.2.3	**Agribusinesses integrating farmers in efficient value chains** (number)	2	640
5.2.4	**Food safety and traceability standards improved** (number)	2	1
5.3.1	**Land improved through climate-resilient irrigation infrastructure and water delivery services** (hectares)	2	17,000
5.3.2	**Farmers using quality farm inputs and sustainable mechanization** (number)	2	–
5.3.3	**Commercial farming land supported** (hectares)	2	–
5.3.4	**Modern knowledge-intensive corporate farming models introduced** (number)	2	–
Operational Priority 6: Strengthening Governance and Institutional Capacity			
6.1.1	**Government officials with increased capacity to design, implement, monitor, and evaluate relevant measures** (number)	16	44,000
6.1.2	**Measures supported in implementation to improve capacity of public organizations to promote the private sector and finance sector** (number)	17	35
6.1.3	**Measures supported in implementation that promote resilience and responsiveness to economic shocks in a timely manner** (number)	1	3
6.1.4	**Transparency and accountability measures in procurement and financial management supported in implementation** (number)	16	19
6.2.1	**Service delivery standards adopted and/or supported in implementation by government and/or private entities** (number)	16	6

ADB Operations Overall (continued)

Indicator		SDG	Results Achieved 2020
6.2.2	Measures supported in implementation to strengthen subnational entities' ability to better manage their public finances (number)	16	23
6.2.3	Measures to strengthen SOE governance supported in implementation (number)	16	14
6.2.4	Citizen engagement mechanisms adopted (number)	16	19
Operational Priority 7: Fostering Regional Cooperation and Integration			
7.1.1	Transport and ICT connectivity assets established or improved (number)	9	9
7.1.2	Measures to improve the efficiency and/or productivity of cross-border connectivity supported in implementation (number)	9	24
7.1.3	Clean energy capacity for power trade installed or improved (megawatt equivalent)	9	–
7.1.4	Regional or subregional mechanisms created or operationalized to enhance coordination and cooperation among DMCs in energy, transport, or ICT connectivity (number)	17	12
7.2.1	Measures to improve execution of provisions in existing or new trade or investment agreements supported in implementation (number)	17	66
7.2.2	Measures to develop existing and/or new cross-border economic corridors supported in implementation (number)	17	8
7.2.3	Measures to improve regional financial cooperation supported in implementation (number)	17	2
7.2.4	Regional or subregional mechanisms created or operationalized to enhance coordination and cooperation among DMCs in trade, finance, or multisector economic corridors (number)	17	12
7.3.1	Measures to improve shared capacity of DMCs to mitigate or adapt to climate change supported in implementation (number)	13	–
7.3.2	Measures to expand cross-border environmental protection and sustainable management of shared natural resources supported in implementation (number)	12	1
7.3.3	Measures to improve regional public health and education services supported in implementation (number)	1	7

LEVEL 2: Results from Completed Operations

Operations Financed by Concessional OCR Loans and ADF Grants (continued)

Indicator		SDG	Results Achieved 2020
6.2.2	Measures supported in implementation to strengthen subnational entities' ability to better manage their public finances (number)	16	12
6.2.3	Measures to strengthen SOE governance supported in implementation (number)	16	14
6.2.4	Citizen engagement mechanisms adopted (number)	16	14
Operational Priority 7: Fostering Regional Cooperation and Integration			
7.1.1	Transport and ICT connectivity assets established or improved (number)	9	6
7.1.2	Measures to improve the efficiency and/or productivity of cross-border connectivity supported in implementation (number)	9	10
7.1.3	Clean energy capacity for power trade installed or improved (megawatt equivalent)	9	–
7.1.4	Regional or subregional mechanisms created or operationalized to enhance coordination and cooperation among DMCs in energy, transport, or ICT connectivity (number)	17	7
7.2.1	Measures to improve execution of provisions in existing or new trade or investment agreements supported in implementation (number)	17	62
7.2.2	Measures to develop existing and/or new cross-border economic corridors supported in implementation (number)	17	4
7.2.3	Measures to improve regional financial cooperation supported in implementation (number)	17	1
7.2.4	Regional or subregional mechanisms created or operationalized to enhance coordination and cooperation among DMCs in trade, finance, or multisector economic corridors (number)	17	8
7.3.1	Measures to improve shared capacity of DMCs to mitigate or adapt to climate change supported in implementation (number)	13	–
7.3.2	Measures to expand cross-border environmental protection and sustainable management of shared natural resources supported in implementation (number)	12	1
7.3.3	Measures to improve regional public health and education services supported in implementation (number)	1	6

LEVEL 2: Results from Completed Operations

ADB Operations Overall (continued)

Indicator		SDG	Results Achieved 2020
7.3.4	Regional or subregional mechanisms created or operationalized to enhance coordination and cooperation among DMCs on regional public goods (number)	17	1

LEVEL 2: Results from Completed Operations

Operations Financed by Concessional OCR Loans and ADF Grants (continued)

Indicator		SDG	Results Achieved 2020
7.3.4	**Regional or subregional mechanisms created or operationalized to enhance coordination and cooperation among DMCs on regional public goods** (number)	17	1

– = no operations in the reporting period targeted results for these indicators; ADB = Asian Development Bank; ADF = Asian Development Fund; DMC = developing member country; ICT = information and communication technology; OCR = ordinary capital resources; SDG = Sustainable Development Goal; SME = small and medium-sized enterprise; SOE = state-owned enterprise; STEM = science, technology, engineering, and mathematics; TVET = technical and vocational education and training.

Notes:

1. "ADB Operations Overall" refers to ADB operations financed by regular and concessional OCR and/or ADF grants.
2. Results delivered as reported in project completion reports, extended annual review reports, and technical assistance completion reports circulated from 16 November 2019 to 15 November 2020.
3. Achieved results over 10,000 are rounded to the nearest 1,000. Values smaller than 10,000 are rounded to the nearest 100. Values smaller than 1,000 are rounded to the nearest 10. Values smaller than 99 are not rounded.

LEVEL 2: Results from Completed Operations

ADB Operations Overall

Indicator			Period	2018	2019	2020
LEVEL 2B. QUALITY OF COMPLETED OPERATIONS						
1.	Completed operations rated *successful* (%) (sovereign)					
	a.	Investment projects	3-year	75	70	68
	b.	Policy-based operations	3-year	89	82	84
	c.	Fragile and conflict-affected situations DMCs	3-year	73	57	50
	d.	Small island developing states	3-year	59	42	56
2.	Completed operations rated *successful* (%) (sovereign)					
	a.	Relevance	3-year	88	82	82
	b.	Efficiency	3-year	74	75	72
	c.	Effectiveness	3-year	74	68	64
	d.	Sustainability	3-year	68	61	62
3.	Completed operations rated *successful* (%) (nonsovereign)					
	a.	Development results	3-year	54	51	53
	b.	ADB's additionality	3-year	63	54	55
	c.	ADB's investment profitability	3-year	74	71	65
	d.	ADB's work quality	3-year	51	40	53
4.	Web-distributed knowledge solutions (number of downloads)		Annual	725,000	834,900	978,229
5.	Engagement on social media (number)					
	a.	Subscribers and followers	Annual	653,788	774,792	921,414
	b.	Active engagement	Annual	1,157,259	391,830	1,090,184
6.	Event participants reporting increased knowledge and/or skills (number)[a]		Annual			
7.	Clients satisfied with ADB's development effectiveness (%)[b]		Every 2 years			75

LEVEL 2: Results from Completed Operations

Operations Financed by Concessional OCR Loans and ADF Grants

Indicator		Period	2018	2019	2020
LEVEL 2B. QUALITY OF COMPLETED OPERATIONS					
1.	**Completed operations rated** ***successful*** (%) (sovereign)				
	a. **Investment projects**	3-year	73	66	64
	b. **Policy-based operations**	3-year	92	83	75
	c. **Fragile and conflict-affected situations DMCs**	3-year	73	57	50
	d. **Small island developing states**	3-year	62	47	53
2.	**Completed operations rated** ***successful*** (%) (sovereign)				
	a. **Relevance**	3-year	89	83	80
	b. **Efficiency**	3-year	76	77	72
	c. **Effectiveness**	3-year	73	64	56
	d. **Sustainability**	3-year	66	59	59
3.	**Completed operations rated** ***successful*** (%) (nonsovereign)				
	a. **Development results**				
	b. **ADB's additionality**				
	c. **ADB's investment profitability**				
	d. **ADB's work quality**				
4.	**Web-distributed knowledge solutions** (number of downloads)				
5.	**Engagement on social media** (number)				
	a. **Subscribers and followers**				
	b. **Active engagement**				
6.	**Event participants reporting increased knowledge and/or skills** (number)[a]				
7.	**Clients satisfied with ADB's development effectiveness** (%)[b]				

LEVEL 2: Results from Completed Operations

ADB Operations Overall (continued)

Indicator		Period	2018	2019	2020
8.	**Completed technical assistance projects rated *successful*** (%) (sovereign and nonsovereign)	3-year	88	86	83
9.	**Completed country strategies and assistance programs rated *successful*** (%) (sovereign and nonsovereign)	3-year	80	87	88
10.	**Impact evaluations completed** (number)	Annual	2	2	2
11.	**Operations with meaningful civil society organization engagement** (%) (number)[c]	Annual			76

LEVEL 2: Results from Completed Operations

Operations Financed by Concessional OCR Loans and ADF Grants (continued)

Indicator		Period	2018	2019	2020
8.	**Completed technical assistance projects rated** ***successful*** (%) (sovereign and nonsovereign)	3-year	88	86	87
9.	**Completed country strategies and assistance programs rated** ***successful*** (%) (sovereign and nonsovereign)	3-year	63	67	71
10.	**Impact evaluations completed** (number)	Annual	2	1	1
11.	**Operations with meaningful civil society organization engagement** (%) (number)[c]				

ADB = Asian Development Bank, ADF = Asian Development Fund, DMC = developing member country, OCR = ordinary capital resources.

Notes:

1. "ADB Operations Overall" refers to ADB operations financed by regular and concessional OCR and/or ADF grants.
2. Success rates of completed operations and country strategies and assistance programs are ratings evaluated by the Independent Evaluation Department based on validations of project and/or program completion reports, project and/or program performance evaluations, country assistance program evaluations, and validations of country partnership final reviews.
3. Technical assistance success ratings are from the technical assistance project completion reports, which are not reviewed by the Independent Evaluation Department.
4. The reporting year is 1 July–30 June and is based on the circulation year of completion reports reviewed. For example, RY2020 refers to 1 July 2018–30 June 2020. Indicators 1–3 and 8–9 are reported by reporting year. Indicators 4–6 and 10–11 are reported by calendar year.
5. Gray shading in cells indicates the column heading does not apply.

[a] Methodology under review.

[b] No client survey was conducted in 2018.

[c] Starting 2020, ADB reports operations with meaningful civil society organization (CSO) engagement based on the percentage of completed projects that delivered meaningful CSO engagement out of the total number of completed projects that had planned to deliver meaningful CSO engagement. ADB defines meaningful CSO engagement as significant information sharing or consultation activities, or any type of collaboration or partnership with CSOs. This replaces the tracking indicator in level 3C. Strategic Alignment: 27. Civil society organization participation, which was based on the number of committed sovereign operations in a year containing elements of activity and/or participation by civil society organizations (CSOs) in any stage of the project and as reflected in the reports and recommendations of the President, as a percentage of the total number of sovereign operations committed during the year. The value reported in 2019 report was 90% for 2019.

Sources: ADB (Strategy, Policy and Partnerships Department; Department of Communications; and Sustainable Development and Climate Change Department).

LEVEL 3: ADB's Operational Management

ADB Operations Overall

Indicator	SDG	Period	2018	2019	2020
LEVEL 3A. DESIGN AND IMPLEMENTATION QUALITY					
1. **Performance of operations at implementation rated *satisfactory*** (%) (sovereign)		Annual		52	64
a. **Output**		Annual		84	86
b. **Contract award**		Annual		75	68
c. **Disbursement**		Annual		75	67
d. **Financial management**		Annual		65	88
e. **Safeguards**		Annual		73	81
LEVEL 3B. DEVELOPMENT FINANCE					
2. **Time from concept approval to first disbursement** (months) (sovereign)		Annual	31.8	30.5	28.3
a. **From concept approval to loan fact-finding**		Annual	14.3	10.8	10.9
b. **From loan fact-finding to approval**		Annual	8.3	7.2	7.5
c. **From approval to commitment**		Annual	3.5	3.3	2.1
d. **From commitment to first disbursement**		Annual	5.7	9.2	8.9
3. **Time from concept approval to first disbursement** (months) (nonsovereign)		Annual	16.4	16.3	14.7
a. **From concept clearance to project approval**		Annual	7.2	8.4	7.3
b. **From approval to signing**		Annual	5.6	3.8	2.6
c. **From signing to first disbursement**		Annual	3.7	4.1	4.7
4. **Overall disbursement** ($ billion) (sovereign)		Annual	9.2	9.5	9.2
5. **Disbursement ratio** (%) (sovereign)		Annual	21.1	19.6	18.5
6. **Approvals** ($ billion) (sovereign and nonsovereign)		Annual	19.3	19.5	29.0
7. **Commitments** ($ billion) (sovereign and nonsovereign)		Annual	21.6	21.6	28.2

LEVEL 3: ADB's Operational Management

Operations Financed by Concessional OCR Loans and ADF Grants

Indicator		SDG	Period	2018	2019	2020
LEVEL 3A. DESIGN AND IMPLEMENTATION QUALITY						
1.	**Performance of operations at implementation rated *satisfactory*** (%) (sovereign)		Annual		53	64
	a. **Output**		Annual		84	85
	b. **Contract award**		Annual		75	69
	c. **Disbursement**		Annual		72	67
	d. **Financial management**		Annual		67	89
	e. **Safeguards**		Annual		75	80
LEVEL 3B. DEVELOPMENT FINANCE						
2.	**Time from concept approval to first disbursement** (months) (sovereign)		Annual	33.2	29.6	28.2
	a. **From concept approval to loan fact-finding**		Annual	15.7	10.6	12.1
	b. **From loan fact-finding to approval**		Annual	8.7	7.0	7.1
	c. **From approval to commitment**		Annual	2.9	2.9	2.0
	d. **From commitment to first disbursement**		Annual	5.8	9.0	8.8
3.	**Time from concept approval to first disbursement** (months) (nonsovereign)					
	a. **From concept clearance to project approval**					
	b. **From approval to signing**					
	c. **From signing to first disbursement**					
4.	**Overall disbursement** ($ billion) (sovereign)		Annual	1.9	1.9	1.9
5.	**Disbursement ratio** (%) (sovereign)		Annual	19.8	15.7	14.6
6.	**Approvals** ($ billion) (sovereign and nonsovereign)		Annual	5.2	3.5	5.5
7.	**Commitments** ($ billion) (sovereign and nonsovereign)		Annual	5.3	4.5	5.4

ADB Operations Overall (continued)

Indicator	SDG	Period	2018	2019	2020
8. **Commitments in concessional assistance countries** (group A + group B) (%) (sovereign and nonsovereign)					
9. **Commitments in FCAS DMCs and SIDS** (%) (sovereign and nonsovereign)		Annual	8	8	10
10. **Private direct mobilization** ($ billion) (sovereign and nonsovereign)[a]		Annual	0.8	1.7	
11. **Sovereign cofinancing** ($ billion) (sovereign)		Annual		4.8	11.1
LEVEL 3C. STRATEGIC ALIGNMENT					
12. **Committed operations that promote gender equality** (%) (sovereign and nonsovereign)	5				
a1. **GEN – sovereign operations**		3-year	8	8	9
a2. **GEN – nonsovereign operations**		3-year	11	13	10
b1. **EGM – sovereign operations**		3-year	44	54	63
b2. **EGM – nonsovereign operations**		3-year	12	16	27
c1. **SGE – sovereign operations**		3-year	23	21	19
c2. **SGE – nonsovereign operations**		3-year	28	35	45
d1. **NGE – sovereign operations**		3-year	25	16	9
d2. **NGE – nonsovereign operations**		3-year	49	35	18
13. **Financing for gender equality** (%) (sovereign and nonsovereign)	5	3-year	41	51	65
14. **Committed operations supporting climate change** (%) (sovereign and nonsovereign)	13				
a. **Mitigation**		3-year	17	16	14
b. **Adaptation**		3-year	28	26	22
c. **Both**		3-year	12	17	22

Operations Financed by Concessional OCR Loans and ADF Grants (continued)

Indicator	SDG	Period	2018	2019	2020
8. **Commitments in concessional assistance countries** (group A + group B) (%) (sovereign and nonsovereign)		Annual	45	40	36
9. **Commitments in FCAS DMCs and SIDS** (%) (sovereign and nonsovereign)		Annual	28	20	36
10. **Private direct mobilization** ($ billion) (sovereign and nonsovereign)[a]					
11. **Sovereign cofinancing** ($ billion) (sovereign)					
LEVEL 3C. STRATEGIC ALIGNMENT					
12. **Committed operations that promote gender equality** (%) (sovereign and nonsovereign)	5				
a1. **GEN – sovereign operations**		3-year	12	13	10
a2. **GEN – nonsovereign operations**					
b1. **EGM – sovereign operations**		3-year	50	60	66
b2. **EGM – nonsovereign operations**					
c1. **SGE – sovereign operations**		3-year	20	18	18
c2. **SGE – nonsovereign operations**					
d1. **NGE – sovereign operations**		3-year	18	9	6
d2. **NGE – nonsovereign operations**					
13. **Financing for gender equality** (%) (sovereign and nonsovereign)	5	3-year	67	71	67
14. **Committed operations supporting climate change** (%) (sovereign and nonsovereign)	13				
a. **Mitigation**		3-year	10	8	7
b. **Adaptation**		3-year	35	36	33
c. **Both**		3-year	14	19	23

ADB Operations Overall (continued)

Indicator	SDG	Period	2018	2019	2020
15. **Financing for climate change** ($ billion, cumulative) (sovereign and nonsovereign)					
a. **Mitigation**		Annual		2.4	3.2
b. **Adaptation**		Annual		0.8	1.1
c. **Both**		Annual		3.3	6.5
16. **Nonsovereign operations as a share of total ADB operations** (%, $) (nonsovereign)		Annual	19.3	17.5	6.2
17. **Operations or transactions supporting inclusive business** (number) (nonsovereign)		Annual	6	8	6
18. **Knowledge products and services delivered** (%)		Annual	84	106	102
19. **Operations that are green, sustainable, inclusive, and resilient** (%) (sovereign and nonsovereign)		Annual		100	100
20. **Operations contributing to each of the seven operational priorities** (%) (sovereign and nonsovereign)					
Priority 1: Addressing Remaining Poverty and Reducing Inequalities		Annual		[75]	[86]
Priority 2: Accelerating Progress in Gender Equality (Categories 1, 2, 3)		Annual		[92]	[97]
Priority 3: Tackling Climate Change, Building Climate and Disaster Resilience, and Enhancing Environmental Sustainability		Annual		[59]	[56]
Priority 4: Making Cities More Livable		Annual		[23]	[23]
Priority 5: Promoting Rural Development and Food Security		Annual		[27]	[23]

Operations Financed by Concessional OCR Loans and ADF Grants (continued)

Indicator	SDG	Period	2018	2019	2020
15. **Financing for climate change** ($ billion, cumulative) (sovereign and nonsovereign)	13				
a. **Mitigation**		Annual		0.1	0.1
b. **Adaptation**		Annual		0.3	0.4
c. **Both**		Annual		0.3	0.8
16. **Nonsovereign operations as a share of total ADB operations** (%, $) (nonsovereign)					
17. **Operations or transactions supporting inclusive business** (number) (nonsovereign)	8				
18. **Knowledge products and services delivered** (%)					
19. **Operations that are green, sustainable, inclusive, and resilient** (%) (sovereign and nonsovereign)	9				
20. **Operations contributing to each of the seven operational priorities** (%) (sovereign and nonsovereign)					
Priority 1: Addressing Remaining Poverty and Reducing Inequalities					
Priority 2: Accelerating Progress in Gender Equality (Categories 1, 2, 3)					
Priority 3: Tackling Climate Change, Building Climate and Disaster Resilience, and Enhancing Environmental Sustainability					
Priority 4: Making Cities More Livable					
Priority 5: Promoting Rural Development and Food Security					

ADB Operations Overall (continued)

Indicator	SDG	Period	2018	2019	2020
Priority 6: Strengthening Governance and Institutional Capacity		Annual		[68]	[72]
Priority 7: Fostering Regional Cooperation and Integration		Annual		[22]	[29]
21. **Operations contributing to social protection** (%) (sovereign and nonsovereign)	10	3-year	5	5	10
22. **Disability-inclusive operations** (%) (sovereign and nonsovereign)	10	Annual		22	32
23. **Operations aligned with SDGs** (sovereign and nonsovereign) (%)					
SDG 1: No Poverty		Annual		35	56
SDG 2: Zero Hunger		Annual		7	16
SDG 3: Good Health and Well-being		Annual		12	27
SDG 4: Quality Education		Annual		8	5
SDG 5: Gender Equality		Annual		51	69
SDG 6: Clean Water and Sanitation		Annual		15	15
SDG 7: Affordable and Clean Energy		Annual		17	20
SDG 8: Decent Work and Economic Growth		Annual		16	37
SDG 9: Industry, Innovation, and Infrastructure		Annual		29	31
SDG 10: Reduced Inequalities		Annual		35	46
SDG 11: Sustainable Cities and Communities		Annual		18	20
SDG 12: Responsible Consumption and Production		Annual		15	18
SDG 13: Climate Action		Annual		62	53

Operations Financed by Concessional OCR Loans and ADF Grants (continued)

Indicator	SDG	Period	2018	2019	2020
Priority 6: Strengthening Governance and Institutional Capacity					
Priority 7: Fostering Regional Cooperation and Integration					
21. **Operations contributing to social protection** (%) (sovereign and nonsovereign)	10	3-year	5	5	11
22. **Disability-inclusive operations** (%) (sovereign and nonsovereign)	10			12	30
23. **Operations aligned with SDGs** (sovereign and nonsovereign) (%)					
SDG 1: No Poverty					
SDG 2: Zero Hunger					
SDG 3: Good Health and Well-being					
SDG 4: Quality Education					
SDG 5: Gender Equality					
SDG 6: Clean Water and Sanitation					
SDG 7: Affordable and Clean Energy					
SDG 8: Decent Work and Economic Growth					
SDG 9: Industry, Innovation, and Infrastructure					
SDG 10: Reduced Inequalities					
SDG 11: Sustainable Cities and Communities					
SDG 12: Responsible Consumption and Production					
SDG 13: Climate Action					

ADB Operations Overall (continued)

Indicator	SDG	Period	2018	2019	2020
SDG 14: Life Below Water		Annual		1	1
SDG 15: Life on Land		Annual		1	2
SDG 16: Peace, Justice, and Strong Institutions		Annual		5	11
SDG 17: Partnerships for the Goals		Annual		5	15
24. **Operations using country procurement systems** (%) (sovereign)		Annual	54	60	76
25. **Contracts using government e-procurement systems** ($ billion) (sovereign)		Annual		4.5	4.6
26. **Innovative operations and technical assistance projects** (%) (sovereign and nonsovereign)[b]					

Operations Financed by Concessional OCR Loans and ADF Grants (continued)

Indicator	SDG	Period	2018	2019	2020
SDG 14: Life Below Water					
SDG 15: Life on Land					
SDG 16: Peace, Justice, and Strong Institutions					
SDG 17: Partnerships for the Goals					
24. Operations using country procurement systems (%) (sovereign)		Annual	35	58	76
25. Contracts using government e-procurement systems ($ billion) (sovereign)					
26. Innovative operations and technical assistance projects (%) (sovereign and nonsovereign)[b]					

ADB = Asian Development Bank, ADF = Asian Development Fund, DMC = developing member country, EGM = effective gender mainstreaming, FCAS = fragile and conflict-affected situations, GEN = gender equity theme, NGE = no gender elements, OCR = ordinary capital resources, SDG = Sustainable Development Goal, SGE = some gender elements, SIDS = small island developing state.

Notes:
1. "ADB Operations Overall" refers to ADB operations financed by regular and concessional OCR and/or ADF grants.
2. "Concessional assistance countries" refers to a subset of ADB DMCs that have access to regular OCR loans, concessional OCR loans, and ADF grants.
3. Gray shading in cells indicates the column heading does not apply.
4. Values presented in square brackets ([x]) were calculated using interim methodologies that will be revised in 2021.

[a] Data were collected with a 1-year time lag.
[b] Indicator methodology under development.

Sources: ADB (Central and West Asia Department; Controller's Department; East Asia Department; Pacific Department; Private Sector Operations Department; Procurement, Portfolio and Financial Management Department; South Asia Department; Southeast Asia Department; Strategy, Policy and Partnerships Department; Sustainable Development and Climate Change Department).

LEVEL 4: ADB's Organizational Effectiveness

ADB Operations Overall

Indicator		Period	2018	2019	2020
LEVEL 4A. ORGANIZATIONAL SYSTEMS AND PROCESSES					
1.	**Capital utilization ratio** (%) (sovereign and nonsovereign)[a]	Annual			69.1
2.	**Impaired loans ratio** (%) (nonsovereign)	Annual	4.9	4.8	4.2
3.	**Weighted average risk rating of the nonsovereign portfolio** (nonsovereign)[b]	Annual	9.6 or B	9.6 or B	9.7 or B
4.	**Internal administrative expenses per $1 million disbursement** ($ '000)	Annual	49.6	49.0	37.8
5.	**Internal administrative expenses per project under administration** ($ '000)	Annual	751	794	771
6.	**Internal administrative expenses per project approved** ($ '000)[c]	Annual	4,559	4,877	4,242
7.	**Procurement time from advertisement to contract signing, $10 million or more** (days) (sovereign)	Annual	269	265	285
8.	**Consulting services recruitment time for ADB-administered contracts, from consulting services recruitment notice to consultant contract signing** (days) (sovereign)	Annual	178	163	185
9.	**Audited financial statements reviewed on time** (%) (sovereign)	Annual		55	76
10.	**Representation of women in the international staff category** (%)	Annual	36.3	36.7	37.7
	a. **Levels 4–6**		35.4	36.7	36.8
	b. **Levels 7–8**		26.1	24.1	29.3
	c. **Levels 9–10**		27.5	29.4	35.6
11.	**Clients satisfied with ADB's responsiveness** (%)[d]	Every 2 years			63
12.	**Stakeholders satisfied with ADB's collaboration with development partners** (%)[d]	Every 2 years			63

LEVEL 4: ADB's Organizational Effectiveness

Operations Financed by Concessional OCR Loans and ADF Grants

Indicator	Period	2018	2019	2020
LEVEL 4A. ORGANIZATIONAL SYSTEMS AND PROCESSES				
1. **Capital utilization ratio** (%) (sovereign and nonsovereign)[a]				
2. **Impaired loans ratio** (%) (nonsovereign)				
3. **Weighted average risk rating of the nonsovereign portfolio** (nonsovereign)[b]				
4. **Internal administrative expenses per $1 million disbursement** ($ '000)				
5. **Internal administrative expenses per project under administration** ($ '000)				
6. **Internal administrative expenses per project approved** ($ '000)[c]				
7. **Procurement time from advertisement to contract signing, $10 million or more** (days) (sovereign)	Annual	378	322	332
8. **Consulting services recruitment time for ADB-administered contracts, from consulting services recruitment notice to consultant contract signing** (days) (sovereign)				
9. **Audited financial statements reviewed on time** (%) (sovereign)	Annual		55	76
10. **Representation of women in the international staff category** (%)				
a. **Levels 4–6**				
b. **Levels 7–8**				
c. **Levels 9–10**				
11. **Clients satisfied with ADB's responsiveness** (%)[d]				
12. **Stakeholders satisfied with ADB's collaboration with development partners** (%)[d]				

ADB Operations Overall (continued)

Indicator	Period	2018	2019	2020
LEVEL 4B. ORGANIZATIONAL CAPACITY				
13. **Digital products completed** (number)	Annual		27	50
14. **Internal training budget** (average $ per staff)	Annual		887	621
15. **Departments with documented and tested business continuity plans in place** (number)	Annual		7	4
16. **Budgeted international and national staff positions in FCAS DMCs and SIDS field offices** (number)	Annual	82	84	86
17. **Operations administered in field offices** (%) (sovereign)	Annual		53	57
18. **Share of operational expenses for operations departments and direct operations support departments** (%)	Annual	83.7	83.8	82.9
19. **Knowledge products and services drawn from k-Nexus** (number)	Annual		301	424

Operations Financed by Concessional OCR Loans and ADF Grants (continued)

Indicator	Period	2018	2019	2020
LEVEL 4B. ORGANIZATIONAL CAPACITY				
13. **Digital products completed** (number)				
14. **Internal training budget** (average $ per staff)				
15. **Departments with documented and tested business continuity plans in place** (number)				
16. **Budgeted international and national staff positions in FCAS DMCs and SIDS field offices** (number)				
17. **Operations administered in field offices** (%) (sovereign)	Annual		55	47
18. **Share of operational expenses for operations departments and direct operations support departments** (%)				
19. **Knowledge products and services drawn from k-Nexus** (number)				

ADB = Asian Development Bank, ADF = Asian Development Fund, DMC = developing member country, FCAS = fragile and conflict-affected situations, OCR = ordinary capital resources, SIDS = small island developing state.

Notes:

1. "ADB Operations Overall" refers to ADB operations financed by regular and concessional OCR and/or ADF grants.
2. Concessional assistance is the subset of ADB's overall operations financed by concessional OCR loans and ADF grants.
3. Gray shading in cells indicates the column heading does not apply.

[a] Starting 2020, ADB reports capital utilization ratio defined as the ratio of the total economic capital used to total available capital. The economic capital covers capital requirement for credit, market, operational, and other risk types. This indicator replaces reporting on equity-loan ratio.

[b] Starting in 2020, ADB reports weighted average risk rating based on outstanding exposure instead of exposure at default. Values for 2018 and 2019 were updated using this new methodology.

[c] Values for 2018 and 2019 have been updated to reflect a correction of the number of projects approved in 2016 (from 140 to 142) and 2019 (from 149 to 148).

[d] No survey was conducted in 2018.

Sources: ADB (Budget, Personnel, and Management Systems Department; Controller's Department; Information Technology Department; Office of Administrative Services; Office of Risk Management; Procurement, Portfolio and Financial Management Department; Strategy, Policy and Partnerships Department; and Sustainable Development and Climate Change Department).

www.ingramcontent.com/pod-product-compliance
Lightning Source LLC
Chambersburg PA
CBHW050042220326
41599CB00045B/7251

* 9 7 8 9 2 9 2 6 2 8 0 7 9 *